NINETEENTH CENTURY
FASHION

NINETEENTH CENTURY
FASHION

NINETEENTH CENTURY FASHION

PENELOPE BYRDE

B. T. Batsford Limited • London

For Prue

First published 1992
© Penelope Byrde 1992

ISBN 0 7134 5546 2

Typeset by Colorcraft Ltd
and printed and bound in Great Britain
by Butler & Tanner Ltd, Frome and London
for the publishers B.T. Batsford Ltd
4 Fitzhardinge Street, London W1H 0AH

A CIP catalogue record for this book is available from the British Library.

Contents

Acknowledgments

I should like to thank the many people who have helped me in the preparation of this book. Firstly, the staff of the libraries, museums, art galleries and photographic collections I have visited and used; in particular, my colleagues at the Museum of Costume and Fashion Research Centre in Bath and the Bath Reference Library. I am grateful to the owners of works of art who have not only kindly supplied me with photographs and allowed me to reproduce them but in many instances gave me invaluable information and advice.

Dr Aileen Ribeiro of the Department of the History of Dress at the Courtauld Institute of Art has given support and encouragement throughout this project, and I am also grateful to Pauline Snelson and Kate Bell at Batsford for their editorial assistance.

To my family and friends I am indebted for their unfailing interest, patience and help of all kinds which have made this book possible.

List of Illustrations

The following illustrations are reproduced by the kind permission of the owners. Pictures without credits are from either the Fashion Research Centre, Bath (by courtesy of Bath Museums Service) or from the author's collection.

List of Colour Plates
(between pages 112 and 113)

INTRODUCTION

Dress in nineteenth-century Britain presents us with a picture which is almost kaleidoscopic in effect; constantly shifting and changing, each style evolving from a previous form to unfold its pattern before submerging into the next, colourful, decorative and full of contrasts. It is in the nature of clothes to absorb and reflect the mood and tastes of the moment, the wearer's status and aspirations, and in the nineteenth century fashions in dress responded as sensitively to their time as in any other period, giving back an image of extraordinary variety and detail.

The nineteenth century is one of the most complex periods in history. It defies generalization and yet has been the subject of countless generalizations. One of the most obvious is the tendency to regard the whole era as 'Victorian', although almost four decades had passed before Queen Victoria ascended the throne in 1837. The opening of the period may be properly described as late Georgian: George III did not become permanently insane until 1811 and died in 1820. His son, the Prince of Wales, acted as Regent during these years and reigned as George IV from 1820 to 1830. He was succeeded by his brother, William IV (another of Victoria's uncles) who, at sixty-three, was to have only seven years on the throne. In matters of taste the 'Regency' style was to predominate for some time after 1820 and,

as a general stylistic term, it is often used to cover the first quarter of the nineteenth century or the years from 1800 to 1830.[1]

While it is possible to use the term 'Regency' with some accuracy, 'Victorian' is inexact and misleading, covering as it does such a long period of time and such a diversity of artistic styles. This is certainly the case in the history of fashion, where each decade seems to project its own particular line and it is impossible to confuse, say, a dress of the 1830s with one of the 1870s. It is, of course, an illusion (and another generalization) that each decade should produce a style of its own, since fashion rarely changes at such well-defined intervals; at the same time, however, it is possible to associate a certain look with each decade in this period because in women's fashions the transition from one line or shape to another tends to take about seven or eight years.

In spite of its many social and cultural nuances and its innumerable paradoxes, there are some general points which can be made about the nineteenth century. It began with Britain's involvement in the Napoleonic Wars and ended with the Boer War in South Africa but, apart from the Crimean War in the mid-1850s, it was largely an era of peace and political stability for this country. The victories of Trafalgar and Waterloo established Britain as a major European power, while commercial success

1 Mr and Mrs Robert Campbell. *H. Raeburn.*

An elegant Scottish couple painted around 1810. The nineteenth century is often identified with the Victorian period but nearly four decades had elapsed before Queen Victoria ascended the throne in 1837.

2 St Martin-in-the Fields. *W. Logsdail, 1888.*

The prosperity and the poverty of nineteenth-century Britain are illustrated in this central London scene of the 1880s. The painter contrasts the impoverished young flower-seller in the foreground with the well-dressed, middle-class woman and child behind her.

society. Industrialization brought riches, especially from textiles and the iron, coal and engineering industries, but with prosperity there also came poverty at the lower end of the social scale. Although by the end of the century living and working conditions for the very poor had begun to improve and a little benefit from the general prosperity was felt, for most of the period there was an immense amount of deprivation and hardship. Much of this stemmed from the uncontrolled growth of towns attendant on the rapid spread of industrialization; living accommodation was inadequate, severely overcrowded and insanitary. The problem was exacerbated by a great expansion in the population during the first three-quarters of the century; growing, for example, from around 10.5 million in 1801 to 26.1 million in 1871.

As a period of change and activity the nineteenth century was remarkable. Even in our own age of sophisticated technology it is hard not to be impressed by the ferment of ideas and high degree of energy that were engendered. It was an age of inventions and technological development which, inevitably, quickened the pace of life and transformed the nature of communications. The building of canals, roads, bridges, railways and steamships, photography, the electric telegraph, the telephone, the phonograph and wireless, the penny post, the typewriter, the sewing machine, the bicycle and, at the very end of the century, the motor car – all these revolutionized different aspects of daily living, as did the introduction of gas, piped water and electricity. Almost everything could be done much faster and much more could be crowded into the day. This added a dynamic quality to the constant awareness of change and perhaps fuelled some of the energy and enthusiasm for work so characteristic of the period.

The hard work or 'concentrated industry', as one writer has aptly described it,[2] of the nineteenth century is one of its notable features and work took on the aura of a religion for many people (without supplanting conventional faiths in this highly religious

had followed the Industrial Revolution. The essential unity of the nation and the flexibility of its parliamentary system helped it to withstand the political unrest which swept through Europe in the 1830s and 1840s. The Reform Bills of 1832 and 1867 extended the franchise and altered the basis of political representation to create a more democratic form of government, no longer dominated by the aristocracy or landed interest. It was a climate which fostered economic expansion, both at home and abroad.

The nineteenth century in Britain was an age of prosperity. Until the last three decades there was not only an enormous accumulation in material wealth but also a significant diffusion of wealth which benefited, in particular, the middle classes in period). Hard work was the foremost of several virtues, now popularly described as 'Victorian values', which included thrift, sobriety and self-help. This essentially middle-class social philosophy was encapsulated in Samuel Smiles' best-selling work, *Self-Help*, published in 1859. One of his favourite maxims was 'the frugal use of time'.

There was a wide range of emotional responses to the challenges of nineteenth-century life. On one hand there was a feeling of optimism: enthusiasm and excitement about change and a faith in progress, an enjoyment of prosperity and the ambition to create more. While this appears, on occasion, to have led to a feeling of complacency, of smugness and philistinism, there were at the same time many people who found the rate of change alarming and were troubled by a sense of insecurity. A number were also shocked and distressed by the inequalities in society, by poverty, disease and the working conditions of much of the population. These were highlighted by artists and writers, of whom Charles Dickens is probably the most famous. The humanitarian impulse and demand for reform were as typical of the Victorian age as its apparent complacency and are illustrated by the number of Parliamentary Acts dealing with such issues as the emancipation of the Roman Catholics and Jews, the Poor Laws, Factories, Education and Married Women's Property.

An earnest moral outlook was applied to every aspect of life. A particular area of concern was the introduction of machinery and coming to terms with the machine-made object. While many liked the modernity, perfect finish and availability of manufactured goods, there were others who deplored their poor design and the public's lack of discrimination, especially over some of the exhibits in the Great Exhibition of 1851. The machine was seen as a threat to the craftsman, sweeping away the knowledge and taste distilled from centuries of experience. The fear of losing social values and traditions and a rejection of the materialism of contemporary life encouraged a nostalgia for the past. Britain in earlier historical periods seemed more stable and secure, with higher ideals and greater virtues. The past was romantically portrayed in literature and in painting and a common feature of both architecture and dress was the revival of earlier styles.

New wealth and opportunities created a more fluid social structure which, though it benefited many who had achieved financial success, tended to blur the old distinctions of birth, breeding and education. In order to strengthen what was perceived as the old order, complicated rules for manners and clothes were developed and etiquette became an important means of distinguishing one class from another. This was also intended to discourage the attempts of the

3 Letter from Papa. *F. Goodall, c. 1855.*

The Victorian ideals of a happy home, loving children and a devoted wife and mother are evoked in this painting.

4 Too Early. J. Tissot, 1873.

Some women's fashions were surprisingly seductive in the Victorian period and evening dresses could be cut with very low necklines slipping off the shoulders. The frothy decoration of frills and flounces helped to create the undulating curves of the 1870s silhouette.

ambitious to ascend the social ladder. The impulse to create a greater uniformity of social behaviour was an outcome of the underlying sense of insecurity.

Another response to the pressures of nineteenth-century life was to place more importance on the home and the family. The home was seen as a safe haven from the unpleasantness of the outside world, to which the men of the family could retreat from their daily work; it was the place where children could be safely brought up and where morality was taught; it was the source of comfort, relaxation and happiness. The ideal of the home served to define the respective roles of the men, women and children within it and within society at large. Men, therefore, were the providers and their work was of great importance; they

were expected to be strong, reliable and businesslike. Women were the creators of the home and the guardians of virtue; they were dependent on men but within their own sphere they could exert an enormous influence for good. Marriage and the bearing of children were thus regarded as the natural and most desirable career for a woman. She was expected to make herself attractive, affectionate, virtuous and submissive to the men in her family. Children were welcomed and large families were usual but discipline was considered important. Although the notion of childhood innocence was widely held, there was an anxiety to preserve it from the corruption of adult sin and to develop moral character.

These are stereotypes which were frequently belied by reality, but as ideals to

5 The Dinner Hour, Wigan. *E. Crowe, 1874.*

In stark contrast to Tissot's glossy image of fashionable society, Eyre Crowe gives a picture of young factory girls taking a break from work. None of them wears a bustle and each has her hair dressed in the netted snood fashionable some ten years earlier.

which many people aspired they point to certain features of nineteenth-century fashionable dress. In men's clothes of the Victorian period there was an increasing emphasis on 'manliness': male dress became uniformly dark and practical, with a gradual elimination of unnecessary shaping and ornamentation. The fashion for beards, moustaches and whiskers underlined a masculinity of appearance. In women's clothes there are obvious conclusions to be drawn from the restricting nature of highly decorative garments, tightly laced corsets and long, full skirts. During the middle decades of the nineteenth century it would seem as if women were imprisoned or made dependent by their clothes, they also appear to be set apart by them; the cage crinoline petticoat and even the bustle putting a distance between them and the approaching male, as if women were unassailable and untouchable. Towards the end of the century this effect disappeared and women began to signal their attempts at independence by

adopting masculine features of dress such as tailored jackets, shirts with collars and ties and hard hats. Children's clothes had a measure of comfort and freedom at the beginning of the century which they were to lose later, and there seems to have been an element of harsh discipline in the very elaborate, stiffly starched 'Sunday best' clothes they were obliged to wear at the close of the period. Very often, though, children's clothes anticipated adult fashions and some of their more informal garments of the late nineteenth century looked towards the easier styles of the present century.

The Victorian era is so often associated with prudery and modesty in dress that some fashions appear surprisingly provocative. While the legs and feet were almost always covered by full-length skirts, the neck and shoulders were often exposed and in evening dress there could be a near-naked effect with a very low-cut neck and a shoulder seam dropped over the top of the arm. In the late 1870s some observers were

21

scandalized by the fashion for tie-back dresses whose tightly fitted skirts revealed a clear outline of the woman's hips and legs. The twentieth-century tendency has been to attribute Freudian theories of sexual repression to such fashions, but if there is an element of truth in this view (which is questionable), these styles may also be open to other interpretations.[3]

As in other periods in the history of fashion, the nineteenth century saw a constant re-shaping of the human figure. The fashionable silhouette underwent more frequent and radical transformation than perhaps at any other time. This was achieved through the widespread use of the tightly laced corset to repress the waist and artificial aids such as the crinoline frame and the bustle to distend the skirt. A corresponding enlargement or tightening of the sleeves helped to create the variety of body shapes, each of which was carefully balanced by the size of the head (which in turn was controlled by styles of hairdressing and head-dresses). The slim, column-like silhouette at the beginning of the century was gradually transformed into the curving, hourglass shape of the early Victorian period, then into the S-shaped profile of the 1870s and 1880s and the distinctive line of the mid-1890s, resembling the letter X, before finally easing out into the narrower, sinuous curves of the turn of the century. Although more marked in women's dress, these shapes were carried through into men's fashions which echoed the prevailing line – for example, by an emphasis on the shoulder line, or by narrowing the waist and widening the skirts of the coat. For most of the period children's garments followed the shape of adult clothes.

Change, prosperity and the new technology of nineteenth-century British life had a profound effect on dress. Fashions began to alter more quickly with the improvements in communications and they were stimulated by the greater demand for fashionable goods that came with increasing wealth. Mechanization in the textile industries brought a wider range of materials at more affordable prices, and the invention of the sewing machine not only made the mass production of clothes a viable proposition in the second half of the century but also enabled the home dressmaker, with the aid of paper patterns, to copy the fashionable styles with more ease. Although most garments continued to be partly made and finished by hand and were therefore less standardized than clothing in our present century, this period saw high fashion becoming available to a much wider section of the population. The poor still depended on the second-hand market for many of their clothes but towards the end of the century wholesale manufacture brought down the prices of new garments to within the reach of many more people.

The aim of this book is to trace the development of fashion in the nineteenth century, examining the evolution of styles in dress for men, women and children, both in relation to the construction of the garments and their social context. The work is confined to the British Isles although some consideration is given to French fashion which for most of the period was a dominant influence. The emphasis has tended to fall on the fashions of the middle and upper classes, partly because when evaluating fashion it is usually necessary to look at it in its purest form, at the source of the style, rather than in its more dilute state when it has filtered down to a wide number of wearers; and partly because the dress of the middle classes reflects one of the most influential elements in British society at the time.

-1-
CLASSICAL INSPIRATION
Women's Dress 1800-1825

The New Silhouette

As the nineteenth century opened a distinctive style of dress for women was already established. Fashionable dresses had a low neckline, a plain short-waisted bodice and a long skirt falling in easy folds to the ground and extending into a train at the back. For evening or formal wear sleeves were generally short and gently puffed; the daytime or less formal version of this dress had long sleeves and the bodice filled in high to the neck. The fashionable colour was white, both for morning and evening wear, and although other colours could be worn white was generally regarded as correct, elegant and refined. The most popular dress fabrics were muslin, lawn and other similar types of finely woven cotton or linen. Their soft, light texture was an important element, contributing to the effect of graceful drapery over the limbs. During the first decade of the century the essential features of this style, the raised waistline and long column-like silhouette, hardly altered apart from a few modifications and they persisted well into the second decade.

Although the purest expression of this form of dress appeared to coincide with the beginning of a new century it had begun to emerge several years earlier and by the late 1790s it had already evolved. By that date

women's dresses were almost invariably made of lightweight cottons in white or pale colours, while the waistline had been rising since the early 1780s. In comparison with the formality of mid-eighteenth century dress with its stiff silks and artificial shapes created by boned stays and hooped petticoats this new style of dress had seemed much simpler and lighter, giving women a new sense of ease and freedom of movement. This may have been an expression, in part, of the atmosphere of political change and reaction against established authority following the American and French Revolutions; and of the romantic mood of the later eighteenth century with its interest in the natural world, the imaginative and the picturesque and its emphasis on informality. The romance of other times and of other places was an important element of this romantic spirit and was to provide a fund of inspiration for fashionable dress in succeeding decades. At the turn of the century the predominant interest was in the classical period and there were conscious attempts to evoke the clinging draperies of antique statues in the long flowing skirts of the fashionable white gown. Although classical in content this was essentially a romantic impulse, and the attraction

6 The Bridges Family. J. Constable, 1804.

The simple white muslin dresses worn by women at the beginning of the century were inspired by the neo-classical taste but had appeared in the dress of young girls several decades earlier. An interesting aspect of fashion in the late eighteenth and early nineteenth century was that children's clothes, rather than following the line of adult styles, were for once a step ahead of them (small boys adopted trousers before they became fashionable for adult men).

lay more in the charm of dressing up as a Greek or Roman maiden than in striving after the cool formality, order and restraint of true classicism. Within a few years, in fact, other sources of inspiration were discovered so that 'Gothic' ornament, expressive of the early and later mediaeval periods, could be seen in close proximity to the neo-classical, together with exotic features culled from oriental dress and European costume, fanciful aspects of pastoral dress and even adaptations of military clothing. It was to be an intermixture of tastes, with the classical leading the field in the first decade of the century but the Gothic gaining ascendancy from thereon.

Under the influence of the neo-classical taste the line of women's dress was gradually narrowed and refined to give the impression of light, flowing drapery. In 1800 this effect had not yet been fully achieved as the gown still retained much of the fullness and roundness that had been characteristic

of the 1790s. During that transitional period the skirt was amply cut, with extra fullness gathered in to the back, and there was an emphasis on the bust with the fashionable 'pouter pigeon' shape of the 1780s and 1790s being created by softly draped cross-over bodices and large muslin neck-handkerchiefs bunched up under the chin. Elizabeth Grant could remember her mother in 1802, for example, 'with dark hair curling all over her head in a bush close to her eyes, white shapeless gowns, apparently bundled up near the chin without any waist visible.'[1] After about 1805 this amplitude was reduced by cutting the skirt a little straighter, with less fullness at the front, so that it fell in a smooth line from just under the bust, and by lightening the layers of underwear beneath. Although in France it was said that women abandoned their stays altogether and most, if not all of their petticoats, the trend was less radical in this country. Certainly there is no evidence of

7 Full Dress. Miroir de la Mode, *1803.*

Trains were fashionable, especially with full evening dress, until about 1806. Also illustrated in this plate are the dress accessories of the period: a long boa of swansdown or fur, silk ribbon 'armlets', long fabric gloves and heelless satin slippers. The small, essential items usually carried in a pocket, such as a handkerchief, smelling-salts and money, were now placed in a handbag or reticule so as to preserve the smooth flow of the skirt. Turban-style caps were often worn in the evening. (In spite of its French name, the Miroir de la Mode *was an English magazine.)*

English women appearing in public with no underwear or that their muslin gowns were dampened to cling more closely to the figure. It would appear that most women continued the eighteenth-century practice of wearing stays although they were now lighter in construction with less boning. There was a more natural shaping over the bust and the stays were lengthened over the hips to give a smoother, more sinuous line under the short-waisted gown. The stays were worn over a long linen shift, the basic undergarment for all women in the nineteenth century, and over this came a petticoat of light cotton (or fine wool in winter). In addition to this it became fashionable with 'full' or evening dress to wear a coloured silk or satin slip under the white muslin gown. This again would have helped to give a smooth line to the dress, while the glossy surface of the silk was an ideal foundation for the fluid lines of the muslin skirt. Elizabeth Ham, recollecting the clothes she wore to a ball in Ireland in the early 1800s wrote, 'I was very particular with my dress that evening. My gown was a very delicate sprigged India muslin over a bodice of blue satin. It sat beautifully about the waist.'[2]

A certain amount of fullness was retained at the centre back of the skirt, gathered into the waist seam, and this allowed the dress to fall in ample folds round the legs. The effect of flowing drapery was enhanced by the addition of trains and these were fashionable until about 1806. Trains were thought to be particularly graceful for evening wear although they required careful management. Susan Sibbald made a point of practising and acquiring the way of sweeping her train 'elegantly around on entering a room to prevent it being caught in the door.'[3] For dancing they could be pinned up, but there are contemporary references to trains sweeping along the floor of the ballroom and accidents sometimes occured. Elizabeth Ham was mortified when she opened a ball in Ireland: 'to enter gracefully, of course, I had dropped my long train. Mary [her sister] was just behind, staring about I suppose, she put her foot on it – crack it all went out

8 Miss Harriet and Miss Elizabeth Binney. J. Smart, 1806.

White was fashionable for formal wear but coloured muslins were also worn. Miss Harriet Binney's dress (left) is blue, trimmed with white. The one-piece, round gown could fasten either in front or behind and the front bodice ties of Miss Elizabeth Binney's dress can be seen on the right. Both girls wear their hair arranged in a 'Grecian' style ornamented with jewelled combs although there was a restrained use of jewellery at this date.

of the waist behind. I gathered my dress up in my hand, as well as I could, and on reaching Mrs Jones begged her to put a few pins in it.'[4]

Short overdresses or tunics, reminiscent of the Greek *chlamys* could also reinforce the classical image, and the hair was carefully cut and arranged in a consciously 'antique' manner. Following the styles of Ancient Greek and Roman busts, short curls and loose tresses were caught up in fillets or bandeaux to look as natural as possible. Decoration on the dress was restrained and, although white embroidery and woven patterns were often used to lighten the monotony of plain white muslin, the designs were delicate and frequently incorporated classical motifs. Nothing was allowed to interrupt the pure line of this fashion during the first few years of the century, and even accessories to dress were kept deliberately plain and simple.

Although the finest-quality muslins with their very soft, light textures could be diaphanous the dress itself was not intended to be transparent. The aim of this style was to create an effect of drapery which would subtly hint at and enhance the natural contours of the famale figure. 'Propriety' and 'neatness', in fact, are two words that appear regularly at this time, not only in the work of Jane Austen but also in contemporary fashion magazines. It is perhaps not surprising that these qualities were admired at a time when fine white muslin was the most fashionable dress fabric. White might recall the statuary

9 Full Dress. The Lady's Magazine, *1808.*

The neo-classical inspiration is evident in this evening dress, with its overtunic in the style of a Greek chlamys, *and the classical motifs used for ornamenting the gown and head-dress. This taste also exerted an influence over children's clothes, encouraging the adoption of lighter, looser garments which allowed them freedom of movement and did not distort the natural lines of their young bodies.*

Engraved for the Lady's Magazine.

London Fashionable Full Dress.

of Ancient Greece and Rome but it could also imply social status and refinement. Although cottons and linens were less expensive than the elaborate dress silks of the eighteenth century, the finest muslins and lawns were still quite costly, especially with the addition of skilful white embroidery. Unlike silk, muslin washed very well, making it possible to indulge freely in the fashion for white; but white gowns were not practical, they soiled easily and only those with means and leisure could afford to change them frequently. Edmund Bertram in *Mansfield Park* thought that 'a woman can never be too fine while she is all in white',[5] but it is evident that white was only considered proper to certain social stations. It was thought pretentious for servants to wear white gowns and even for ladies when their circumstances did not warrant it. In Susan Ferrier's novel *Marriage* the Douglas aunts disapproved of their great-niece's upbringing in Scotland: 'it was a shame to hear of a girl of Mary's age being set up with tea to

her breakfast, and wearing white petticoats in winter – and such roads too!'[6] In the evening white was always correct but coloured gowns were often worn during the day. Barbara Johnson's album, a collection of fabric samples of the clothes she wore between 1746 and 1822, reveals a surprising number of brightly coloured and boldly patterned materials used for dress in the first two decades of the nineteenth century.[7]

Muslin dresses appear to have been worn into the winter season but warmer fabrics such as heavier cottons and linens, fine wool and silk were acceptable for daytime and evening dress in the very cold months. Slips or underdresses and flannel petticoats could give extra warmth without spoiling the effect of the gown, and out of doors the spencer and the pelisse gave additional protection. The spencer was a very short jacket cut on similar lines to the bodice of the gown; it had long sleeves and fastened high to the neck. As a light covering it was probably warmer than it might appear, especially if it was made of woollen cloth, because Jane Austen mentions that her 'kerseymere Spencer is quite the comfort of our Evening walks' in June 1808.[8] Spencers had been fashionable since the 1790s and were made both of silk and wool in a wide range of colours. The pelisse was a coat-like garment and like the dress it had a raised waistline and a long, narrow skirt. It had first appeared in England in 1799 and was already fashionable by the late autumn of 1800.[9] Short versions of the pelisse, to the hip or the knee, were common during the first decade of the century but after 1810 it was usually ankle-length and followed the lines of the dress. In later years, from around 1817 to 1850, the pelisse robe was a fashionable type of coat-dress which could be worn both in and out of doors. Suitable footwear was made to correspond with day dresses and outer garments. Ackermann's *Repository of Arts* in spring 1810 advised: 'With the evening costume, the Grecian slipper, sandal, and simple shoe of queen silk, satin, or kid, is at your choice. In the morning habit, the half-boot prevails over every other,

10 Cheltenham Summer Dress. La Belle Assemblée, *1809.*

The romantic appeal of pastoral dress can be seen in this plate. The description reads: 'A Flushing hat of white Italian chip, a cap of the same material appearing underneath, ornamented with a wreath of oak-leaves and acorns, bound round the edge with blossom-pink ribband. Round dress of jaconet muslin . . . slashed Spanish front . . . Gaitered slippers of blue kid and yellow jean. Gloves of York tan . . . Gold hoop earrings.'

and is most fashionable when formed of materials similar to the pelisse or mantle.' Later that year, the magazine said, 'we generally appear till dinner in half-boots of silk, the colour of our ribbons or pelisses.'[10]

During the first two decades of the century ladies' magazines make references to the 'Grecian' and 'Roman' aspects of fashionable dress, but these are not as fully explored as one might expect. Perhaps the clearest exposition of this style came with the scholarly works which were quite independent of the fashion periodicals and appeared just as the classical inspiration was on the wane. These included Thomas Hope's *Costume of the Ancients* published in 1809, *Designs of Modern Costume* illustrated by Henry Moses for Thomas Hope in 1812 and a lesser-known work, Thomas Baxter's *An Illustration of the Egyptian, Grecian and Roman Costume,* with forty 'outlines from the Antique', published in 1814 (with a dedication to the painter Henry Fuseli, dated July 1810). These books were intended to be

a reliable source of information and inspiration to artists and designers as well as a guide to the correct interpretation of antique costume when creating new styles in modern dress. Ackermann's *Repository* considered Hope's *Costume of the Ancients* to be an extremely important work and in June 1809 thought it was to this that 'the late change in dress' was principally to be attributed: 'indeed, to the exertions of this gentleman almost all our modern improvements in taste may be referred. It is hoped the publication alluded to will become the *vade-mecum* and toilet-companion of every lady distinguished in the circles of fashion.'[11] No doubt some ladies followed this advice, but by this date the fashion commentators had already become distracted by other lines of thought.

The romantic appeal of pastoral dress was a legacy of the later eighteenth century and was still evident during the early years of the nineteenth. There are frequent references in the *Lady's Monthly Museum,* for instance, to 'gypsy' bonnets and hats (made of straw, with a low crown and wide flat brim often tied down under the chin) trimmed with flowers and ribbons, 'cottage' and 'woodland' bonnets and 'gypsy' cloaks (perhaps a fanciful name for the traditional scarlet cloth cloak with a hood worn by women of all classes in the British Isles during the eighteenth and well into the nineteenth century). Something of the potential incongruity of this fashion is suggested by Elizabeth Grant when she described a friend in 1809: 'Grace Baillie was with us with all her pelisses, dressing in all the finery she could muster, and in every style; sometimes like a flower-girl, sometimes like Juno; now she was queen-like, then Arcadian, then *corps de ballet,* the most amusing and extraordinary figure stuck over with coloured glass ornaments, and by way of being outrageously refined.'[12]

The charm of foreign parts and 'peasant' dress also had its appeal, partly heightened by the campaigns of the long war with France. The light cloaks and mantles fashionable for outdoor wear lent themselves to a variety of different styles and names such as the 'Spanish' and 'Vittoria' cloaks or the 'Pyrenean' mantle. Other articles of dress were variously described as 'Tyrolese', 'Polish', 'Hungarian', 'Russian', 'Algerian', 'Turkish', 'Egyptian' and 'Circassian'. 'Chinese' parasols in the fashionable pagoda shape reflected a general and long-standing interest in oriental art but probably the most significant fashion from the East was the shawl. Long scarves, of all kinds of fabrics, were worn as a light wrap inside and out of doors but the most costly and highly prized were the genuine Kashmir shawls imported from India. These were made of the very finest and warmest wool with embroidered or woven borders in the traditional pine or cone pattern. Examples in painted portraits of the period are displayed by their wearers with

obvious pride and as Ackermann's *Repository* remarked in June 1809, 'Shawls are much worn; they are admirably adapted to the promenade, as they afford, in the throw and arrangement, such fine opportunities for the display of the wearer's taste.'[13] The soft, graceful folds and draping qualities of real Indian shawls were also ideal for creating a neo-classical effect. In time the shawls were copied and manufactured elsewhere, most notably at Norwich, Edinburgh and Paisley. A more fanciful version of the scarf was the long and narow boa – or tippet as it was often called – made of swansdown or fur, which was fashionable from 1800 to 1810 (and again from the later 1820s). Very large feather muffs were also seen during the early years of the century, but the 'sudden and entire abandonment' of this fashion was noted at the end of 1811.[14]

The classical was by no means the only historical period to suggest itself to the romantic imagination of the early nineteenth century. During the second half of the eighteenth century the neo-classical taste in the fine and decorative arts had been followed by an interest in the Middle Ages, generally referred to as 'Gothic'. By the early 1800s the Gothic taste was just beginning to penetrate fashionable dress, and its terms of reference were wide enough to include the Tudor and Elizabethan periods and sometimes even features of earlier seventeenth-century Stuart costume. Indeed, these were more noticeable than allusions to purely mediaeval dress, although the adoption of very long sleeves reaching over the knuckle may have been inspired by the late fifteenth-century fashion in northern Europe. By 1803 the long plain sleeve of daytime dress had lengthened to well beyond the wrist (flaring at the end to accommodate the width of the hand), and it did not shorten again until the early 1820s.

Another convention of daytime dress was to fill in the low square neckline of the gown with a neck-handkerchief, tucker or chemisette. The chemisette, also known as the habit-shirt, was a sleeveless blouse open at the sides and fastened at the waist.

11 Full Dress. Ackermann's Repository of Arts, *1810.*

By 1810 the Gothic taste had begun to penetrate fashionable dress. The lady's ruff-like collar with vandyke points, laced stomacher front and paned sleeves take their inspiration from the early seventeenth-century period. The little girl wears a plain white muslin frock tucked at the hem and the boy an all-in-one skeleton suit with a frilled shirt. Both girls and boys wore their hair cut in short, natural styles.

12 Hyde Park Walking Dress. La Belle Assemblée, *1810.*

During a period of war women's fashions were influenced by military styles. This dark cloth pelisse with its caped collar and decorative braiding looks like an officer's uniform, as does the bicorne hat trimmed with a large ostrich feather. Even the fashionably huge fur muff has a curious resemblance to a bearskin head-dress. In the winter of 1816 Elizabeth Grant noted that 'an ugly colour called Waterloo blue' was seen everywhere.

devices to suggest the late sixteenth or early seventeenth century period and by 1808 the 'Marie Stuart' or 'Mary Queen of Scots' shape of cap, dipping to a peak at the centre front, was very fashionable. In spite of the short waist of the gown it was possible to add a longer, pointed stomacher to the front of the bodice. 'In full dress', reported the *Lady's Monthly Museum* in January 1809, 'the antique stomacher has again made its appearance, and is likely to be generally adopted, it is chiefly composed of satin, with gold or silver embroidery, and suitable cords and tassels.'[16] This kind of ornament was to become increasingly popular and the war encouraged a borrowing of military trimmings. Spencers and pelisses in particular were decorated with frogging, braid, cords and tassels. In December 1811 ladies were recommended a 'hussar coat, of green Merino cloth, ornamented on each side with dark silk frogs, lined and trimmed with skin', to be worn with a 'military helmet cap composed of the same materials';[17] and in 1815 Elizabeth Grant said she had walked out in Edinburgh 'like a hussar in a dark cloth pelisse trimmed with fur and braided like the coat of a staff-officer, boots to match, and a fur cap set on one side, and kept on the head by means of a cord with long tassels. This equipment was copied by half the town it was thought so exquisite.'[18]

This heady variety of inspiration was greeted with enthusiasm, and by 1812 the classical taste, though still prevalent, was just beginning to seem a little dull. The Gothic taste was gaining ground and as it did so the purity of the earlier line began to disappear; it was interrupted by ornamentation on the bodice, sleeves and skirt, which lost much of its fluidity to become straighter and more angular. For several years, at the height of the war with France and the Continental blockade, Britain was cut off from news of French fashions, and in her isolation tended towards a Gothic eccentricity in dress (which foreigners have always regarded as a national characteristic). The waistline fluctuated, and on several occasions between 1808 and 1814 it was

Separate or attached collars, neck frills and ruffs of pleated muslin, lawn or lace were also worn. Susan Sibbald remembered this fashion for ruffs 'something like Queen Elizabeth's' but with hers, 'only one frill fully quilled stood out round the neck, another much wider lay down on the shoulders.'[15] The 'Medici' collar was another variation which was open at the front to reveal the throat. Simulated slashed or paned sleeves in segmented puffs and vandyked lace collars and cuffs (that is, with a dentilated edge) were two other favourite

13 Walking Dress. Ackermann's Repository of Arts, 1814.

This fashion plate was described as: 'A lilac sarsnet petticoat, full flounce round the bottom . . . high plain body, made of white sarsnet, or jaconet muslin, buttoned behind; long full sleeve, confined at the wrist, and trimmed with a lace ruffle. Full lace ruff. Lilac scarf sash, worn in braces, and tied behind in bows and ends. A Russian bonnet . . . ribbed stockings with lace clocks. Sandals of lilac kid; gloves to correspond.'

becoming increasingly elaborate – silk or satin was often used as an edging or trimming to them. The added weight pulled the skirt into a straighter line and, as it widened towards the hem, it assumed more of an inverted cone shape. The clinging drapery of earlier years soon disappeared and firmer-textured cottons and fine silks were beginning to replace the soft, open-weave muslins. White was still worn but could be combined with strong colours in striking contrast. Again, Jane Austen noted this rather sprightly tendency when she was in London in September 1814: 'I am amused by the present style of female dress; the coloured petticoats with braces over the white Spencers and enormous Bonnets upon the full stretch, are quite entertaining. It seems to me a more marked *change* than one has lately seen.'[21]

Jane Austen was quite correct in noticing a marked change in fashion by the autumn of 1814. The first Peace of Paris in May of that year had allowed British travellers to visit France once again, and they were surprised to find the French fashions had moved along different lines from their own: waists were much higher and skirt hems wider and more extravagantly trimmed. The French, in turn, professed amazement at the British lack of style and did not hesitate to caricature this in a series of engravings. Horace Vernet in *Le Bon Genre*, in particular, gives us a picture of the British as seen through French eyes: with long waists and bodices made ungainly by stiff, jutting corsets, plain dull skirts of a bulbous shape narrowing at the ankle and small flat hats. These features were greatly exaggerated, but British fashion was quick to take the hint and follow the lead of France by adopting the high waistline, highly trimmed and flared skirt and large bonnets of the kind to be seen in such elegant French fashion plates as the 'Costumes Parisiens' of the *Journal des Dames et des Modes*. The Congress of Vienna, which opened in November 1814 and lasted for almost a year, brought together the rulers, statesmen and leaders of European society. This brilliant

lowered quite considerably. Jane Austen remarked on this to her sister in January 1809 when she supposed that Cassandra's six weeks' absence from home 'will be fully occupied, were it only in lengthening the waist of your gowns';[19] and in 1812 many fashion plates illustrated a waistline only two or three inches above the natural level. In October 1813 another significant change was noted by Jane Austen when she told her sister that a Miss Chapman 'had a double flounce to her gown. You really must get some flounces. Are not some of your large stock of white morning gowns just in a happy state for a flounce, too short?'[20] Frills and tucks were now added to the hem of the gown and soon began to spread up the skirt,

*14 Costumes Anglais.
Le Bon Genre, 1814.*

*During the war on the
Continent Britain was
cut off from French
fashions and when the
first visitors arrived in
Paris after the peace
treaty of 1814 their
clothes appeared out of
place. The French were
quick to ridicule the
British for their
seemingly long-waisted
gowns, stiff corsets,
bulbous skirts and fussy
ornaments.*

gathering and the attendant social activities gave a new impetus to the fashion industry and helped to disseminate an international style in high fashion.

A vivid description of the clothes worn by a young woman coming out in Edinburgh society at this time is given by Elizabeth Grant in her *Memoirs of a Highland Lady*. In the spring of 1814, she writes, 'I was furnished with a new occupation. My mother told me that my childhood had passed away; I was now seventeen, and must for the future be dressed suitably to the class "young lady" into which I had passed. Correct measurements were taken by the help of Mrs Mackenzie, and these were sent to the Miss Grants of Kinchurdy at Inverness, and to aunt Leitch at Glasgow [i.e. to dressmakers in Inverness and Glasgow]. I was extremely pleased; I always liked being nicely dressed, and when the various things ordered arrived, my feeling rose to delight. My sisters and I had hitherto been all dressed alike ... I now burst out full-blown into the following wardrobe. Two or three

gingham dresses of different colours very neatly made with frills, tucks, flounces etc. Two or three cambric muslins in the same style with embroidery upon them, and one pale lilac silk, pattern a very small check, to be worn on very grand occasions – my first silk gown. A pink muslin for dinner, both prettily trimmed, and some clear and some soft muslins, white of course, with sashes of different colours tied at one side in two small bows with two very long ends. In the bright, glossy, pale auburn hair no ornament was allowed but natural flowers ... The best bonnet was white chip trimmed with white satin and very small, very pale, blush roses, and the new spencer was of blush-rose pink. Then there were pretty gloves, neat shoes, silk neckerchiefs, and a parasol. Fancy my happiness.' For her début at Inverness, she went on to say, 'new dresses had come for my decoration, and beautiful flowers ... There were white muslin with blue trimming, shoes to match, and roses; white gauze, pink shoes and trimmings, and hyacinths; pearl-grey gauze and pink, and a

Bacchus wreath of grapes and vine leaves, for we had three balls, dinners before the first two, and a supper after the last. With what delight I stepped into the barouche which was to carry us to this scene of happiness!'[22] Most of Elizabeth Grant's clothes were made by Scottish dressmakers, but she and her mother also had dresses from a fashionable court dressmaker in London and were able to follow fashion quite closely.

This account gives an idea of the range of a woman's wardrobe in the first decades of the century. By 1800 the one-piece gown had become usual although it was still possible to wear a two-piece gown open at the front to reveal a 'petticoat' or underskirt in the eighteenth-century manner. The one-piece gown had its origins in the loose, flowing chemise dress which had become fashionable in France in the 1780s and soon spread to the rest of Europe. Popularized by Queen Marie Antoinette, the *chemise à la reine* was a new, informal garment which particularly lent itself to the lines of the neo-classical taste.[23] As its name implied, it was a simple, shift-like garment, cut all-in-one and put on over the head; it fastened with drawstring ties at the neck and waist or sometimes just with a sash tied under the bust. For most tastes, this style was too suggestive of undress wear to be suitable for formal occasions and by 1800 a more structured version had evolved. This was cut with a separate bodice and skirt joined by a waist seam and was similar in appearance to the white muslin or lawn 'frocks' which had appeared in the dress of young girls as early as the 1760s. These low-necked, short-sleeved dresses with waist sashes were originally worn by infants but were then carried on into the second or third year and by the 1780s girls were wearing the dresses well

15 The Arrival of Country Relations. *A. Carse, c. 1812.*

This domestic scene by a Scottish painter shows the ladies in day dress. The low neckline of the one-piece gown is filled in with a habit-shirt or chemisette and sleeves are long. The elderly lady wears a cap and shawl, carrying over her arm the scarlet hooded cloak worn out of doors by women of all social classes in the British Isles during the eighteenth and early nineteenth century.

16 The Cloakroom, Clifton Assembly Rooms. *R. Sharples, 1817.*

In 1816–17 the waistline reached its highest point and the skirt began to flare out in a smooth A-line. The use of firmer-textured silks and added ornament at the hem gave the dress a more conical shape. However, the lady on the far left illustrates the characteristically hunched look which resulted from a very narrow bodice and skirt fullness at the level of the shoulderblades.

into their teens.

The one-piece dress was referred to as a 'round gown' in British fashion periodicals of the 1790s and Barbara Johnson's album records one made for her in December 1798. Jane Austen also described in great detail a round gown she was having made by a Bath dressmaker in May 1801.[24]

Bodices, Waistlines and Bonnets

The fastening of a round gown could be at either the front or back. From 1800 to 1810 front fastening arrangements, surviving from the eighteenth century, were common. In effect, the dress could have a bib or fall front, which was lifted up and fastened on the shoulders with pins or fabric-covered buttons while the skirt was secured by ties at the waist. The ties usually passed round the back and were brought forward to fasten in a bow at the front which can be seen in many contemporary portraits. A separately cut bodice gave a certain amount of support to the bust and a more secure fit was achieved by an arrangement of two flaps inside, attached to the bodice lining; these were crossed over the bust and pinned in place under the bodice. In another version of this gown the bodice was joined at the shoulders and fastened at the centre front but the skirt had a fall front and was lifted and fastened separately round the waist like an apron. This form was not much used after 1810 but the former was to be found up to 1820. From about 1815 hooks of flattened copper or brass wire could be used for back fastenings and after 1820 this style of dress was usual.

The shape of the bodice altered during the first two decades of the century. At first there was an emphasis on width and prominence: the neckline was low and square, cut in a straight line across the bust, the shoulder sections were narrow and the sleeves were set far back into the bodice towards the centre back. During the second decade this narrow-shouldered effect was eased and the back widened. The neck opening could also be cut in a V-shape or a cross-over bodice might be worn, but in general the low wide neck was preferred. The front of the bodice could be plain and fitted or full, with extra fabric gathered across the front. In 1813 the gored bodice was introduced and its shaped panels gave a smoother and tighter fit over the bust.

With the resumption of regular contact with Parisian fashion at the end of the

17 Evening Dress. La Belle Assemblée, *1825.*

A low neck and short sleeves remained usual with evening dress although long, transparent oversleeves were also worn. Pleated bands of material and trimming applied to the bodice drew the eye downwards and accentuated the narrowness of the waist.

Napoleonic Wars in 1815 Britain continued to follow the high waistline worn in France. During the next three or four years, in fact, the waistline was pushed up to its highest level, settling almost immediately below the breasts in 1816 and 1817. As with many fashions, the line having been explored to its limit it began to lose its interest and a re-action set in. It took a number of years to effect a change and progress was unsteady, but a lower waistline (as much as two inches below the bust) was appearing in fashion plates of 1818 and 1819. By 1820 the waist was undoubtedly descending and it dropped inch by inch to reach a more or less natural level by 1825. An increasing amount of orna-mentation on the bodice helped to push the waistline downwards. With the waist at its highest level there was little room for de-coration, but neck frills, pleated ribbon or ruched fabric were all applied to this area. As the waistline dropped it tightened, and a narrower line was created by the closer fit of the bodice set into a waistband about two inches deep (rather than joined directly to the skirt by a seam). Sashes and belts also began to be worn. After a relatively long period of obscurity the natural waist was emerging as the focus of attention, and a neat, slim line was the new ideal. By 1821 the trim belt was further accentuated by a waist buckle and Maria Edgeworth wrote to her sister: 'No long ends to your sashes at your peril – Steel buckles to belts in the morning gold in the Evening preferred to sashes.'[25]

It was usual for short sleeves to be worn with evening or 'full' dress but from time to time the long sleeves of the daytime seem to have been acceptable for formal wear. In January 1810 the fashion eidtor of Ackermann's *Repository* noted: 'the short sleeve has by no means established itself as I had expected; even in full dress, the long sleeve of lace or of some article of a trans-parent fabric, is generally adopted.'[26] By 1815 the decoration applied to the bodice and skirt was spreading to the sleeves and the shoulders began to widen. By 1818 the sleeve-head was larger and its size might be

18 Dress of checked taffeta, c. 1823.

By the early 1820s the waistline was dropping and sleeves were fuller over the shoulder. The elaborate decoration on the skirt had a three-dimensional quality and hems were often padded and stiffened. Patterned silks returned to fashion for both day and evening wear.

pointed the way to a further enlargement of the sleeve and the distinctive *gigot* or 'leg of mutton' shape which was emerging by 1825.

A transformation in the shape of the skirt was also taking place during these years. It had already begun by 1813 when frills and tucks were added to the hem and by 1815 these had become highly decorative. They multiplied in number, growing deeper and wider as ornament was applied to the flounces themselves in the form of embroidery, scalloped or vandyked edgings and lace trimming. This gave an increasingly three-dimensional character to the decoration. Maria Edgeworth wrote to friends in March 1819 that 'all the fashionable trimmings are of that rolled sort of flounces', going on to say that hems were run with packthread to stiffen them.[27] The additional weight and bulk of the hem encouraged it to shorten but the fall of the skirt was improved by the introduction of gores which enabled it to flare out smoothly in an A-line from the high waist. At the back, however, the extra fullness was retained, being finely gathered into the waist and supported by a small pad or 'bustle' worn under the skirt. The early 1820s saw a continued widening of the skirt and from 1823 the hems of silk dresses were often padded with cotton wool. Dresses as well as sleeves could be of transparent gauze, tulle, or lace with silk trimmings, and these were worn over a brightly coloured silk or satin slip to create a shimmering effect. This fashion was made possible by the development of machine-made net after 1809, although hand-made bobbin lace continued to be admired. Blonde, a creamy and lustrous bobbin lace made from silk rather than linen thread was becoming particularly popular.

In the years following 1815 there was a less controlled use of colour and ornament in dress which required skill in handling. Maria Edgeworth was made aware of this when she visited Bowood House in September 1818 in the company of the ladies Bathurst. 'The simplicity of their dress indeed struck us particularly after all the

accentuated by decorative shoulder-pieces or epaulettes called 'mancherons'. For evening dress in the early 1820s it was very fashionable to add transparent, cuffed oversleeves of gauze or net, either worn over the short sleeve of the gown or attached to the lower edge of it. These oversleeves

19 Promenade Dress. Ackermann's Repository of Arts, *1825.*

The sleeve had begun to swell into the gigot *or leg of mutton shape by 1825. The waistline on fashionable dresses had almost returned to the natural level and the skirt was becoming more bell-shaped. A veil hangs from the brim of the lady's straw bonnet. In sunny weather the parasol offered further protection for the face.*

turmoil the Bath ladies and Bath dress-makers make in vain about this business – plain French white silk frocks with a plain short full sleeve…and plaited blond round the neck and a blond flounce and that's all – a crescent of white gilly-flower or scarlet carnations on the head – morning dresses more shewy – young ladies with a profusion of flowers in straw bonnets and matrons with blond caps and crape bonnets and [more] profusion of lace than anything my poor countrified imagination could have conceived.'[28]

Six months later Maria Edgeworth was

again remarking on bonnets which she thought 'very pretty and elegant but far too large both in crown and leaf'.[29] The tall-crowned French bonnet with a brim spreading round the face had come into fashion in 1814 replacing the generally smaller and lower hats and bonnets worn in Britain until then. The most usual styles for outdoor wear were the 'gypsy' hat with a flat crown and brim, the 'Spanish' hat with a round, flat-topped crown and brim turned up at the front, and a bonnet with a deep brim continuous with the crown and projecting well beyond the face. This often had long ribbon ties crossed over the crown to fasten under the chin. After 1815 the bonnet steadily increased in size and the height of the crown could be further emphasized by ostrich feather plumes or other forms of decoration. Net or lace veils were often worn attached to the bonnet brim to hang over the face, both to give protection from the sun and dust and to provide an attractive trimming. Hats and bonnets could be made of any number of materials, but straw was usual for the summer and for walking. Fine Leghorn or Dunstable straws were used and the bonnets were only lightly trimmed. In the winter, and for more formal wear, bonnets were made of silks, crapes, velvets and even muslins stretched over a framework of cane or wire and these were more generously trimmed. Indoors, married and older women wore white muslin or lace caps, often gathered into a full crown and tying under the chin. These became more elaborate, in line with other fashionable garments, after 1815. In the evening young girls wore simple wreaths and flowers in the hair, but for women well-trimmed evening caps were usual and for more elderly ladies the turban or beret style of cap was thought to be suitable.

-2-
THE ROMANTIC SPIRIT
Women's Dress 1825-1850

Extravagance and Individuality

The first ten years of this period, from 1825 to 1835, marked an individual era in the style of women's dress, and the period was perhaps the most lively, imaginative and extravagant of the nineteenth century. The Romantic Movement was at its height and its effect on dress can be seen in the taste for fantasy and lack of restraint characteristic of the fashions.

The new features of women's dress established by 1825 were explored and developed to their fullest extent: the skirt continued to widen (changing from the inverted cone to a rounded bell-shape); the waist tightened and was made to appear still narrower by the full skirt, oblique V-shape of the bodice and enlarged shoulders. The greatest attention was focused on the sleeves, which expanded rapidly. By day the long sleeve took the full *gigot* shape and by night the short sleeve widened into the aptly named beret shape. The horizontal line across the shoulders was further exaggerated by spreading cape-like collars. By 1835 the sleeve had become so gigantic that it could expand no more, its fullness began to sag, and a change of shape became imminent.

Despite the increasing bulk in women's gowns the effect was by no means heavy. Lightweight dress materials in bright, clear colours and graceful patterns were worn, and less ornate decoration was applied to skirts. Long, fluttering ends of ribbon from the hat or bonnet and waistband of the dress were particularly fashionable and, combined with the shimmering gauzes and blonde lace, there was a feeling of constant movement, buoyancy and exuberance in women's clothes when at their best. At their worst, however, these styles could appear wild, fussy and nonsensical, and the balance was not always easy to maintain.

The form of garments worn by women during the period remained largely unchanged, although there were alterations in cut and construction. The one-piece gown was usual for day and evening wear: it fastened behind and had no train, but there could be several variations in the bodice and sleeves. After 1825 the pelisse robe, a front-fastening dress with a large collar derived from the pelisse, became popular especially as a carriage or walking dress and was usually referred to as a *redingote* in fashion journals. It could also be worn in the evening, as *The Ladies' Pocket Magazine* reported in 1825: 'A fashionable dress for the theatre is a white satin pelisse robe, with the corsage, sleeves, and front, trimmed with large bows of satin at equal distances.'[1] The

20 The Lily. E. T. Parris, 1832.

The Romantic Movement was at its height in the early 1830s. 'The Lily' group of family figures celebrates youth in a consciously charming and sentimental manner. Women's fashions looked back to earlier historical periods for inspiration and in this example the girls' ringlets, low-cut bodices, lace collars and puffed sleeves are reminiscent of the later seventeenth century.

concealed front fastening (generally hooks and eyes) ornamented by a series of ribbon bows was a usual form. By 1831 it was reported that 'gowns of the pelisse form are universally adopted in home-dress.'[2] The pelisse itself as an outdoor garment declined in use as it became increasingly difficult to wear a fitted coat over enormous sleeves. Capes, cloaks and mantles proved more suitable and light wool or silk shawls, which did not crush the puffed sleeve, continued to be worn indoors and for the evening. The shape changed from the long, narrow stole to the more versatile square (folded cornerwise) and it grew larger in size to accommodate the increasing width of the sleeves and skirt. Less practical long scarves were often worn over the shoulders with the ends twisted and hanging down the front of the dress, and fur boas were also fashionable again.

Collars, shoulder capes and fichus were amongst the most distinctive accessories to dress from the mid-1820s to the mid-1830s and they played a part in emphasizing the horizontal lines of the gown. Both separate and attached collars increased in depth and width during the 1820s until they resembled small shoulder capes. This type of collar was, in fact, known as a pelerine, and the fichu-pelerine had long ends which could be secured beneath the waist belt or crossed over the bust to tie round the waist. The pelerine collar was usually made of fine white cotton or linen delicately trimmed with white embroidery or lace, but it could also be of the same fabric as the dress and was often several layers deep. Many collars were attached to chemisettes and, although the spreading collar was customary, tuckers, neck frills and pleated ruffs remained in fashion and filled in the neck opening of the day dress or pelisse robe. One other dress accessory in this category was the canezou, a type of sleeveless bodice of lawn or muslin worn over the dress.

The Rise and Fall of the Sleeve

As in most periods, the area of dress most sensitive to fashion was the sleeve, and these years saw an extraordinary variety and ingenuity in the creation of the required shape. The most characteristic style was the leg of mutton which appeared in a recognizable form in 1824–5. Ackermann's *Repository* mentions sleeves *en gigot* and the *gigot de mouton* shape, 'the upper part being very large, and small towards the wrist', in both these years, and the fashion was well established by 1826. The sleeve was cut in one piece on the cross-grain of the material to give a very large, almost circular sleeve-head which was gathered into the armhole. The sleeve-head steadily increased in size, reaching its fullest extent in the years 1830–33, and its fantastic aspect was reflected in some of the other names given to full sleeves: 'balloon', *à l'imbécile* or *à la folle*. There were other variations on this shape, including sleeves *à la giraffe* which had 'a band round the arm a little

39

21 Pelisse Robes.
Townsend's Parisian
Costumes, *1827.*

*The pelisse robe, a type
of coat-dress, was
particularly
fashionable in the 1820s
and 1830s. Sleeves
were cut in the leg of
mutton shape and
caped collars
emphasized the width
at the shoulderline.
Large and highly
trimmed hats and
bonnets were worn out
of doors. The lady on
the left carries a
patterned shawl for
additional warmth.*

*22 Dinner Party Dress
and Bridal Dress.* La
Belle Assemblée, *1828.*

*The late 1820s saw an
extraordinary variety
and ingenuity in the
design of women's
sleeves. Besides the*
gigot de mouton *or leg
of mutton shape there
were full sleeves caught
in at intervals, known
by such names as* à
l'imbécile, à la folle *and*
à la giraffe.

above the elbow, and another a few inches above that, the space between these two bands is occupied with a *bouffant* [puffing] which prevents the transition from the fullness of the gigot to the tightness of the sleeve from the elbow to the wrist, from appearing too *brusque*.'[3] Full sleeves required support by the end of the 1820s, and when a stiffened lining of book-muslin or buckram proved inadequate, separate sleeve supports were worn. These took the form of down-filled pads, attached to the arms, or a cotton foundation with whalebone hoops.

The gigot, being long, was of course a day sleeve; the alternative for evening wear was a short, full sleeve which extended sideways as far as possible. The so-called beret sleeve achieved this effect by being cut from a complete circle; an opening was made in the centre for the arm and the outer edge was gathered into the armhole. Although short sleeves were usually worn with formal dress, these could be covered by long, almost transparent oversleeves of silk gauze or finely embroidered net. These had appeared in the mid-1820s and were very fashionable; in January 1831 Maria Edgeworth wrote to her step-mother from London: 'I to Miss Gerrard about white blonde gauze sleeves, without which there is little possibility of living – decently.'[4] These were cut suitably full, in the gigot shape, and contributed to the feeling of roundness about the arm. Width could be added to both day and evening sleeves by ornamenting the shoulder line with decorative tabs, epaulettes or mancherons, vandyke points and ribbon bows.

The bodice continued to be draped and trimmed to emphasize its essentially triangular shape – the base of the inverted triangle forming the horizontal line across the shoulders. Pleated or applied bands of material, tucks and piping were applied to the bodice to converge at the centre front of the waistband and suggest a downward movement. Although in theory the level of the waistline had returned to normal by the mid-1820s, in practice – to judge by

23 Queen Adelaide. *W. Beechey, 1831.*

The consort of William IV wears very fashionable blonde lace oversleeves with her velvet evening dress and the waistline is clearly emphasized by a belt. Her hair is elaborately curled and arranged in a variation of the 'Apollo Knot' style.

decade it was not until the late 1830s that a long, pointed line was to become general.

The appearance of the skirt altered during this period, for not only did it steadily increase in width but it also lost much of its former ornament at the hem and ceased to be gored after about 1827–8. Although hems continued to be wadded (that is, a thin layer of padding was inserted at the hem to a depth of about six inches), flounces, frills and rouleaux were abandoned at this date and decoration was confined to deep false hems, horizontal or serpentine bands of embroidery and applied trimming much higher up the skirt, often at knee level. This helped to break the vertical line of earlier years which was also eroded by the addition of gauze, net or lace overskirts to evening dresses. At the same time the skirt began to be made from straight widths of dress fabric pleated or gathered into the waistband rather than from shaped panels widening at the hem. The result was a more rounded bell-shape, and this blunter feel was carried through to the square toes now in fashion for shoes. The skirt was short enough to reveal both the feet and the ankles and this tended to give women a youthful, flirtatious air.

As the skirt widened and the waist narrowed women's underclothing became more important in creating the shape of fashion. Tightly laced stays were almost indispensable beneath the close-fitting bodice to achieve the desired effect of a neat slim waist; they were shaped to the figure with gussets over the bust and hips to create the necessary curves. The stays were boned (pieces of whalebone being inserted between the layers of stout cloth which were reinforced with rows of stitching) and they were still laced at the back. Shoulder straps were also retained until the 1840s but sometimes these had button fastenings 'which enables the wearer, by unbuttoning them, to dress her hair in an evening with perfect ease.'[5]

Full skirts needed the support of more than one waist petticoat (worn over the chemise and stays) and the number in-

surviving specimens in museum collections – many dresses continued to be made with a short-waisted bodice until at least 1835. But in all dresses of this period the waist itself was always indicated by a waistband or separate belt several inches deep, often with a large metal buckle fastening at the centre front or to the side of it. Until the late 1820s the waistline was round, but in 1828 some fashion plates began showing waists dipping to a point at the front; there were also Swiss belts with points above and below the waist. Although fashion magazines were advocating the lower waist at the close of the

creased as the skirt grew larger. To create a firmer foundation one of the petticoats would be made of a stouter cotton or linen with several rows of cording or piping at the hem. Also important to the general shape of the skirt was the bustle, which supported the extra fullness at the centre back and created a slight projection. The bustle consisted of a small, semi-circular pad or an arrangement of stiff cotton flounces tied round the waist by tapes. 'They should not be too large', said *The Workwoman's Guide* of 1838, 'or they look indelicate, and in bad taste.'[6]

The years 1829–33 saw a continuing variety in women's dress while the fashionable line was explored to its limit, but there was no real change in style. The trend of the previous decade towards brighter colours, bolder patterns and different dress materials became a feature of the later 1820s and early 1830s. In 1824 the use of silks and satins in British dress had been encouraged by the reduction of import tariffs from 30 per cent to 15 per cent (foreign silks had been available earlier – often smuggled in from France – but they were very expensive). By 1826 the prohibition on luxury goods was lifted, so that silks and various costume accessories manufactured abroad could be imported in large quantities. The firm, crisp texture of silk was particularly suitable to

the changing shape of dress which required a certain amount of body even when supported by several layers of petticoats. Light woollen cloths, wool muslins and silk and wool fabrics like challis (with a silk warp and fine wool weft, sometimes woven with a satin strip) were also fashionable, and many of these were imported from France. For morning wear and during the summer months, however, cotton was still in demand and clear white muslins were worn for many years to come, especially by young girls, as *The Ladies' Pocket Magazine* pointed out in 1825: 'Dresses of clear India muslin, profusely trimmed with lace, are much worn at dinner parties by very young ladies; yet white is not likely to be so much in favour as the beautiful chintzes and coloured printed muslins now so much in vogue.'[7] A number of the cottons and light wool fabrics were printed in striped, floral patterns and bright – though not brilliant – colours. In the mid-1830s there was a fashion for patterns printed in bright colours on a black or very dark ground.

Patterned fabrics, with either woven or printed designs, were tending to replace applied ornament on the dress, but white embroidery on muslin remained a favoured form of decoration and lace was much admired. Blonde lace in particular was worn on dresses and its lustrous quality was well suited to the taste of the period. In Emily Eden's novel *The Semi-Attached Couple* (written around 1830) the heroine, Helen, 'came in, looking like a genuine angel, so soft and white and bright. It is difficult for the unlearned to explain the component parts of a becoming dress, but some of the party observed that the embroidery of her silk pelisse must have been done at Lyons ... There was also a quantity of shining lace, ordinarily, I believe, termed blonde, floating about.'[8] Helen's husband, Lord Teviot, also brought back a parcel of 'fine lace' he collected for her on a mission to Lisbon and a piece of this – a black guipure lace shawl – was presented to Helen's maid for services rendered. Black laces and nets (of either

Newest Fashions for Sep.ʳ 1831 — Evening and Morning Dresses.

silk or linen thread) were fashionable in the 1830s and 1840s and were often used for evening dresses over a silk foundation in such colours as rose pink and citron yellow.

Perhaps the feature which contributed most to the fanciful and dramatic appearance of women during the period was the arrangement of the hair, which, for evening coiffures, was at its most inventive and ornamental. The hair was often massed to one side of the head, built up in a high chignon or large loops and curls, stiffened with gum arabic or wire, and decorated with combs, flowers, ribbons or 'trembling' ornaments on long glauvina pins (similar to large hatpins with ball heads and decorative chains). The elaborate 'Apollo Knot' was probably the most fashionable of these hair arrangements but there were many variations, including the quieter 'Madonna'

26 Miss Elizabeth Potts. *W. Etty, 1834.*

Etty described his sitter as 'the young lady with tresses like the moon!' and Miss Potts has managed to avoid the worst extravagances of the fashionable coiffures. Her cameo brooch, bracelets, waist buckle and long neck chain (called a sautoir) *illustrate the great liking for jewellery at this date.*

style with a centre parting and the hair smoothed flat over the temples. The extravagance of some coiffures was not wholly approved by contemporary observers, and Emily Eden shows that in well-bred circles a lack of restraint was regarded as bad taste. When Sarah and Eliza Douglas (who were considered a little vulgar) were invited to dine with Lord and Lady Eskdale, Sarah overheard remarks about her sister: 'Mr Trevor came up to Lady Eskdale and said, looking at the flowers and the silver comb in your hair, "Don't you think those silver *épergnes* full of flowers would look better on a dining-table than walking about a drawing-room? I know nothing of dress, but is not that a little in the May-day line – rather chimney-sweeperish?"' Back at home Sarah realized how very pretty Lady Helen had looked, 'She had no flowers in her hair … and her hair was braided quite smooth'; and she 'gave a desperate tug at a highly frizzed set of bows which she had built up on the top of her head with some pride.'[9] Lady Helen would have been more in line with French fashion and it was reported in 1831 that in Paris: 'Many young ladies have no other ornament in their hair than a large tortoiseshell comb; the gallery of which is excessively high and very curiously carved.'[10]

During the day, and when wearing a cap or bonnet, the hair was arrranged in a less ornate manner. From the mid-1820s sausage-shaped side curls spread across the temples and ears from a centre parting (following the horizontal line of the current fashion) and the hair was drawn back in a knot on the crown. Here again the less sophisticated could fall into the trap of overdoing the fashion, as Mary Russell Mitford noted in *Our Village.* Miss Phoebe, daughter of the landlord at the Rose Inn was 'the belle of the village … all curl-papers in the morning, like a porcupine, all curls in the afternoon, like a poodle, with more flounces than curl-papers, and more lovers than curls.'[11] Indoor caps increased in size after 1827 and were profusely trimmed with ribbons, lace and frills to correspond with the taste in dress.

27 The Bridesmaid, The Bride. The Court Magazine, *1833.*

During the day and when wearing a cap or bonnet the hair was arranged in a less ornate manner. The simpler 'Madonna' style, with the hair smoothed flat over the temples from a centre parting, can be seen here. Hats and bonnets were growing smaller by the early 1830s and the upturned brim of the bonnets began to follow a narrower, oval shape.

Another novel set in the 1830s, George Eliot's *Scenes of Clerical Life,* speaks of Mrs Amos Barton's caps, which 'would have been pronounced, when off her head, utterly heavy and hideous – for in those days even fashionable caps were large and floppy; but surmounting her long arched neck, and mingling their borders of cheap lace and ribbon with her chestnut curls, they seemed miracles of successful millinery.'[12] In the evening some caps were little more than an intricate arrangement of large ribbon loops, but for married and older women turbans and berets were the most fashionable style. These were made of silk, satin, velvet or gauze, elaborately trimmed and often tilted to one side of the head, echoing the asymmetric line of formal hair styles. Very large dress hats were also worn, trimmed with ostrich or marabout feathers and wide ribbons in loops, bows or streamers.

The hat was one of the characteristic fashions of this period, possibly because its spreading brim could more successfully create an impression of width than the bonnet drawn down to tie under the chin. Bonnets continued to be worn, and often the distinction between bonnet and hat was very slight. Both had deep crowns and wide, open brims, while many hats of the later 1820s had long loops of ribbon hanging to well below the waist at the back or front of the dress; these were, in effect, bonnet ties that were left loose and uncut. Hats and bonnets had reached an enormous size by 1828, but in the early 1830s they were growing smaller and the upturned brim of the bonnet began to follow a narrower oval shape.

The love of ornament so prevalent during these years coincided with a great liking for jewellery, which often formed part of the dress itself. Paired bracelets, for instance, were frequently worn over the wristband of the long sleeve and could create a decorative finish to gauze oversleeves. These bracelets tended to be broad and often contained an oval miniature or cameo; matching bracelets of velvet ribbon and bead embroidery were also popular. Another fashion of this period was the *ferronnière*, a band or fine chain of precious metal or ribbon worn round the head and crossing the forehead, sometimes with a pendant jewel or ornament at the centre. Long neck chains suspending a watch, eyeglass or scent bottle (which could be tucked into the waistband), necklaces, earrings, jewelled clasps and brooches were also worn in some quantity.

By 1835 the exuberant, billowing lines of female fashion had reached a climax, and during the next two years a change of mood began to be reflected in the increasingly sedate and subdued character of women's clothes. From 1836 dresses lost much of their exaggerated shaping, they became less cluttered with ornament and jewellery and adopted softer, more subtle colours. As sleeves collapsed the waistline lengthened and skirt hems dropped to floor level; women seemed to droop, losing the sprightliness of the earlier 1830s. The new line concentrated on smooth curves and angles in a late flowering of the Gothic taste, and these were to be reflected in the neat, flat shape of the head, sloping shoulders and sharply pointed waistline.

In Britain this change of direction and the sense of a new era opening was identified with Queen Victoria's accession to the throne in June 1837. Although the new

28 Queen Victoria.
A. E. Chalon, 1837–8.

The young Queen's accession in 1837 coincided with a change in mood and a much quieter taste in dress. The hair was dressed very simply and the enormous sleeves had begun to collapse. A popular accessory to dress in the 1830s and 1840s was the apron, worn for decorative rather than practical purposes, although it did save the skirt from soiling. Aprons of black silk or cashmere embroidered in brightly coloured silks were particularly fashionable.

Queen was young, pretty and light-hearted her outlook was essentially serious and she proved an ideal figurehead to the general reaction against the more disreputable, irresponsible or frivolous aspects of social behaviour associated with the reigns of her uncles, George IV and William IV. The mid-1830s also saw the emergence of the middle classes in society as a dominant force in the political, economic and social lives of most European nations; in Britain especially the middle classes were to benefit from political reforms (most obviously from the Reform Bill of 1832) and increasing industrial expansion. What came to be considered as middle-class virtues – hard work, self-improvement, respectability – were the ideals of the Victorian period, and the Queen and Prince Consort were able to set an example in their own domestic arrangements.

In dress, anything which appeared bold or sophisticated was now carefully avoided. The desire to conform, to appear genteel or at least respectable was to some extent the result of the fluid social structure. Gentility was at a premium, and this was one element which contributed to the fashionable image of women in the 1840s; another was the ideal of womanhood being formulated by both men and women at this time. This held women to be dependent on men and that their role in life was a passive one, confined to the sphere of the home and family. The ideal woman was sweet, modest, gentle, shy and serious and her essential goodness was manifest in her pretty looks. The image was later most succinctly summed up by the title of Coventry Patmore's poem of 1854, *The Angel in the House*, whose heroine was 'all mildness and young trust'. These ideas were fostered by the general tendency towards sentimentalism, a symptom of the Romantic Movement in the later 1830s and 1840s. Also symptomatic of the Romantic spirit and of a feeling of insecurity in the wake of rapid industrial progress was a nostalgia for the fashions of earlier periods, in particular those of the seventeenth and eighteenth centuries. These were to prove a source of inspiration for women's hairstyles and the shape and decoration of bodices and skirts.

The change of direction in women's dress in the late 1830s was heralded by the deflation of the sleeves. It was apparent, by 1835, that the sleeve could grow no larger and in that year the immense fullness began to sag slightly. In 1836 a reduction in size came about fairly rapidly and was well-grounded by 1837, although large sleeves were doubtless retained by less fashionable women for a few more years. The process began with the fullness dropping to the level of the elbow and the sleeve tightening in the upper arm, the loose fabric being vertically pleated, ruched or gathered in; the sleeve also fitted closely from below the elbow to the wrist. As usual the new line was introduced in stages and this first phase accustomed the eye to the new shape of the shoulder without abolishing the full sleeve

29 Day and Evening Dresses. Modes de Paris, *1837.*

By 1837 the fullness in the upper part of the sleeve had dropped and the loose material was gathered in to the arm. The waistline was lengthening, dipping to a sharp point at the front, while the skirt continued to widen. The turban-shaped cap continued to be a fashionable evening head-dress for married women.

altogether. For evening dress, the short sleeve similarly shrank in size but the relative plainness of the new shape was relieved by some kind of ornament such as double or triple rows of lace flounces or ribbon. Tight upper sleeves in day dresses of 1837 could be decorated in the same way. Sometimes, reported *Modes de Paris*, 'they are furnished with such an abundance of volans, ruches, bouillons and bows of ribbon, that they are in appearance as voluminous as the bouffant sleeves' but the writer thought it 'in good taste to take the *juste milieu* between all extremes.'[13] By 1840 the fullness round the elbow was much reduced and some day sleeves could be quite tight, but headed by a small oversleeve or mancheron at the shoulder. The short, straight, tight sleeve with trimming was usual with evening dress and by 1845 this was frequently covered by a deep collar or flounce of lace falling from the neck opening. Day dresses by 1845 showed a smooth, sloping shoulder line with the tight sleeve set into a small armhole. A little width lower down the arm was still permissible and after 1843 the sleeve mouth on some dresses flared open to reveal short white lace or muslin undersleeves.

Structural Innovation

A low-cut neck opening on day dresses was quite common until the early 1840s, when a higher bodice was adopted, often trimmed with a small round collar of white cotton or linen. The spreading collars of the earlier 1830s passed out of fashion, although a separate pelerine or shoulder cape matching the dress was often worn. In the evening the bodice had a low *décolletage*, baring the shoulders; the neck opening could be cut straight across, in an oblique V-shape or curved to a point at the front, *en coeur*. As the neckline widened and dropped over the top of the arms the corset (as it was

30 Mrs Bacon. *W. C. Ross, 1841.*

In the evening the bodice had a low décolletage which bared the shoulders. The neck opening was often trimmed with a deep collar or flounce of lace. Mrs Bacon wears her hair in a flat, smooth style from a centre parting, with ringlets falling free on either side.

the figure to the fashionable shape – but in particular they prevented horizontal creasing on the bodice which was especially important when the waistline lengthened. Shaping over the bust was sometimes improved by the insertion of soft pads in the bodice lining to fill the hollow below the collar bone. A useful innovation in the early 1840s was the use of dress-protectors of chamois leather and India rubber under the arms.

An even rounder, fuller skirt was made possible by several means during these years. There was a new method of pleating the skirt and joining it to the bodice which successfully and evenly accommodated an increased amount of material set into a lower, pointed waistline. This was called gauging: the top of the skirt was turned over and drawn up by running stitches into very fine cartridge or organ pleats, which were stitched to the lower edge of the bodice at every alternate fold. This was introduced in 1841 as an alternative to the earlier method of flat pleating or gathering and was used until about 1846, when the bodice and skirt began to be made separately. The jacket bodice which fastened at the front with hooks and eyes or buttons was at first used for day dresses and, although the separate bodice and skirt had become general by the end of the 1840s, the back closure was retained for evening bodices which also tended to have more deeply pointed waistlines. The separate skirt was now pleated (or gathered, if a fine material such as muslin was used) into a waistband concealed by the lower edge of the bodice. The method of close gauging was abandoned in favour of flat pleating and the skirt continued to widen. One of the advantages of the separate bodice and skirt was that an even tighter waist and fuller skirt could be achieved. The Princess Robe, with the bodice and skirt cut in one piece, was tentatively put forward in 1848 but did not meet with success, probably because the shape was not right at that moment.

Constant thought was applied to the problem of stiffening the petticoat well enough to support the swelling skirt, since there

now called) lost its shoulder straps. Until the mid-1840s the dress was made in one piece and fastened at the centre back with brass (rather than copper) hooks and eyes. Very occasionally a skirt might be made with two bodices, one for day and one for evening wear, stitched to the skirt each time when used, but the separate bodice and skirt did not become common until 1846. The waistline was steadily lengthening; it dipped to a sharp point at the centre front between 1836 and 1838 and continued to drop in the early 1840s. The hard, angular line of the bodice, reminiscent of an inverted Gothic arch, was emphasized by single or double rows of stiff piping along the seams and by flat pleats or folds in a pronounced V-shape from the shoulders to the centre point of the waist. A rather similar form of decoration to be found on many surviving dresses of this period was a loose panel pleated fan-wise across the front of the bodice and secured over the shoulders and at the waist. Boning was now usual at the centre front seam (which appeared on most bodices), along the darts on either side of it, in the side seams and sometimes in the back seam as well. The bones helped to create a smooth tight fit, firmly moulding

31 The Bromley
Family. *F. M. Brown,
1844.*

*The three young women
on the right are
fashionably dressed for
the mid-1840s but the
older lady on the left
still wears the frilled
cap and sausage curls
of a decade earlier. A
posy of flowers, in a
metal or paper holder,
was a popular
accessory to evening
dress.*

was a limit to the number of layers that could be worn. A partial solution was found at the very end of the 1830s with the introduction of a horsehair cloth petticoat – of stout linen woven with horsehair and called 'crinoline' (from the French *crin*, horsehair, and *lin*, linen). This was the true crinoline petticoat and the later hooped version is more correctly called an 'artificial' or 'cage' crinoline or crinoline frame. The crinoline petticoat, worn with several ordinary ones, dispensed with the need for the bustle, which was now abandoned. Drawers were in common use by 1840 when *The Workwoman's Guide* mentioned that 'these are worn by men, women and children of all classes, and almost all ages, under the different names of trousers and drawers … Drawers for ladies and children are usually made of calico, twill and cambric muslin.'[14] They took the form of two tube-shaped legs open along the inside seam and linked by a band round the waist.

A device which created the illusion of a wider skirt was the flounce. In the early 1840s flounces were usually only added to evening dresses, but by the end of the decade they were also worn during the day and could be several layers deep, scalloped at the edge or trimmed with piping or embroidery. A variant of the flounce was the double skirt – a dress with a shorter overskirt, often of net or lace – which had become popular for evening dresses by 1842 and for day dresses by 1845. A fashionable way of trimming the front of the skirt in the 1830s and 1840s was *en tablier*, with a panel of decoration in the shape of a long apron. This could also recall the effect of an eighteenth-century open robe, revealing a contrasting petticoat or underskirt at the front. The skirt lengthened after 1836 and as the hem began to sweep the floor again it became usual to add an edging of wool braid to protect the silk from dirt and wear.

32 The Governess.
R. Redgrave, 1844.

Redgrave's poignant portrait of a young and evidently lonely governess illustrates the very modest and demure appearance of women's dress in the 1840s. Her dark, plain clothes and the black-bordered letter she holds suggest that she is in mourning.

The Feminine Ideal

33 Fashions for April 1846.

Loose-fitting mantles and jackets were an alternative to the shawl for outdoor wear. Flounces were added to skirts in the 1840s and emphasized their width. By the second quarter of the nineteenth century children's clothes were beginning to lose their appearance of freedom and simplicity; girls' dresses were following the lines of adult clothes and making more use of woollen cloths, silks and velvets in darker colours.

The quiet, demure aspect of women's dress by 1840 was partly created by the adoption of softer colours and plain or delicately patterned fabrics. Although black was still quite often used in contrast with other colours, the preferred range was in pastel hues. There was a subtler emphasis on texture and the play of light as applied ornament was gradually withdrawn, and this resulted in a particular liking for 'shot' or 'changeable' silks where the warp and weft were of two different colours. Plain silks could be enriched in the evening by the addition of lace, and genuine antique pieces were assiduously collected. Lace was used for deep flounces and bertha collars in the style of women's dresses of the 1660s. An interest in the dress of earlier periods extended to the use of brocaded silks in the eighteenth-century style – original silks, in fact, were often used and a number of eighteenth-century dresses were remade during the years 1835–45.

In 1847 Lady Eastlake considered that the really well-dressed woman 'deals in no gaudy confusion of colours – nor does she affect a studied sobriety; but she either refreshes you with a spirited contrast, or composes you with a judicious harmony. Not a scrap of tinsel or trumpery appears on her. She is quite aware, however, that the garnish is as important as the dress; all her inner borders and beadings are delicate and fresh, and should anything peep out which is not intended to be seen, the same scrupulous care is observable.'[15] Immaculately fresh white collars and undersleeves were an important feature of fashion and gave day dresses of the 1840s and 1850s a refined and dainty air. The shawl could also invest a dress with ladylike qualities: its graceful drapery was thought to enhance a costume and the way it softly enveloped the back and shoulders added to the air of modesty and sobriety in women's clothes. Improvements in weaving, dyeing and printing techniques made a wider choice available, and the *Belle Assemblée* was able to report in November 1838: 'There is really quite a mania for shawls, besides those of Cashmere, which still maintain their ground, we have velvet shawls, satin, and *peluche* ones, and a great variety of fancy shawls.'[16] Light wool or cashmere was preferred for the spring and autumn while lighter-weight fabrics such as muslin or lace were used for summer shawls.

In colder weather the most common forms of outerwear were the full-length cloak and half- or three-quarter-length capes or mantles. These were made in different styles, some semi-fitting and some with sleeves, and they were called by a confusing variety of names, but the general term *pardessus* was often used. The immense popularity of the polka in London in 1845 gave its name to many garments including a form of short tight jacket which a few years later could be simply referred to as a 'polka'.

There was little change in the form of

women's footwear. The plain, heel-less slipper was worn indoors and was made in black or white satin for formal wear, while half-boots of leather, or leather with cloth tops, were still usual for walking. Less of the foot was seen when the hemline dropped in 1836 and 1837 but when it did appear it was expected to look as small and as narrow as possible. This was partly because small hands and feet were associated with gentle birth and partly because it suited the ideal image of women. In 1854 Mary Merrifield was to complain of 'poets and romance-writers' who encouraged women to 'pinch their feet into small shoes'.[17]

Hair arrangements became less fanciful. The Apollo knot had passed out of fashion in 1836 and, as if echoing the line of the deflated sleeves, the fullness at the top of the head drooped downwards from a centre parting. Long loose curls or ringlets hung over the ears and neck while the rest of the hair was tightly coiled into a knot at the back. Ringlets were particularly fashionable from the late 1830s well into the 1840s although

an alternative Madonna-like arrangement, dressed very flat and close to the head with the hair on either side plaited or looped over the ears, was also favoured and was usual by the mid-1840s. The new shape of the head was also reflected in the cap and the bonnet which, like the sleeve, began to shrink in 1836. Day caps, worn indoors, were shaped closer to the head by the early 1840s and later in the decade some younger married women began to leave off wearing them altogether, replacing them with a knot of ribbon. During the late 1830s the wide brim of the bonnet, which had been worn at an angle to the crown, was tilted downwards and in time assumed the funnel shape so characteristic of the 1840s poke bonnet. The deep brim, made continuous with the crown, projected beyond the face and dipped down at the sides. While this shielded the head and reinforced the image of modesty, it was a hampering fashion, making it difficult for women to look about from side to side, as if they were blinkered.

-3-
PROSPERITY AND EXPANSION
Women's Dress 1850-1875

The third quarter of the nineteenth century, from 1850 to 1875, falls within the mid-Victorian period in Britain, a time of expansion in almost every sense of the word. Prosperity and self-confidence increased, especially in the middle classes, British industry and trade were flourishing, the railways opened up new lines of communication and further advances in technology were being made. In 1851 the Great Exhibition in London afforded comparisons to be made between 'our progress as a nation, and that of our continental neighbours, in those various useful and elegant arts which contribute so much to the comfort and enjoyment of life. In many branches of industry the English need not fear competition with any nation...'.[1]

Continental neighbours had been less fortunate in 1848 – the year of revolutions – but fashion was to benefit from the establishment of the French Second Empire in 1852. A glittering court was created by the Emperor Napoleon III and his stylish wife, the Empress Eugénie. After nearly two decades under the lacklustre Orleans monarchy Paris re-emerged as the fashion centre of Europe, and the French Empress herself set a high standard of taste in dress. From the date of her marriage in January 1853 to the outbreak of the Franco-Prussian War in 1870 the British press commented almost daily on her clothes and her appearance. From 1860 much of her wardrobe was made by Charles Frederick Worth, whose career was interrupted, but essentially undamaged, by the war in France and the fall of the Empire in 1871. While Eugénie retired into exile in Britain, Worth resumed his business in Paris; his fame and influence was greater than it had been under the Empress's patronage and ensured the dominance of French fashion until the end of the century.

34 The Great Exhibition Building. *L. Haghe, 1851.*

The Great International Exhibition held in London in 1851 marked a high point in Britain's prosperity and prestige abroad. Women's dress seemed to adapt itself to the mood of the times and there was a sense of increasing size, growing opulence and almost competitive display.

The Expanding Skirt

During the first part of this period, from 1850 to 1865, women's dress seemed to adapt itself to the mood of the times and there was a sense of increasing size, growing opulence and almost competitive display. The skirt continued to widen and was the focal point of fashion. The earlier method of supporting the skirt with multiple layers of petticoats and decorating it with rows of flounces was replaced in 1856 by the 'artificial' or cage crinoline petticoat, and by 1860 skirts had reached their widest extent. The steady expansion of the skirt was complemented by a higher, rounder waistline and wide, open-mouthed sleeves which flared towards the wrists in the pagoda shape. These features pointed to a modification of the essentially vertical and angular line of the 1840s which was gradually softened and blurred, while flounces and other ornaments emphasized the horizontal nature of the silhouette. By the late 1850s men's clothes were also reflecting a more relaxed and easy line with their loosely cut coats and trousers.

Female fashions continued to stress the contemporary ideal of womanhood: form-fitting bodices, tightly laced corsets and swelling skirts which not only enhanced the natural contours of the feminine form but also underlined women's dependent status. After 1850, however, there were some signs that a woman's role might possibly be more active and less home-bound in the future. A few more practical forms of dress began to be introduced such as the looped-up skirt for walking, tailored jackets or cloaks with matching skirts for country wear, and an easy-fitting bodice or blouse with plain dark skirt for informal occasions – ideas which often drew their inspiration from masculine fashion and were to be developed further in following decades. With the invention of the first synthetic or aniline dyes from 1856 a new range of bright colours became available and by the early 1860s women's clothes were presenting a bolder, sometimes even rather aggressive appearance.

The nineteenth-century tendency to seek inspiration from the arts and dress of earlier historical periods or of other countries was a feature of fashion in these decades. The eighteenth century had a particular appeal and there were frequent references to the styles of Louis XIV, XV and XVI throughout this period, but it was in the late 1860s and early 1870s that the eighteenth-century revival found its purest expression. The fullness of the skirt had been gradually swept towards the back and by 1868 was being draped up over the hips in the style of the 1770s polonaise (supported by a 'dress improver' or bustle). Long fichus crossed over the bodice, and ruffled sleeves and straw hats in the shepherdess style completed the image. The early 1870s were characterized by a preference for soft and almost frothy drapery and trimmings which overlaid the foundations of a new line: by 1875 the fashionable silhouette was perceptibly longer and narrower and a vertical emphasis had completely replaced the horizontal line of the mid-1850s.

The late 1840s had seen the introduction of two distinctive features which were to

36 To Let.
J. Collinson, 1857.

Two distinctive features of women's dress in the 1850s were the front-fastening jacket bodice and the flounced skirt. Though fashionably dressed, this rather florid landlady would have appeared vulgar to contemporary eyes with her bold stare at the spectator and her side ringlets which were only worn by young girls by this date.

dominate fashionable women's dress in the 1850s. These were the front-fastening jacket bodice with basques (that is, with an extension which flared out at the hips, sometimes giving the impression of a flounce at the top of the skirt) and the flounced skirt. By 1850 it was usual for the dress to have a separate bodice and skirt and often a silk dress was made with two bodices: one for day wear with long sleeves and a high or medium-high neck opening, and one for the evening, cut low over the shoulders and with short sleeves. The appearance of the day bodice could be varied by the use of small white collars of lace, muslin or cambric with matching undersleeves, or by filling in a lower, V-shaped neck opening with a chemisette. 'Fine linen is more than ever

the true criterion of elegance', commented one fashion writer in September 1850 and in the following spring said: 'All dresses are worn with the body open in front, and wide open sleeves, so as to show in all their beauty the chemisettes and undersleeves, which daily increase in richness and elegance. English embroidery [i.e. *broderie anglaise*] is in high fashion.'[2]

Two variations of the jacket bodice and chemisette were the 'waistcoat corsage' and the jacket worn with a contrasting skirt. The waistcoat had first appeared in 1846 and was fashionable during the late 1840s and early 1850s, despite its masculine connotations. It could be either a real waistcoat beneath the jacket bodice or a stimulated waistcoat front attached to the bodice – and it might be worn with quite formal dress. Jackets of different kinds, for both informal and semi-formal wear, were popular until well into the 1860s. A short, bolero-style Turkish jacket appeared in 1852 for instance (one of several 'Turkish' fashions which were given further impetus by the Crimean War of 1854–6). 'To guard against the chill of evening', it was advised in July 1853, 'Turkish vests are made to put on after dinner, over a light dress. These vests or jackets are rather short, and have no waist … they are worn black, and may, for the sake of elegance, be braided in the same colour, and a single thread of gold may be added. These jackets may also be worn of lighter colours, appropriated to the colours of the dress.'[3]

The jacket bodice with basques gave the waistline a blunter appearance than in the previous decade and there was a noticeable easing round the waist from 1850 to 1855, with less boning in the bodice. The waistline decreased in length and although it was still pointed in evening dress it began to be more rounded in the day bodice. This was probably felt to be allowable because the waist continued to appear small in comparison with the width of the skirt over the hips. Shorter, wider sleeves whose 'Chinese' or pagoda shape echoed the line of the skirt reinforced the impression of dresses expanding and opening up during the 1850s.

The most extreme version of this style appeared in 1857 with the creation of a sleeve from a large square of dress fabric pleated into the armhole and hanging loose from it. This was also described as a sleeve in the 'Greek' form, 'demi-long and wide, and slit open in the front of the arm'.[4] All open-mouthed sleeves of the 1850s were worn with separate undersleeves (or *engageantes* as they were sometimes called) which were tacked on to the sleeve lining or its inside edge, just below the elbow. Undersleeves could be made in the same material as the dress, but more often they were of fine white linen or cotton which was easily laundered. From 1855 the closed 'bishop' sleeve was an alternative shape but the pagoda style remained fashionable until 1860.

Increasing fullness in the skirt was a constant preoccupation, and until the crinoline frame was marketed in 1856 women were obliged to rely on as many as six layers of underpetticoats for support. An illusion of width could also be created by double skirts and flounces which steadily grew in popularity after 1845. In the early 1850s flounces printed or woven *à disposition* were introduced and these emphasized the horizontal line of the skirt. The technique was to print or weave flounces 'in position', as it were, so that the border pattern lay correctly across the skirt (earlier flounces cut on the cross grain showed the pattern in diagonal). The number of flounces could vary from three to seven; three was considered suitable for morning dresses while more could be worn in the evening.

The fuller, rounder effect of women's clothes was completed by the way the hair was dressed and head-dresses worn. A new

37 'Which Looks the Most Ridiculous?' Punch, *1853.*

In 1853 Punch *made fun not only of women's bonnets which were worn so far back as to appear to be falling off but also of men's hats with their very tall crowns and narrow brins (on which 'a lady-bird can about settle, and that is all'). Bonnets were fastened under the chin with broad silk ribbons tied in a large bow. A silk* bavolet *or curtain covered the back of the neck.*

WHICH LOOKS THE MOST RIDICULOUS?

hairstyle, which was popularized, though not invented, by the Empress Eugénie in 1853, gave the face a more open look. Hair *à l'Impératrice* was folded back over softly rounded pads from a centre parting to reveal the temples and ears. Many women continued to dress their hair in the flat, Madonna-like manner but even Queen Victoria modified her style. Lady Eastlake saw her at the Queen's Ball in May 1854 and 'her head-dress was quite new for her – her hair put back, not *à l'Impératrice*, but so far as to show her fine temples and ears – tight to her head, with a level wreath of flowers and diamonds.'[5] Young girls could still wear long ringlets but these were out of fashion for older women by 1852.

Women threw off their blinkered appearance of the 1840s as the bonnet brim opened up and shrank back over the crown. In 1850 the fashionable shape was wide and oval; by 1853 the flared brim had slipped so far backwards it looked as if the bonnet was in danger of falling off altogether (pushed back, to some extent, by the hair puffed out at either side). 'Bonnets are worn very low behind, very wide in front, and are trimmed inside with all kinds of ornaments, which fill up the space between the bonnet and the cheeks.'[6] The new open shape gave women a more confident and inquiring look and fashionable indoor caps revealed very similar features. In 1854 evening head-dresses of flowers were 'becoming displaced by gold and silver, and coloured ribbons; they are placed far back on the head, and they fall down very low on the shoulders.'[7]

For outer wear, shawls were more popular than ever, and their size increased to accommodate the width of the skirt. A fashionable alternative was the mantle, a semi-fitting, three-quarter-length coat. A number of different styles in these loose outer garments continued to be known by the general terms 'pardessus' and 'paletot'. In the evening, the burnous (an adaptation of the Arab garment) was often worn and its distinctive, tasselled hood offered welcome protection against the cold night air.

Problems with the Hoop

The fashion column of *The Illustrated London News* noted on 28 January 1854 that skirts were so full 'that it would be impossible to augment their amplitude, unless hoops such as were worn in the time of Louis XV should be introduced'. Mrs Merrifield in her book *Dress as a Fine Art*, also published in 1854, suggests that these were already in use: 'some ladies of the present day have returned to the old practice of wearing hoops to make the dresses stand out at the base. These are easily recognized in the street by the "sagging" – no other term will exactly convey the idea – from side to side of the hoops, an effect which is distinctly visible as the wearer walks along. It is difficult to imagine what there is so attractive in the fardingale [sic] and hoop, that they should have prevailed in some form or other for so many years ... Who could imagine that there would be an attempt to revive the hoop petticoat in the nineteenth century?'[8] But this was an idea which must have suggested itself some years earlier since a registered design for an 'inflatable rubber petticoat' to distend the skirts of fashionable dresses was officially registered in 1848. Possibly it was this, or another like it, which was parodied by *Punch* later that year and in both illustrations rubber tubes were shown for inserting at the hem of the petticoat.[9] However, an artificial support of this kind does not appear to have come into general use until 1856, the year in which the metal cage crinoline was patented and marketed in the United States, Britain and France by the American, W. S. Thomson. During the summer of 1856 crinoline jokes and cartoons began appearing in *Punch* and its first illustration of an actual crinoline frame was published on 23 August.

In its earliest form the cage crinoline was a cotton or linen petticoat reinforced with hoops of cane or whalebone. The Bessemer steel process of 1856 made it possible, by the following year, to use sprung steel or

38 Woman's underwear and crinoline frame, 1850–60.

The many layers of mid-nineteenth-century underwear can be seen here: chemise, corset, corset cover, drawers, crinoline frame, separate pocket and a decorative waist petticoat. The crinoline frame was a light, pliable and relatively inexpensive structure. By 1859 Sheffield was producing wire to make half a million crinolines each week.

watch-spring to create a light, pliable, durable and relatively inexpensive structure. The petticoat foundation itself was discarded, leaving the concentric steel hoops simply linked by vertical bands of broad webbing. An opening was left at the front to allow the frame to be put on and tied round the waist with tapes. At the bottom, the widest hoop was usually covered with a flounce of stout material which could be removed for washing and this also prevented the sharp edge of the steel from damaging the wearer's boots.

The crinoline frame was extremely impractical: it took up a great deal of room, it knocked over small objects, it could tilt up embarrassingly and, more seriously, could cause skirts to catch fire near candles and open grates; but it was also immensely popular and was quickly adopted by women of all ages and every level of society. Its main attractions were that it successfully created the desired shape of fashion and it was comfortable to wear. The cage was light and left the legs free to move easily, unlike the multiple layers of underpetticoats which must have seemed heavy, hot and restricting by comparison. Although it needed careful management as it swung out, it could give the skirt a buoyant and graceful effect which induced a feeling of ease and freedom in the wearer. There are many contemporary references to the crinoline's pleasing aspects and even Mrs Amelia Bloomer, the American campaigner for the reform of women's dress, accepted it as a sensible alternative to layers of underpetticoats; all that a woman now needed was the frame itself and one decorative petticoat to wear over it. Beneath it, of course, a chemise was always worn, and drawers were considered essential (a few years later, scarlet flannel knickerbockers were recommended to ladies 'fond of gardening, and standing about in the open air'[10]). Some ladies disapproved of the crinoline – most notably Queen Victoria and Florence Nightingale – but a skirt without this kind of support soon looked quite wrong and few women cared to make themselves so conspicuous. The relatively low price of the frame (some as little as six or seven shillings each) made it accessible to virtually every social class and it was, in effect, the first high-fashion garment to be universally adopted. At the same time its potentially ridiculous aspects were quickly seized upon and the crinoline became the butt of innumerable jokes and cartoons in *Punch* and elsewhere. Many of these exaggerated its size and effect and are probably not an entirely accurate reflection of it. Commenting on the 'amplitude of dresses and the circumference of hoop skirts' in December 1857 *The Illustrated London News* reported that 'five yards is

39 Fashion plate, 1856.

The crinoline was ridiculed by Punch *and many other cartoons which exaggerated its size and inconvenience. This fashion plate has no comic intentions but it is interesting to note how the gentleman is dwarfed by the immense size of the ladies' skirts. Flounces with a border pattern,* à disposition, *were very fashionable in the mid-1850s. Flounces were also deliberately stiffened to stand out farther from the skirt.*

considered a moderate degree of amplitude, and six by no means infrequent.' Although six yards are often mentioned in the fashion periodicals, surviving specimens in museum collections rarely measure as much as this and many crinoline frames are of three yards' circumference or less.[11]

Contraptions and 'Rigging'

A practical method of dealing with the skirt in muddy weather was described in *The Lady's Newspaper* in 1856: 'Some inventive genius has contrived a handy "rigging" for ladies, whereby, as they go up or down stairs, enter or quit a carriage, or step across a gutter or puddle, they can pull up their dresses ... There are four small pulleys attached to the waist, underneath the dress, over which are roven small cords, one of which is attached with diaper pins, severally to the front, rear, and sides of the skirt, at about the height of the knee. The other ends terminate in loops which are let into the pockets on either side.'[12] By the following year this was becoming a popular fashion and looped-up dresses were widely adopted for walking and other sporting activities. It was necessary to wear with them a decorative petticoat or underskirt and many of these were scarlet or brightly coloured, trimmed with braid and embroidery at the hem; they were often combined with coloured and barrel-striped stockings. This style contributed to the rather more assertive and sprightly appearance of women's dress in the late 1850s and early 1860s. Military-looking boots with low heels and practical hats, rather than bonnets, added to this impression. During the 1850s hats became popular for younger women as informal daytime wear, especially in the country and at the seaside, although they were regarded as rather 'bold' by some and the bonnet remained essential for church, in the drawing room and on other formal occasions. In 1854 the straw hat with a low round crown and wide, flat brim with

ribbons to tie under the chin was very fashionable at summer resorts, but other styles could be worn such as a hat with a smaller brim turned up at the sides, the so-called Tudor hat, the pork-pie shape and even an adaptation of the Scotsman's Glengarry bonnet.

When it was first introduced the cage crinoline had given the skirt a rounded, dome shape, but towards the end of the decade this altered to become more pyramidal, with less fullness over the hips and more width at the hem. Flounces began to disappear and by 1858 basques, too, were being abandoned and 'they are now worn only with dresses suitable for negligé, and are never seen in evening costume. A waistband of a colour (or in various colours) harmonizing with the dress is very fashionable. It may be fastened by a brooch or buckle in front of the waist. A broad ribbon sash, fastened in a bow and long ends in front, is also very fashionable.'[13] These were to be a feature of dress in the early 1860s.

A noticeable increase in trimming characterized the dress of the 1850s, and apart from the flounces there was a freer use of lace, ribbon, braid, passementerie and fringe. Silk fringe, in particular, was a favourite addition to the bodice, sleeves and skirt of dresses and jackets. Technological advances led to the expansion of the machine lace industry and lace trimming was now within the reach of most women. A good deal of snobbishness was attached to the possession of real, handmade lace but in fact it was not always easy to distinguish from the machine-made examples. Large scarves and stoles of fine lace and tulle were worn in the evening and gave a measure of warmth to bare shoulders without crushing the full, gauzy skirts of ball dresses. This fashion is strikingly depicted in many portraits of the period by the Court painter Franz-Xaver Winterhalter; the clouds of diaphanous white tulle give his sitters an immensely flattering, almost ethereal appearance.

Apart from the lavish use of trimmings a general air of greater luxury and display in

40 HRH The Princess of Wales, photographed c. 1863.

Skirts were looped up over a coloured or braided underskirt and a crinoline petticoat for walking, croquet and other sporting activities in the late 1850s and early 1860s. Princess Alexandra is also equipped with a braided cloth jacket, port-pie hat and walking stick. (Her mother-in-law, Queen Victoria, was an enthusiastic walker.)

41 Making a Posy. *W. P. Frith, 1856.*

Frith's painting reflects a contemporary ideal of young womanhood: sweet, gentle, modest and pretty. However, this image was beginning to change in the late 1850s as bolder colours and more practical garments were introduced. Broad-brimmed straw hats were a fashionable alternative to the bonnet for informal wear.

women's dress was the result of silk becoming more usually worn by day. In 1850, one writer thought 'there never was a time when silken materials were so rich and splendid as at present.'[14] *Moiré antique* or watered silk was a great favourite with older women but it was always used for plain skirts as it was too stiff to wear in flounces. Also very popular were brocaded silks and the chiné or warp-printed fabrics with their blurred patterns which complemented the softer, easier lines of fashionable dress. The emphasis was on prettiness and when the materials and ornaments were tastefully arranged the effect could be charming. John Ruskin described a dress his young wife wore in Venice in 1852 as 'very simple – but

quaint, white, with little rosettes or bows or knots of divers coloured riband fastened over it, on the gothic principle of no one colour being like the next to it. It was Carnival time, and she looked as if she had just sustained a shower of sugar plums. She received many compliments.'[15]

New Colours

Effie Ruskin, however, had a father-in-law who disapproved of her 'want of quietness of Dress' and he felt, in 1851, that his son's and daughter-in-law's society would have been still higher and better had

42 The Landing of HRH Princess Alexandra at Gravesend. *H. N. O'Neil, 1863.*

This painting depicts the Danish-born Princess Alexandra arriving in Britain for her marriage to the Prince of Wales in 1863. By this date, the pyramidal effect of the gored skirt and the spoon-shaped bonnet transformed the female silhouette into a wide-based triangle with a small, neat head at its apex.

Effie's taste been for less gay colours. The Highest Ladies in London are remarkably sensitive about quiet colours, especially out of doors. They have quite a dread of Red and Yellow.'[16] Certainly, quiet colours and delicate pastel shades had been prevalent during the 1840s but Effie, who was young and fashionable, was aware that more definite tones and added ornament were coming back into favour. By the summer of 1852 it was noted that 'embroidery is used for all articles of ladies' dress: it cannot be too heavy or too rich'; and in 1856, 'in silk, rich, dark hues will be among the fashionable colours of the coming season.'[17] It was in this year that the first aniline dye was marketed and within a few years a range of brilliant new colours had become available. Dyes such as magenta, mauve, bright blue and bright green produced different shades from those obtained from natural dyestuffs and they were able to respond to the steadily increasing demand for more intense colours. In the early 1860s the Frenchman, Hippolyte Taine, was repeatedly struck by the 'outrageously crude' colours and 'want of taste' in the dress of British women. His *Notes on England* lists 'violet dresses, of a really ferocious violet'; 'purple or poppy-red silks, grass-green dresses decorated with flowers, azure blue scarves'; and 'dresses of purple silk, very shiny so that they reflect the light dazzlingly, or of stiff tulle on a substructure of skirts, bristling with embroidery; immense shawls of black lace falling to the heels; immaculate white or bright purple gloves … the glare and glitter is brutal.' Taine came to the conclusion that 'there

can be no doubt that there is something peculiar in the condition of the English retina'.[18]

Changing tastes in colour and ornamentation corresponded to alterations in the shape and form of the dress. By 1860 the skirt had reached its maximum width at the hem but it had a smoother, narrower line over the hips. The bulk at the waist, the result of straight lengths of fabric being pleated into the waistband, was eliminated by the introduction of gores or shaped panels which gave the skirt a more triangular, fan-like aspect. Gores began to appear at the very end of 1859 and by August 1860 *The Englishwoman's Domestic Magazine* advised that 'all skirts should be slightly gored (one breadth on each side is just enough to set them out well)'. A few months earlier the magazine had reported that evening dresses 'are worn so long behind that they form quite demi-trains, but in front they are made only ordinary length, just to touch the ground'.[19] During the next five years this line was explored and developed so that the skirt gradually narrowed and flattened at the front while fullness was swept towards the back. The waistline was cut straight and round and rose above its natural level, thus easing out the curves of the fashionable silhouette. The sleeves on day bodices were now close-fitting and plain, in a flattened 'bishop' shape with a curve over the elbow. This straighter and severer line put people in mind of the fashions of the French First Empire period, although in reality the skirt remained very bulky and required the support of a crinoline frame until 1867. Far from resembling a tall slim column, the fashionable woman was more of a wide-based triangle with a small, neat head at its apex. The size of bonnets, hats and caps was carefully contained and from 1861 to 1864 the distinctive spoon-shaped bonnet gave the head a pointed look. The bonnet brim rose up at the front with its sides cut away and the crown sloped backwards into a deep curtain or bavolet. During 1864 the high brim disappeared and a small, flat bonnet with no bavolet was worn.

The Demise of the Crinoline

The appearance of the gored skirt in 1860 had prompted speculation about the crinoline. In April 1864 *The Englishwoman's Domestic Magazine* felt that 'a considerable diminution in the amplitude of the skirts must be noted with satisfaction; indeed, the employment of steel crinolines seems to be altogether on the decrease'; and in March of the following year *Punch* published 'Rhymes to Decreasing Crinoline' ('There will soon be room for us / In the public omnibus').[20] The revival of the double skirt may have encouraged this belief since this new form of dress was an established fashion by the beginning of 1865. A shorter overskirt could be looped up on each side to form an apron or *tablier* effect at the front and puffs at the back in the manner of the eighteenth-century polonaise, while the underskirt lengthened to form a train at the back. The impracticalities of trained skirts were featured by *Punch* on several occasions in 1865 and an *Illustrated London News* report of the latest Paris fashions in June 1866 found that 'the majority of robes were with trains of considerable length ... if the spectacle which Longchamps presented may be regarded as any indication of the coming mode, the days of crinoline are certainly numbered. The majority of the more elegantly dressed women seem to have entirely abandoned it.' The following month a *Punch* cartoon showed a servant being reprimanded for imitating her superiors and leaving off her crinoline.[21]

Although by 1867 the skirt was looking relatively narrow the majority of women continued to wear the crinoline petticoat in a modified form. The upper hoops were removed, leaving only three or four steels at the bottom but, as *The Ladies' Treasury* noted, 'as dresses are apt to fall in and look hollow with this arrangement two petticoats are worn above it.'[22] A shorter skirt, without a train, could be worn for walking, but many day dresses and all evening gowns had long, trained skirts. Even with the support of a

43 Maids of All Work.
J. Finnie, 1864–5.

*The crinoline was the
first high fashion
garment to be worn by
all social classes but the
frames worn by these
maidservants were
probably not very good
quality and reveal an
ugly ridge at the hem.
The mid-1860s practice
of removing some of the
upper steel s to create a
more triangular shape
had the unfortunate
effect of making dresses
'fall in and look hollow'.*

44 The Fashions. The Englishwoman's Domestic Magazine, *1867.*

By 1867–8 the narrower, gored skirt no longer required the support of a crinoline frame. Fullness was swept towards the back, extending into a short train and double skirts were fashionable. The hair was arranged in a chignon at the back of the head. Knicker-bocker suits for young boys appeared in the late 1850s and by the late 1860s the knicker-bockers could be either open or closed at the knee.

modified crinoline petticoat these skirts were extremely impractical and late-1860s taste tended more towards the bouffant style of the eighteenth century than the flowing, neo-classical draperies of the early nineteenth century. Before long, the ample skirts and trains were being looped up at the back and arranged over the hips in a conscious imitation of the dress of a hundred years earlier. Loose-backed gowns, in the style of the eighteenth-century sack dress, were also adopted and called the 'Watteau toilette'. As *The Englishwoman's Domestic Magazine* commented in March 1868: 'We are far from the scant, unbecoming dress of the First Empire. Skirts are gored, it is true, but they are ample and flowing. Crinolines, far from being left off, have merely changed their shape; they are plain in front, but puffed out on either side so as to remind one strongly of the hoops or *paniers* of the last century. This together with the looped-up or double skirt *à la Watteau*, flowing open sleeves, very low bodices, and

fichus crossed over the bosom, contributes to make a modern lady of fashion bear much outward resemblance to those who flourished before the French Revolution.'[23]

This back drapery called for some additional support and by January 1869 *The Englishwoman's Domestic Magazine* was describing the *paniers tournures* worn in Paris over 'rather scant' half-crinolines. These were overlapping frills of horsehair cloth 'bound with braid and stiffened with steel bands' which tied round the waist to give the skirt its necessary back projection. The French term *tournure* was also known in Britain as a 'dress improver' or 'bustle', and in time other means of constructing the support were invented. All fashionable dresses continued to have double skirts or a polonaise in one form or another (that is with the bodice extended at the back and sides to form an overskirt); they were looped up, as one writer put it in December 1869, 'after the fashion of window curtains'. Flounces and pleated frills made a return to

45 The Fashions. The Englishwoman's Domestic Magazine, *1870.*

By 1869 double skirts and trains were being draped up over the hips and required the support of a tournure *or bustle. The late eighteenth-century inspiration for this fashion can be seen in the bouffant shape of the skirt, lace flounces and ribbon bows.*

dress trimmings and were added to most dresses of the early 1870s. The soft, undulating curves of the new line were further achieved by a revival of tight lacing, and women were careful not to lose sight of a neat slim waist amongst the frothy decoration of the upper skirt.

The Grecian Bend

During the period when the cage crinoline had been in fashion, from the mid-1850s to the mid-1860s, there had been less emphasis on tight lacing and women's clothes had responded to the shortening and easing of the waistline. By the 1850s all corsets were front-fastening and shoulder straps had disappeared. Once the skirt began to lose its all-round bulk at the waist,

flattening at the front and lying more smoothly over the hips, there was a less marked definition at the waistline and this called for tighter control once again. During the second half of the 1860s the corset became a heavier, more inflexible foundation garment and at the end of the decade steam moulding was introduced. By this means highly starched corsets were dried out on metal shapes into which steam was forced. In 1873 the 'spoon busk' appeared: the metal bar at the centre front of the corset, carrying the hooks and stud fastenings, lengthened and curved gently over the stomach in a narrow spoon shape.

The new line of women's dress with its bustle projection at the back called for a characteristic posture which was popularly known as the Grecian bend. This served to accentuate the rear fullness by throwing the head and bust forward and the hips backwards. This stance was induced in part by the shape of the longer, tighter corset and also by the higher heels now in fashion. It was not until the 1850s that boots and shoes acquired low heels and these rose to a height of about two and a half inches in the 1860s. By 1871 *The Queen* was commenting with some disapproval on the 'Dangers of High-Heeled Boots. Everyone who has noticed the height to which the heels of women's boots is now carried, must have marvelled much how the wearer could maintain her equilibrium, walking on stilts is nothing to it. It may be questioned how far the "Grecian bend" has become fashionable from a certain power it gives the wearers of the "high heel" to balance themselves.'[24] Women were unused to wearing very high heels and the long, tightly furled umbrella which was a fashionable dress accessory of the early 1870s must have been a useful aid to walking.

As if to counterbalance the bulk of the skirt, the hair was arranged in a massive chignon at the nape of the neck. The chignon had become fashionable in the early 1860s as the long back hair loosened out of the bun. The hair could also be enclosed in a net or snood made from silk or

46 *'The Dolly Varden Farewell Kiss'. G. du Maurier,* Punch, *1871.*

The Dolly Varden costume was another eighteenth-century revival and was a fashionable informal dress in 1871–2.

THE DOLLY VARDEN FAREWELL KISS.

A DELIGHTFUL OPERATION, BUT A DIFFICULT ONE TO PERFORM SUCCESSFULLY.

chenille thread. From 1862 the chignon was worn fuller and higher on the crown, sometimes necessitating artificial aid, as was noted by *The Englishwoman's Domestic Magazine:* 'Formerly a little repugnance was felt in making use of false hair, when more simple coiffures were in vogue; now this is no longer the case, when, on account of the voluminous nature of dress generally, elaborate head-dresses are absolutely necessary.'[25] By 1864 coiffures were perceived as very fanciful and in the evening the hair was 'drawn off the face and raised very high behind, much in the style worn during the

First Empire – a kind of Greek style, in which is a mixture of small plaits and curls. This is almost indispensable when one has a dress gored at the hips and a sash which makes the waist appear short.'[26] The Greek style in time gave way to a more eighteenth-century image as the chignon loosened and spread over the back of the head, often bulked out by false hair. Sometimes the chignon was braided or simply massed in loose ringlets. The height and fullness of this hair arrangement was not unlike the tall styles of the 1770s and tended to push bonnets, hats and caps forwards, tilting them at an angle over the forehead.

One version of the eighteenth-century revival was the Dolly Varden fashion of 1871–2. So-called after a character in Charles Dickens' novel *Barnaby Rudge* (which dealt with events at the time of the Gordon Riots in 1780), it consisted of a polonaise of a striped or printed cotton (usually brightly coloured flowers on a dark ground) looped up over a plain underskirt and worn with a cap or a straw hat in the *bergère* or shepherdess style. This was intended for informal wear and was particularly popular in Britain although it was also known in France under the name of the 'Dubarry' costume.

Contemporary opinion of the Grecian bend, the bustle, high heels and the chignon was mixed. Though fashionable and widely adopted these features were seen by many as unnatural and highly artificial. Apart from the lampoons in *Punch* a number of writers condemned the fashion. Describing his heroine in *The Eustace Diamonds* (1873), Anthony Trollope wrote: 'There was no unclean horse's tail. There was no get up of flounces, and padding, and paint, and hair, with a dorsal excrescence appended with the object surely of showing in triumph how much absurd ugliness women can force men to endure.'[27]

The short-waisted bodice remained in fashion for evening dresses but during the early 1870s the day bodice with its basques or polonaise steadily lengthened and tightened. By 1874 it reached well over the hips and was given the apt name of a 'cuirass' bodice. Beneath this, longer well-boned stays were worn. At the same time the skirt began to lose some of its full, floating drapery at the front and sides and a narrower line was just beginning to emerge. From 1874 dresses could be drawn back against the legs by a series of tapes inside the skirt.

47 Poor Relations. *G. G. Kilburne, 1875.*

The bodice lengthened and tightened during 1874, reaching well over the hips. The 'waistcoat corsage' on the left is combined with a polonaise (a bodice extending into an overdress which could be looped up at the back and sides). The young girl in this evidently quite prosperous middle-class household is fashionably dressed with a 'bustle' projection at the back of her skirt.

-4-
FIN DE SIÈCLE

Women's Dress 1875-1900

Women's Changing Role

An extraordinary variety of styles in women's dress during the last quarter of the nineteenth century reflects the accelerating pace of fashion and changes in the social pattern, the most notable of which was a revaluation of the traditional role of women. It was a period of paradox, even in a paradoxical century, for on the one hand it was looking forward to a new era of more practical and comfortable clothes for women and on the other it saw some of the most restricting and irrational fashions of the entire period. There were four major changes in the fashionable female silhouette during this twenty-five-year period: the long narrow line of the later 1870s and early 1880s, characterized by the Princess line and tied-back dresses; the exaggerated bustle shape of the mid-1880s with its rigid projection at the back and heavy draperies at the front of the skirt; the horizontal emphasis of the 1890s with its return to huge leg of mutton sleeves and adoption of a plain and stiffly flared skirt; and in the last three years of the century a softer, more sinuously shaped bodice and skirt, echoing the sweeping curves of the emergent Art Nouveau taste. Each of these distinctive images was to evolve from the style of dress which preceded it, a process which took several years, but even so the rate of change appears to be comparatively fast.

During this period a new type of woman began to take the lead in fashion and set the style in beauty. Stage actresses and so-called 'professional beauties' like Lillie Langtry and Sarah Bernhardt (both of whom were dressed by Worth) were now studied and admired by the fashion magazines and their readers, challenging the traditional leaders of society – royalty and the aristocracy. Lillie Langtry, in particular, caused a sensation in the 1880s: 'never since the days of the Gunnings had such universal worship been paid to beauty. The Langtry bonnet, the Langtry shoe, even the Langtry dress-improver, were widely stocked and as widely bought; photographs of Mrs Langtry papered London.'[1]

Other changes were coming about and although the basic form of women's clothes remained the same (the two-piece dress, with fitted bodice and full-length skirt over a tightly laced corset was worn until the end of the century) there were new elements which were to have a far-reaching effect, leading to what might now be called 'modern' fashion. One of these was the development of the tailor-made costume, a practical dress or skirt with matching jacket and sometimes a waistcoat, tailored in plain woollen cloth. By the 1890s both this and the less formal tailored skirt and contrasting blouse were becoming ordinary daytime wear, suitable for a variety of occupations. The jersey of the late 1870s and early 1880s, although a relatively short-lived fashion, was another item which was to look forward to the easier and more versatile clothing of the next century. Practical clothes for sports (especially cycling, walking, yachting and golf) were developed, and the masculine

48 The Jersey Lily. *E. J. Poynter, c. 1878.*

Lillie Langtry was a 'professional beauty' whose looks and clothes were much admired. The dress she wears here was a picturesque fashion of 1878, the slashed sleeves owing their inspiration to the Renaissance period. 'Copy almost any old costume of the three last centuries and you will scarcely go wrong,' said Cassell's Family Magazine *in August 1878.*

49 Tailor-made Costumes. The Queen, 1897.

The 'New Woman' of the 1890s adopted more practical, mannish clothes. The tailored costume was particularly suitable for walking and outdoor pursuits – even climbing the Alps as suggested here.

features of some of these reflected their serious attempts to be functional. With more women entering the labour market the need for a sensible form of working dress became apparent. Rhoda Nunn, a type of 'New Woman' of the 1890s, who taught typing and practical business skills to young unmarried women who needed to earn their own living, wore for example, 'a black serge gown with white collar and cuffs'. Rhoda is vividly portrayed by George Gissing in his novel *The Odd Women* as a highly professional and independent young woman, 'quite like a man in energy and resources' and yet remaining feminine and attractive to men.[2] The 'New Woman' was a subject of interest and concern during the 1890s. Many writers

were less sympathetic than George Gissing but even *The Lady's Realm* of 1896, which doubted that 'this feminine Frankenstein be indeed among us', conceded 'the gentlewomen of today are the daughters of an alert and self-reliant age, in which marriage is no longer the simple solution of every girl's life ...'[3] The demands for greater female emancipation were spreading and many women openly disputed their traditional role of passivity and dependence. The tendency to adopt some more practical forms of dress and to incorporate 'masculine' elements (such as stiff-collared shirts, ties, tailored jackets and mannish hats) reflect this undercurrent of thought in the 1880s and 1890s.

A dissatisfaction with what were seen as the ugly, irrational and unhygienic aspects of fashionable dress had begun to be voiced as early as the 1850s but it was during the late 1870s and early 1880s that such opinions were coherently expressed in a demand for the serious reform of dress. Ideas were put forward for a more 'artistic' or aesthetic alternative to fashionable styles and also for a form of 'rational' dress; both of these condemned the practice of tight lacing and other restricting features of contemporary clothes. This movement had a minority following and was hardly a real challenge to fashion, but in the longer term many of its ideas were to gain acceptance. It was not until the first decades of the twentieth century that tight lacing was abandoned and divided skirts or trousers were accepted for women, but already by the 1890s fashionable dresses had incorporated the softer shoulderline and more natural silhouette advocated by the dress reformers.

By 1875 a new line had clearly emerged in fashionable women's dress. It had begun in 1874 with the introduction of the longer, tighter cuirass bodice which smoothed away any bulk over the hips and pushed the bustle projection downwards at the back of the skirt. As the skirt itself lengthened and tightened the bustle merged into a fall of drapery which spread into a train. The Princess dress with its long narrow line without

50 The Fashions. The
Englishwoman's
Domestic Magazine,
1875.

*A narrower line had
begun to emerge in 1874
as the bodice
lengthened and
tightened and skirts
were pulled back
against the legs. The
bustle disappeared into
a fall of drapery and a
spreading train at the
back. The narrow line
was emphasized by
vertical stripes and
contrasting sleeves
which gave the bodice a
sleeveless appearance.*

a break at the waist was an ideal style for the new silhouette, and by 1876 it had become extremely fashionable. It usually buttoned or fastened at the front, and a long row of buttons or decorative bows could add to the vertical effect. The polonaise (a bodice with attached skirt) was also worn but by early 1876 this had 'no drapery or poufs at the back, but a straight-cut, with three long seams down the back'.[4] An apron-like effect of drapery remained popular but a wide sash wrapped about the hips was another style fashionable from 1875–9. By 1876 all the fashion pages of magazines were stressing the narrowness of the line, with the skirt draped tightly round the legs. *The Ladies' Treasury* thought these tight skirts 'in front look like the wrappings of an Egyptian mummy, whilst at the back they fall in the longest and fullest of trains ... Ladies almost all look infinitely better in these long and straight draperies, than they ever did in the tucked-up skirts and tunics, which made them look like Dresden China Watteau figures.'[5]

The cuirass bodice did indeed have the appearance of a piece of armour. Its tight fit was achieved by cutting it with five seams at the back, from the top of the shoulder and

slanting towards the waist, while the darts in front were short and close together. The bodice was well boned on the inside to ensure a perfectly straight, smooth line which would not wrinkle or crease and it was sometimes laced at the back to create an even better effect. From around 1877 to 1882 the cuirass bodice was cut high over the hips, dipping to a low point at the front and back. The neck opening was usually cut round and high but if it had a lower V-shape this was filled in with a chemisette or material to match the dress. Sleeves were generally plain and narrow, trimmed at the wrist with a simulated cuff, although there was a particular fashion for slashed puffs at the shoulders and elbows in 1878. During the late 1870s the sleeve began to shorten and by 1883 it was three-quarter length even for ordinary daytime wear. Gloves lengthened to correspond and covered the forearm. Another distinctive fashion of the late 1870s was to make the dress in two contrasting materials so that the sleeves might be a different colour and texture (such as a combination of two shades of satin and velvet). This gave the bodice the appearance of being sleeveless, which helped to underline its narrowness.

The great object was 'exceeding slimness' but women on the whole were not at ease in a completely plain skirt, so a narrow effect had to be created in other ways. In Paris, for instance, 'the dresses you see worn by the élégantes are made long and very flat to the figure, not tied back as they are in England, but so cut and shaped about the hips that no such tying is required.'[6] Most dresses combined both methods, but tying back the skirt, by a series of interior tapes which pulled the front flat across the legs, was the most common means of giving a sheath-like impression. It was to be expected that this fashion would be widely caricatured and many cartoons suggested the impossibility of sitting down or walking in such skirts. In reality the skirts were not as narrow as they might appear and a measurement of three to three and a half yards wide was considered correct in

SIC TRANSIT!

ALAS, FOR THE PRETTY JERSEY COSTUME! 'ANDSOME 'ARRIET, THE 'OUSEMAID
HAS GOT IT AT LAST, AND IT FITS HER JUST AS WELL AS HER MISSUS.

51 'Sic Transit!' G. du Maurier, Punch, 1880.

The jersey bodice became fashionable in 1879 and was ideal for creating a very tight, smooth fit. The tied-back skirt also revealed the natural lines of the figure and underwear was reduced to a minimum.

Combinations were adopted in place of the bulky chemise and drawers.

December 1876. Skirts now looked tight in comparison with those of the earlier 1870s and it was noted that: 'Plaitings are still the fashionable trimming for skirts, either kiltings or box-plaitings, but they are all pressed down and tacked in their place, not being allowed to fly free as of yore.'[7]

One of the most obvious effects of the tied-back dress was to reveal and define the natural lines of the figure. It became important to eliminate any bulk beneath the clothes so the undergarments had to be modified. 'Slimness being so essential for the present modes, many and various are the contrivances to produce it, such as satin stays moulded to the figure, made as long as

comfort will permit', said *Cassell's Family Magazine* in April 1878. The writer went on to say: 'all that can be is placed beneath the stays, instead of over them ... All under-clothing is inclined to be made of thinner material than formerly; nainsook for full-dress under-linen, even cambric and lawn, and écru silk being favourite materials for the purpose.' Even more effective was the introduction of combinations, in 1874, as an alternative to the separate and bulky under-garments of chemise and drawers. Combinations had become generally accepted by 1878 and were commended not only for their contribution to the slender line but also 'because the weight of combination garments is suspended from the shoulders instead of from the waist'.[8] This saving of weight might appear to be negligible, but the heaviness of clothes was to become an increasing preoccupation in the 1880s, and it was perhaps hardly surprising in view of the amount of drapery on the skirt.

As the line narrowed so the bustle gradually disappeared, but a flounced petticoat was generally required to support the water-fall of drapery and train at the back of the skirt. Trains on both day and evening dresses were fitted with an interior flounce to protect them from inevitable dirt and damage and perhaps also to enhance their appearance. 'Those who are economically inclined', it was reported in April 1878, 'will be pleased to hear black muslin is sometimes used for these flounces, or *balayeuses* as they are called.'[9] By the end of the year, however, trains were beginning to pass out of fashion. The hem was rising and skirts for walking dresses were made without trains; by 1880 the train was only seen on evening dresses and the skirt had assumed a more tubular shape.

In some respects the complex dresses of the late 1870s were very versatile. The fashion for combining different colours and materials and for multi-layered skirts meant that the bodice, polonaise or Princess tunic of one dress might be worn with the skirt or underskirt of another. This was particularly useful for the economically minded woman who might wish to make alterations to her wardrobe or extend the life of some garments with the minimum of outlay. An innovation of 1879 was the jersey bodice which could be worn with several different skirts. At first these tight fitting and back-fastening bodices of silk or wool jersey fabric were generally seen on informal occasions, worn with a serge or flannel skirt (or one of linen or cotton in the summer) and they were regarded as suitable for tennis; but later they were accepted for more formal wear. One of the jersey's undoubted advantages was its smooth, tight fit which perfectly achieved the narrow line with the minimum of discomfort.

The Silhouette Alters

Women were clearly prepared to suffer a certain amount of discomfort and it was hardly denied that the fashionably long and tight corsets required some effort to wear; but a temporary relief from the rigours of high fashion was openly welcomed. It was no coincidence that the late 1870s saw the emergence of a new form of dress in which women could relax elegantly. This was the tea gown which was, in effect, a more formal version of the easy-fitting morning gown or wrapper which women had worn about the house since the beginning of the century. Its relatively loose, unboned bodice – often made in the form of a lightly fitted front and flowing Watteau-pleated back – allowed it to be worn without a corset and it was adopted for that period in the afternoon between changing out of afternoon costume and into formal evening dress. This coincided with the new, fashionable practice of taking 'five o'clock tea'.[10] Friends of both sexes might be entertained to this meal and the tea gown, though ostensibly a comfortable and informal garment was quickly turned into a highly decorative item (but it was only thought suitable for married ladies to wear). In its issue of 27 April 1878 *The Queen* had illustrated the front and back of 'The

Louis XV Tea Gown' and from this time on the fashion magazines were full of directions for making tea gowns and advice on how they should be trimmed. By 1889 the tea gown was considered dressy enough for the mistress of the house to dine *en famille*.

The well-defined lines of the narrow silhouette called for a change in the style of outer garments. The soft, loose folds of an all-enveloping shawl had already proved unsuitable with the dresses of the earlier 1870s, interfering with the back projection and front drapery of the skirt. In the later 1870s fitted jackets with basques and narrow, three-quarter-length coats were preferred, although semi-fitting jackets or mantles could also be worn. One particular style was the dolman which had loose sleeves cut in one with the sides of the garment, making it half-coat, half-cape. Shawls might now be out of fashion but it was impossible to halt production all at once and many new (as well as valuable old ones) were turned into fitted wraps of some kind – if possible without cutting and spoiling the material. For the winter, short jackets of fur and especially sealskin were popular and fur was used to trim both dresses and mantles. Also from the 1870s there was a marked increase in the use of feathers to decorate millinery and other parts of dress. The feathers of many endangered species and even whole birds were now used for hats and evening bonnets, hair ornaments, muffs (made entirely of feathers or stuffed with eiderdown), fans, and for trimming the corsage.

Millinery itself was growing smaller and was worn farther back on the head. By 1876 velvet bonnets in the toque form, without a brim, had become general but there was also a fashion which lasted several years for so-called picturesque hats with brims, such as the 'Gainsborough', 'Rembrandt' and 'Beefeater' styles. The names of leading French milliners were now appearing in magazine reports of Paris fashions and those of Reboux and Virot led the field. A small, neat head complemented the slender line of dress and the chignon gradually

52 Mrs Catherine Chapple-Gill and her Children. *J. Tissot, 1877.*

Mrs Chapple-Gill wears an easy-fitting and very decorative indoor dress of a type which was to become known as a tea gown in the late 1870s. For children, white remained a favourite for formal wear but by the late 1870s girls began to wear black or dark brown stockings rather than white, even with the lightest of dresses.

front, swathing round the hips or scarf-like draping mounted on a foundation skirt. A popular version of this was an overskirt turned up at the front in what was called the *laveuse* or washerwoman style, also known as the 'fishwife' tunic. This had come into fashion by 1878 but was a style more characteristic of the early 1880s. Pleating and gathering of every kind was used to ornament the dress, from the well-regulated kilt pleating round the hem to the softer shirring and gauging across the front of the bodice and top of the skirt, especially popular from 1880 to 1882.

A new form of skirt drapery appeared in 1881–2, giving additional fullness over the hips. The so-called panier puffs were usually created by looping up a long polonaise bodice at the sides in what was thought of as a late-eighteenth-century manner or the 'Louis XV' style. Before long the *tournure*, as it was still politely called, was considered to be an indispensable support to the skirt and, as in the early 1880s, it could take several different forms. Stiffened flounces, half-crinolines or steel petticoats and cushion-like pads were all worn, but unlike the earlier version, many more dresses of the mid-1880s had their own bustle built in, created by inserting horizontal bands of steel or whalebone in the back skirt lining and drawing them up into half-hoops by tapes tied across the inside of the dress. The bustle in its second phase was at the height of fashion from 1883 to 1887. It differed from its earlier form by being more pronounced in shape, generally narrower and more sharply projecting at the centre back. In its most extreme form it resembled a large, domed bird-cage concealed beneath the skirt. More than one observer commented on its unfortunate tendency to 'wobble, and nothing appears more ungainly than a dress moving from side to side with every step or movement of the wearer.'[11]

Although the bustle appeared to be a cumbersome appendage it was almost always collapsible, and the skirt afforded greater freedom of movement now that the legs

dropped and shrank back into a smooth coil at the nape of the neck. At the front the hair could be cut short in a curled fringe, a style which became fashionable during the later 1870s and was popularly associated with the Princess of Wales.

From 1880 to 1882 the sheath-like silhouette remained in fashion, but at the same time as it reached its most extreme form new elements were introduced to modify and then alter this line. The stark appearance of the Princess dress of 1876 had already been challenged by the alternative form of double skirt with complex drapery; most dresses had some form of apron

54 Petticoat and Bustle, 1884.

In its second phase, from 1883 to 1887, the bustle was more pronounced in shape, generally narrower and more sharply projecting at the back. However, many dresses of the mid-1880s had their own bustle built in. 'Good dressmakers', said The Ladies' Treasury *in January 1883, 'always provide the skirt with the exact* tournure *that is required for it; and then no under-crinoline or skirt is required.*

were freed from tying-back and long trains. The 1880s skirt was more voluminous but materials were heavier and less highly trimmed. The drapery fell in sculptural folds over a foundation skirt and from 1883 there was a decided preference for asymmetrical effects. The apron front continued to be popular but was often looped up on one side. The similarity between skirt drapery and furnishing fabrics had been remarked upon by at least one writer in the late 1870s, and women's dresses of the 1880s seemed to reflect the contemporary taste in interior decoration. There was a liking for rich, dark colours and imposing effects, with the continuing preference for combining contrasting materials in one costume. An example is the description in *The Ladies' Treasury* for January 1882: 'Some very handsome embossed dresses are composed of plush, with reliefs of Venetian leather – or of cloth, with reliefs of velvet or plush ... Contrasts of colour are seen on many of Worth's new costumes. He trims dark blue satin for instance, with brown plush, or green velvet

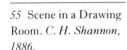

55 Scene in a Drawing Room. C. H. Shannon, 1886.

Evening dresses of the mid-1880s were cut very low in th bodice and skirts fell in heavy, sculptural folds over a tournure *or bustle. Sleeves were short and were worn with very long gloves reaching well over the elbow.*

*56 The Ornithologist.
J. E. Millais, 1885.
The length of girls'
dresses varied but they
were always shorter
than adult styles. The
girl on the left wears a
practical, dark print
gown with black
stockings and shoes.
The sailor suit was one
of the most popular
styles for children and
was worn by both girls
and boys throughout the
year.*

with brown fur. Coats intended to be worn with black or dark coloured skirts, he makes of rich tapestries, or of brocaded satin, with plush reliefs on them. Dark red plush coats are also worn over handsome black skirts for dinner and evening wear.'[12] Plush, a type of cotton velvet with a long, shaggy pile, was probably the most characteristic fabric of this decade, used in equal quantities for household furnishings and articles of dress (from gowns and mantles to bonnets, hats, bags and muffs). Brown was a favourite colour and a rich, reddish shade called 'Etna' was fashionable in the late 1870s and early 1880s.[13]

The bodices of day dresses were tight-fitting and well-boned, cut close to the neck with a high stand collar. By 1885 the collar was felt to be almost too high for comfort: 'Of course they look elegant, and protect from the cold, stiff neck, and sore throat; but they are very uncomfortable for those who read or write much, and even produce an affection of the throat, which feels as though there were always a ball in it.'[14] Sleeves, however, were rather short and only reached the elbow for semi-formal wear, while for full evening dress they were almost non-existent or had 'merely a little epaulet for sleeve'.[15] Formal evening gowns were also cut with a very low *décolletage* at both back and front, often in a V-shape during the mid-1880s.

The final decades of the nineteenth century saw the introduction of more practical and comfortable clothes for children but it was also a period when they were obliged to wear very elaborate and uncomfortable styles of dress. There was a marked distinction between the clothes worn for everyday and those for 'best' or Sunday wear. White

57 *Winter Novelties by Redfern.* The Lady, *1885.*

Dresses tailored in plain woollen cloth became fashionable in the 1880s for smart day wear. 'So popular are these dresses that even modistes make them in what they are pleased to call tailor-fashion,' wrote The Lady *in April 1885; 'but it needs no experienced eye to detect the genuine article, for the gown made by the tailor has that unmistakeable style that no dressmaker can copy.'*

58 A Silk Muslin Tea-Gown. The Illustrated London News, *1897.*

'A model tea gown for summer wear, made of finest silk muslin trimmed with lace and diamanté embroidery'. By the late 1880s and 1890s tea gowns and tea jackets had become elaborately-wrought confections of thin silk, lace and ribbons. Accordion pleating added to their decorated appearance.

the hips in imitation of the *laveuse* or fishwife tunic. The inclusion of so many adult features reflects an increasing attention to children's clothes and the fashion periodicals of the 1880s have a much greater number of plates devoted to girls' dresses.

Less restricting clothes were worn on informal occasions, especially during the summer and at the seaside. The sailor suit had first appeared as a summer and seaside fashion for small boys but was adapted for girls (who wore the sailor's blouse with a pleated skirt instead of knickerbockers or trousers) and by the last quarter of the century it was a style to be worn throughout the year. In summer the suit was usually made of white cotton drill trimmed with navy braid and worn with a straw sailor hat; in winter, versions apppeared in navy blue serge with white, red or black trimmings and cloth caps or tam-o'-shanters. Another seaside fashion which spread to ordinary wear was the knitted jersey, similar to the traditional garments worn by fishermen. These were seen on children as early as the 1860s and 1870s but did not become an established fashion until the early 1880s, when the jersey bodice was popular for women. Jerseys were worn by both girls and boys.

Any costume which was comparatively plain and practical, such as a tailor-made dress or coat and skirt, was described as 'masculine' in the 1880s and the decade saw a developing taste for this type of women's dress. Since the beginning of the century, and for some time earlier than that, it had been possible for women to wear riding habits for walking and travelling; these costumes expertly tailored, in a closely woven woollen cloth which was warm, durable and almost waterproof, proved to be both functional and stylish. The 1850s had also seen the emergence of a matching jacket and skirt in plain cloth for informal, country or holiday wear, and although these were much easier-fitting than the traditional riding habit, they established a taste for a comfortable, sensible but attractive kind of daytime dress. In the 1870s and 1880s the tight and narrow line of fashion was more in

remained a favourite for formal wear but by the late 1870s girls began to wear black or dark brown stockings rather than white, even with the lightest of dresses. The length of girls' skirts varied but they were almost always shorter than the adult styles; it was not until a girl left the schoolroom that she adopted the full-length skirt (and she was allowed to put her hair up). The shape of girls' dresses continued to follow adult fashion and the double-skirted 'bustle' style of the earlier 1870s gave way to a narrower line at the end of the decade with the introduction of the Princess dress. During the 1880s skirts were elaborately draped round

sympathy with the style of the riding habit, the bodice of which fitted like a second skin. By tradition, it was men's tailors who made women's habits, their skill based on centuries of experience working with woollen cloth, and it was to the tailors rather than dressmakers that women now looked for the provision of a well-fitting cloth costume – hence the name of tailor-made for such garments. From the start the tailor-made gown was seen as 'essentially an English garment, both in make and origin, and has conclusively shown that when left to our own devices we are able to produce dresses that are both useful, elegant and becoming ... our productions in this especial line have so enhanced our reputation that English tailor-made costumes are eagerly bought by Americans and foreigners of distinction.'[16] The Queen of Portugal 'like many another Foreign Sovereign' was reported to have ordered hers from Redfern, a leading maker who supplied the tailor-mades for Princess Beatrice's trousseau in July 1885. Other notable firms were Creed, Busvine and Messrs Doré of George Street, Hanover Square.

At first, the tailor-made costume consisted of a two-piece dress – in other words, a separate bodice and skirt – and the bodice might take the form of a jacket with a waistcoat or waistcoat front. For example, in 1885 'many tailor gowns of plain cloth in blue, brown, green or black are now made with two or three waistcoats of different colours. These are very useful when visiting or travelling, as the gown may be so varied by its vest – especially if you have also a hat to match each – that it has all the appearance of a fresh costume.'[17] As the tailor-made grew more popular it also became more versatile so that by 1889 'such costumes are worn in London at the smartest weddings and afternoon parties, and would not be out of place in a long country walk across stubble-fields, or for a tour abroad.'[18] In most cases, however, there tended to be a distinction between a tailor-made gown of a light smooth cloth for smart wear and one of a heavier, rougher serge or tweed for the country.

Some tailor-made bodices were worn over a habit-shirt or thin blouse, as were riding habits. From the late 1880s the blouse began to assume a more important role, becoming in the 1890s a decorative garment in its own right, worn with a plain tailored skirt for informal day wear, or with a two-piece costume of a tailored coat and skirt. This marked a further stage in the development of the tailor-made costume which by the mid-1890s had become the clear forerunner of the twentieth-century woman's suit.

For relaxation, the tea gown continued to be a popular indoor garment and by 1889 it was joined by the semi-fitting tea jacket which could be worn over a skirt in place of a tight bodice. In the 1890s this was also known as a *matinée* jacket but, although closely allied to the tea gown, it was not considered its equal 'in either youthfulness or beauty.'[19] Until the end of the century tea gowns and tea jackets were elaborately wrought confections of thin silk, lace and

59 Fashion plate, 1886. The dolman was the most popular version of the semi-fitted mantle in the 1880s and it was skilfully cut to spread out over the centre back projection of the skirt. Tall-crowned hats gave a vertical emphasis to the female silhouette in the latter part of the decade. The importance of clean, well-fitting gloves and shoes was often stressed and the phrase 'well groomed' came into common currency at this time.

ribbons. Their decorative nature was given a further dimension by the introduction of accordion pleating in the late 1880s. In October 1889 for example, it was reported that 'The London Depot of the According Pleating Company, 228 Euston Road, is just now a more than usually busy one, for dressmakers from all parts are sending material to be pressed into the delightfully elastic accordion kilts, which are used alike for mantles, dresses, and tea gowns.'[20]

Mantles were an inportant feature of outer wear in the 1880s. With the return of the bustle in its exaggerated form it was difficult to wear long, tight-fitting coats, and even short jackets had to be cut with a basque at the back to accommodate the skirt projection. Most satisfactory were the many

60 Satin Carriage Dress, 1889.

In 1889 a new line emerged in women's dress. The skirt lost its elaborate cross draperies and was gored to flare out in a simple A-line while the sleeve head loosened to form a puff at the shoulder. There was a fashion for waistcoat fronts on day bodices of the 1880s which tended to emphasize the bust.

versions of the dolman which were made to fan out over the bustle from a shaped back. The longer front edges hung down flat and straight while the semi-fitted sleeves allowed a certain amount of room for movement. For more practical use, in bad weather or for travelling, a female version of the Ulster had appeared in the later 1870s and this was in general use by the mid-1880s.

Millinery echoed the hard-edged lines of the decade. Small bonnets were still correct for formal wear but hats were very popular in rather masculine styles, with tall crowns and moderately wide brims; toques were also worn and were favoured by younger women. A noticeably vertical emphasis in the mid- to late 1880s was reflected in the Tyrolean and postilion-style hats with conical crowns and curved brims, while the hair began to be dressed on the top of the head. Indoor caps were worn by older, married women but the taller hairstyles presented problems and caps were gradually dropped towards the end of the century. In 1885 *The Lady* commented that 'caps are as indispensable for matrons as hats for young girls, and yet it is difficult to get a really tasteful cap that does not perch on the top of the head and form a more or less Philistine excrescence.'[21]

In 1889 the mood changed fairly abruptly and a new line began to emerge in women's dress. It was almost as if the top layer of elaborate cross draperies and the projecting bustle were sloughed off to reveal a plainer, straighter skirt beneath. In fact, there was much talk of a return to the 'Empire' style of dress for as the bustle diminished in size skirts evidently felt narrower and more clinging round the legs. In reality, the resemblance to early-nineteenth-century dress was slight because bodices remained long-waisted and the new plain skirts were gored to flare rather stiffly at the hem. Although the steel bustle was rejected in favour of a more natural line over the hips, a small pad was worn under the skirt for several more years. This supported the residual fullness at the back which now formed a short train. Nevertheless, the new economy of line

61 *Latest Paris Fashions*. The Queen, 1894.

Sleeves swelled out in the leg of mutton shape, reaching an enormous size by 1895. Sleeves were still large enough at the time of Queen Victoria's Diamond Jubilee for reviewers of the past sixty years in fashion to find comparatively little difference between the styles of 1837 and 1897. One writer thought, 'we have gone back to early Victorian modes in everything'. The blouse steadily increased in popularity and was worn with a tailored skirt and jacket at the seaside and for smart, daytime wear in the 1890s.

seemed to be revolutionary and by March 1890 *The Young Ladies' Journal* saw a very great difference between 'the present fashions and those of a twelvemonth ago. All traces of *tournure* have now entirely disappeared; the skirt is scant and plain, falling loose and slightly trailing on the ground ... There are, properly speaking, no draperies at all.'[22]

The word 'revolution' was also applied to the shape of sleeves and *The Lady* said in July 1889, 'very few are worn plain; the so-called plain sleeve now being fulled over the shoulder almost in the fashion of a pouff.'[23]

This puff gave a narrow, pointed look to the head of the sleeve until 1892 when the fullness began to spread out sideways; the shoulder kick-up, together with the long waist and narrower skirt contributed to the characteristically vertical line at the beginning of the 1890s. Although it appeared a small change at first, it was a significant development and marked a shift of emphasis from the skirt to the bodice. The skirt in the 1890s, though carefully cut and shaped, remained essentially plain while the bodice became more elaborate. From 1892 to 1895 the upper part of the sleeve swelled out into a leg of mutton shape very similar to that of the 1830s. For the evening a short, balloon-like shape was worn but this was not thought to be very flattering when combined with the new off-the-shoulder style for evening dresses. In Paris, it was reported, evening sleeves were either small or replaced by jewelled shoulder straps; an alternative style was a shoulder strap with an additional small sleeve falling over the top of the arm. In general, though, there was a marked horizontal emphasis at the shoulder line and large sleeves made it almost impossible to wear fitted coats and jackets out of doors. The short, circular cape came into its own for both day and evening wear. It had a high, curved collar, echoing the deep neckband fashionable on day dresses, and as it flared out from the shoulders it contributed a little more width to the silhouette.

Achieving the 'Rustle'

One of the advantages of these extremely large sleeves was to make the waist appear small by comparison. For the past five decades it had tended to be an enlargement of the hips – either by the crinoline or the bustle – which had performed this function, but now there was no distortion and the skirt fitted smoothly over the hips. To counterbalance the shoulder width the skirt widened at the hem – an effect achieved by gores or shaped panels and some additional

62 Miss Mary Burrell.
J. Lavery, 1895.

*A short, balloon-like
sleeve was worn with
evening dress and by
the mid-1890s the plain
skirt was stiffly flared
at the hem. Fashionable
accessories to evening
dress were a shoulder
cape, long white gloves
and an ostrich feather
fan.*

fullness pleated in to the centre back. By 1895 *The Lady* advised anyone aspiring to be fashionable 'to make up their minds to wear very wide, full skirts. Many of the latest designs in skirts measure eight or nine yards round the bottom, but this is quite unnecessary fullness, as a very good effect can be obtained with a width of four-and-a-half or five yards if the skirt is properly cut.' Although skirts were plain, petticoats were more 'fanciful and elaborate than ever. It is advisable to choose them with plenty of flounces at the edge, to hold out the skirts at the bottom. Some of the flounces are edged with stiff piping-cords, which stand them out stiffly.'[24] Skirts themselves might be stiffened with interlining and lined with weighted silk which not only produced the required shape but created the enticing rustle much loved at the time.

New Sophistication: Underwear and Cosmetics

Underwear in general was becoming much more decorative and luxurious with an increasing use of white embroidery, pintucking, ribbon and lace insertions and silk fabrics. Corsets had begun to be elegantly treated in the 1880s and the best corsets for evening wear were made of coloured satin, patterned silks or (by the 1890s) black silk with coloured top-stitching. For more ordinary wear plain white or buff coutil was usual. In the late 1870s a suspender belt to which the stockings were attached appeared as an alternative to garters and by the 1890s the suspenders could be fixed to the lower edge of the corset. Another significant change was the appearance of the disposable sanitary towel which was advertised by Southall's as 'a new invention for the health and comfort of ladies' in January 1889.[25]

Although there had been a considerable amount of criticism of tight lacing since the late 1870s the practice continued almost unchecked to the end of the century. If any-

thing, the waist was required to be smaller than ever in the 1890s and even the relatively informal fashion of a blouse and skirt depended on a very tight, firm understructure. No such rigid foundation was apparent on the surface of women's clothes and the bodice was usually overlaid with some form of decoration which looked deceptively soft. There were various devices to emphasize width at the shoulders and narrowness at the waist, such as square yokes, false lapels and revers; another effect, appearing in 1895, was a bodice 'with front drooping over the belt, giving a "bag" or "pouch" effect. The drooping front is arranged on a perfectly tight bodice as well as on the full blouse.' Early versions of this style could be pouched at both the back and the front but by 1897, when it was becoming more fashionable, the bodice was 'brought tighter down the back and under the arms, and only permitted to overhang the belt obtrusively in the front.'[26] In 1897 it was also fashionable to wear a short bolero or zouave jacket.

The blouse had been steadily increasing in popularity during the 1880s and was very generally worn at the seaside and in the country with a contrasting skirt. More practical styles, often with turn-down linen collars, cuffs and bow ties, were adopted for sportswear and cycling and were usually referred to as 'shirts'. Both the blouse and the shirt were, in effect, alternative forms of the bodice, and although they gave the appearance of fullness they were often mounted on a boned and fitted lining. But where a bodice was usually made to match one particular skirt to form a 'dress', the blouse was a versatile garment which could be worn with several different skirts or tailored costumes. It could be made in a variety of light materials and colours and highly trimmed.

The 1890s taste for luxurious and traditionally feminine decoration extended to jewellery, with pearls in particular being lavishly worn. The high neckbands of daytime wear were echoed by the pearl chokers or 'dog collars' worn with evening dress. 'For smart dressing, even for the pro-

63 Fashions for Late Spring. The West-End, *1899.*

Left: Gown of fine cream lace over pale green chiffon, bodice trimmed with black Chantilly lace. Black straw hat with ostrich feathers.

Right: Walking gown of white cloth trimmed with black chenille thread embroidery. Straw hat with scarlet poppies and black feathers.

menade, a certain amount of jewellery is needful', commented a writer in 1899. 'Many women would not be seen at any time of the day without the string of pearls that fashion dictates at the moment, and a few good brooches and bangles are equally indispensable. More jewellery still is worn at the Casino of a foreign watering place in the evenings; while for country-house visiting, where dressing for dinner and impromptu dances are the order of the day, a full supply of ornaments is needed.'[27]

By the last quarter of the nineteenth century a discreet use of cosmetics was becoming generally acceptable. The Empress Eugénie's use of black eyeliner in the 1850s and 1860s had seemed very foreign and rather 'fast' to Englishwomen, but by the end of the century many were at least wearing face powder and rouge. At Balmoral in October 1896 Lady Lytton thought that 'the Princess of Wales looked lovely at dinner when the Carringtons dined and she is so wise to put even a little help to give her a good colour.' In the same year, Lady Lytton also noticed that Alexandra, Empress of Russia 'was at the height of her beauty, having just done away with her unbecoming fringe.'[28] From the mid-1890s the hair was dressed in a softer, fuller style, off the face. *The Graphic* described 'coiffures in Paris' in March 1897 as 'extremely pretty. The hair is turned back slightly waved from the face, and all gathered up in a simple knot on the top of the head, sometimes with breezy little curls and an Early Victorian look about it, but with none of the stiffness and hardness of that period. It is all soft, fluffy and exceedingly becoming.'[29]

In response to this enlargement of the head, big hats became fashionable (bonnets were still shrinking in size and were now only worn by elderly women). Wide-brimmed picture hats were often loaded with trimming. 'It really seems as if the one idea in millinery is to see how much can be crowded on a single hat', observed a writer in 1897 and there continued to be some concern about the use of whole stuffed birds on the front of hats and toques.[30] Feathers were also used for boas, which had returned to fashion. Feather boas were worn as a light wrap round the neck and shoulders in the summer months, while fur boas were reserved for winter wear.

The later 1890s saw an increasing preference for softer, lighter dress fabrics in pale colours. The plain, firm-textured silks which had been suitable a few years earlier for the stiffly flared skirt were giving way to thinner, more openly woven materials with much more surface trimming. 'Never was dress more elaborate – nor, be it added, more expensive', it was said at the time of the Jubilee celebrations in June 1897. 'True, many of the loveliest gowns seem simple enough – delicate muslins and lawns, airy grenadines, thin silks – but the frills and laces, the embroideries and the silken linings, reduce the apparent simplicity to a minimum.'[31] By the following year it was reported that white was to be 'immensely worn, also pale blue and mauve, together or separately, but the inclination is far more towards pale, indefinite colours and less gaudiness than last year's fashions showed.'[32] Other popular shades were heliotrope and chartreuse.

The changing taste in materials reflected a more fundamental change in the fashionable silhouette which became apparent in 1897. During the year, sleeves lost their immense fullness at the shoulder – firstly by flopping over and then by shrinking back to a small puff or epaulette. Gradually the upper part of the sleeve was made to fit the arm in a smooth line, but some residual fullness was allowed to drop to the level of the wrist in a form of bishop sleeve. The bodice now curved smoothly over the bust with extra fullness gathered into a pouched front to drop over the waistband or belt, giving the bodice a long-waisted look. The shape of the skirt was 'guileless of stiff lining'.[33]

The fluid, curving line of dress and the use of soft, pastel shades were expressions of the Art Nouveau taste which had begun to dominate the decorative arts and architecture from about 1890. In fashion, the style is usually associated with the Edwardian period in Britain from 1901-10 but in fact it had emerged four years before the death of Queen Victoria. It was the Diamond Jubilee in 1897, rather than the formal ending of her reign in January 1901, which saw an important change in direction; thus the last three years of the nineteenth century were also the first three of a new fashion cycle which brought it well into the twentieth century.

-5-
SENSE AND SOBRIETY
Men's Dress 1800-1900

Democratic Understatement

The history of nineteenth-century dress is marked by increasingly pronounced differences between the aims and effects of male and female fashions. Until the final decades of the eighteenth century men's and women's clothes shared many of the same colours and materials; the form of their garments was very different but essentially they complemented each other. In the nineteenth century, the general adoption of dark cloth and the utilitarian aspect of men's clothing gave a different impression: men now seemed to be acting as a foil to the magnificence of women's clothes and no longer indulged in decorative effects which might rival female fashions. This was particularly noticeable in men's evening dress which, by the mid-century, had settled into an unvarying pattern of black and white. Understatement and sobriety were combined with a generally practical approach to dress. Men's work in large cities, offices and factories demanded hard-wearing, comfortable but respectable-looking clothes. However, fashion was not altogether ignored and the male silhouette can be seen to alter in sympathy with the fashionable line of women's dress.

The inevitable tendency towards uniformity created a mixed response in the latter half of the nineteenth century. For some, it had the advantage of giving men a more 'democratic' appearance. In 1874 *The Tailor and Cutter* felt sure that: 'About twenty-five, or fifty years ago, the different classes of society were more clearly and distinctly marked than they are at the present day; on the street, the promenade or other place of resort, a man's position in society could more easily be traced from his dress and appearance than now. In these days, the clerk with a very moderate salary can appear on the promenade with all the airs and appearance of those very much his superiors.'[1]

For others, modern male dress, though rational, was disappointing in its lack of colour, shaping, variety or any kind of picturesque quality, and there were some serious attempts to reform it in the 1880s and 1890s (most famously by Oscar Wilde who for a brief period advocated knee-breeches instead of trousers and wore velvet suits, a 'cavalier' cloak and other colourful accessories for evening dress[2]). In spite of the complaints, the dress reform movement had little real success and most men seemed unwilling to alter their image.

It could be argued that the restraints of men's dress led to a greater refinement and elegance. In 1896 Max Beerbohm, for one,

64 Henry, 1st Baron Brougham and Vaux. *T. Lawrence, 1825.*

This early nineteenth-century portrait of the distinguished politician, Lord Brougham, points the direction in which men's dress was heading. The restraint of plain cloth and the stark contrast between a dark coat and white neckcloth were in keeping with the classical ideal but also suggest a more utilitarian approach to dress as a new and serious interest in business followed the Industrial Revolution. By the mid-nineteenth century men were content to act as a dark foil to the colour and splendour of fashionable women's dress.

praised its virtues and considered that: 'The costume of the nineteenth century, as shadowed for us first by Mr Brummell, so quiet, so reasonable, and, I say, emphatically, so beautiful; free from folly or affectation, yet susceptible to exquisite ordering; plastic, austere, economical, may not be ignored.'[3]

1800–1825

During the first decade of the century the neo-classical taste was evident although the fashionable male suit was essentially a smart version of late-eighteenth-century riding

jersey fabric or woollen cloth cut on the cross-grain to achieve a close fit, and they were often pale in colour, verging on a skin tone. The effect was to outline the shape of the legs, almost as if they were unclothed, in the manner of a Greek or Roman statue. The restraint of the plain woollen cloths now in fashion and the stark contrast between dark coat and white neckcloth was also in keeping with the classical ideal.

This distinctive style had taken some time to develop and, like women's dress, had just emerged from a period of transition in the 1780s and 1790s. Whereas women had abandoned rich silks in favour of light cottons and linens, men had replaced them with woollen cloth. Until the last two decades of the eighteenth century coloured silks, satins and velvets had been used for formal dress for men, although more practical items of day wear and sports dress were made of fine, plain broadcloth. Increasingly the easier, more informal styles of country wear were preferred and in this post-revolutionary period there was a rejection of elaborate clothes and such 'aristocratic' features as expensive lace ruffles and jewelled buckles. Wigs and powdered hair were also abandoned by young men, who emulated a more fashionably natural look.

The general adoption of cloth had a profound effect on the design of men's dress and its aims were now very different. The matt surface of woollen cloth did not depend on the play of light for its decorative effect nor did it call for surface decoration and trimming, but it could be cut and tailored to fit the body perfectly in a way which silk could never do. Colour, pattern and ornament were no longer important elements in male fashion and they were replaced by a new interest in the subtle qualities of cloth and excellence in the making of men's clothes. Cloth was not adopted at the expense of elegance but it was undoubtedly more practical than silk, being warmer, harder-wearing and more comfortable. It suggested less formality and a more utilitarian approach to dress, which was in keeping with a new and serious interest in

dress: a single or double-breasted tail coat of dark cloth, a light-coloured waistcoat and tight-fitting knee-breeches or pantaloons worn with riding boots (or silk stockings and shoes for the evening). The most noticeable feature of classical inspiration was the hair, cut short and arranged in natural curls close to the head *à la Titus* or *Brutus* as the fashionable styles were called. Short side-whiskers completed the resemblance to an antique bust, especially in profile, and this image was reinforced by the expanse of white linen wrapped round the throat which seemed to detach the head from the body. The long, narrow line of women's dress was echoed in the slim fit and high waist of the male coat and the tightness of the knee-breeches and pantaloons tucked into high boots. Breeches and pantaloons could be made from soft pliable leather, warp-knitted

65 A Gentleman and Two Children. H. Edridge, 1799.

As the nineteenth century opened, young boys had already adopted trousers and these could be worn with a short waistcoat and jacket over a white shirt with a frilled collar. Men still wore knee-breeches with a tail coat – essentially a smart version of riding dress. This very British fashion had been copied and, as a result firmly established, by the French in one of their rare phases of Anglomanie in the 1790s.

66 Morning Walking Dress. Le Beau Monde, 1806.

The caption to the plate in this English journal reads: 'Morning dress is a plain single-breasted frock of brown or olive colour . . . pantaloons, drabs of all degrees, in general worn with hussar boots.' The riding hat, with a tall hard crown and round brim was usual for day wear.

business following the Industrial Revolution. An air of restraint and even of discipline in the use of dark cloth may also have owed something to the influence of military uniform in this time of war.

In the early decades of the nineteenth century it was not usual for the fashionable man's suit to be all of the same cloth or colour (although professional men, such as clergymen, lawyers and doctors continued to wear all-black suits as they had done during the eighteenth century). The coat was usually tailored in dark cloth but shades of blue, green, claret and brown were worn besides black for both day and evening wear.[4] Blue and black coats with velvet collars be-

came generally preferred for evening dress and eventually, by 1825, black alone was worn, setting the pattern for the remainder of the century. At this period, however, the formality of a suit was distinguished by the cut of the coat rather than by its colour.

Coats

Until 1815, when the frock-coat made an appearance, the two versions of the tail coat were the main styles worn by day and in the evening. The so-called dress coat (which could also be worn for 'undress' or informal wear during the first half of the century) was cut in across the front at waist level, with what remained of the divided coat skirts forming a pair of 'tails' at the back. The 'cut in' across the waist was often an inverted U-shaped curve rather than the straight, horizontal line which became the usual form after about 1815. A closer fit was achieved by the introduction of darts under the arms and a horizontal one across the waist and in time these became seams (with the tails cut separately).

An alternative tail coat was the riding or morning coat (riding being a gentleman's normal morning occupation). Like the dress coat, it could be single or double-breasted but the front edges were sloped back at the sides rather than cut in. Both the dress coat and morning coat had a high, turn-over collar and the lapels were notched in either a V- or M-shape to allow them to lie flat. The distinctive M-shape appeared around 1800 and was well established by 1803; it was eventually superceded by the V-notch but was still in use for formal coats until 1850. The single- and double-breasted fastenings used both self-covered and metal buttons. Gilt buttons were particularly fashionable with dark blue and black coats for formal wear during the first two decades of the century. Sleeves were cut with a little fullness at the shoulder and had a deep cuff; they were made long enough to cover the wrist and often reached as far down as the

67 Sir John Hay and his Sister. *J. A. D. Ingres, 1816.*

Painted in Rome in 1816, Sir John Hay wears a long, informal coat with straight, overlapping front edges, a high 'Prussian' collar and military-style, frogged trimming. This is an early version of the frock-coat which became fashionable after 1815. Most men wore their hair short and unpowdered in a style which appeared both suitably classical and romantically casual and windswept, but many elderly men continued to wear wigs and powder for formal occasions.

knuckles, resembling the fashionable sleeve of women's spencers and pelisses.

A third style of coat emerged for informal day wear after 1815. This was called the frock-coat but was quite different from the eighteenth-century version with the same name. The nineteenth-century frock-coat was similar in shape to the topcoat or great-coat from which it probably developed and it had straight, overlapping, knee-length skirts. A military-looking version of the frock-coat had a high, standing 'Prussian'

68 Londoners Gypsying. *C. R. Leslie, 1820.*

The young man on the left wears a dark frock-coat, light trousers, white stockings and black shoes. The older, less fashionable man on the right is in knee-breeches worn with long, buttoned gaiters, a country fashion. He has removed his neckcloth and coat for comfort. Small boys wore dresses, with surprisingly low-cut necks and short sleeves, over matching, ankle-length trousers, until the age of about four. These picnickers are evidently only playing at being gypsies and have brought their smart hats and bonnets with them.

collar and braid or frogging across the front, but the more usual style was with a turn-over collar and a plain single- or double-breasted fastening. A heavier-weight greatcoat was worn over the dress coat, morning coat or frock-coat out of doors and for travelling.[5]

The knee-breeches, pantaloons and trousers worn with these coats were, as a rule, a lighter colour and material. Cream breeches and stockings (with flat, buckled shoes) were usual with a blue or black coat for the evening but black breeches and stockings could also be worn. In the daytime knee-breeches were seen with riding boots of black leather with brown tops. The breeches had a buttoned flap or fall-front opening and fastened at the knee with two or three buttons and a buckle or ties. A fashionable alternative, since the 1790s, had been pantaloons worn with hessian boots (distinguished by their heart-shaped tops

with a tassel at the centre front). Pantaloons were long, fitted breeches reaching to well below the knee, as far as mid-calf or ankle and fastening with ties. Like the knee-breeches they could also be worn in the evening with stockings and shoes.

Very similar to the pantaloons were the early trousers which were also long and narrow with a slit and button fastening at the ankle. Trousers were already familiar wear for small boys in the later eighteenth century but it was not until the early years of the nineteenth that they became acceptable informal wear for adult men. Nankin (a stout, buff-coloured cotton) was much used for loose-fitting summer trousers and possibly the popularity of Brighton as a seaside resort encouraged this fashion. By July 1808 the magazine *Le Beau Monde* was showing nankin trousers with a green dress coat as 'half full dress'. In general, fashionable

69 George Bryan
Brummell. *J. Cook.*

69 George Bryan
Brummell. *J. Cook.*

*Beau Brummell's
understated approach
to the existing fashion
was a reflection of the
social attitudes of a
period when great
value was placed on
good taste, good
manners and good
breeding. One of his
general maxims,
according to his
biographer Captain
William Jesse, 'was
that the severest
mortification which a
gentleman could incur,
was to attract
observation in the street
by his outward
appearance . . .'*

trousers were straight and ankle-length, but by 1817 they reached the instep and were kept in place by a strap passing under the foot. George Brummell is credited with the introduction, if not the invention, of the trouser strap which gave the garment a smooth, taut line. Trousers steadily gained in popularity and by 1825 had virtually replaced pantaloons for daytime wear, but were not yet accepted for full dress wear. As they were worn with low-heeled, lace-up shoes or half-boots, the longer riding boots and hessians began to pass out of fashion.

The third piece of the suit was the waistcoat, which for informal wear might be coloured, checked or striped but for evening was usually plain white or cream or a light striped silk. On some occasions two waistcoats were worn. The waistcoat followed the lines of the coat, either single or double-breasted, but it could be made with or without a high collar and revers. Until about 1820 the lower edge was at the natural waist level or slightly above it, adding to the short-waisted effect of men's fashion. The waistcoat buttoned low enough to reveal part of the shirt front and the frill that concealed the centre front opening of the

shirt. By 1806 this frill was beginning to be replaced by a pleated, buttoned front for day wear but the eighteenth-century frill remained the more usual form with evening dress.[6]

The shirt had a high neckband or collar which rose up to the chin (the points sometimes overlapping the jaw) and round this was wrapped the neckcloth. The fashionable neckcloth was the cravat, a large square of lawn or muslin folded cornerwise into a band and variously arranged about the neck to tie in a knot or bow at the front. Plain white cravats were correct for day and evening dress but patterned white or coloured neckcloths could also be worn on informal occasions. Careful attention was paid to the quality and arrangement of the neckcloth, which was a focal point of men's fashion at this time. Several manuals on the art of tying the cravat were published and Beau Brummell was noted for the freshness, whiteness and exquisite ordering of his cravats, which he lightly starched to improve their appearance.[7] The stock, a made-up, stiffened band of silk or linen which fastened at the back of the neck, could also be worn but this was more confined to military and sporting wear until after 1822, when a black silk stock was popularized by George IV.

Unlike women, men did not look to Paris or the Continent for the lead in fashion at the opening of the nineteenth century. The skill of British tailors was beginning to be appreciated abroad and Britain itself seemed to be setting the standard in fashionable male dress. This is thought to have been due, in some part, to the influence of George Bryan Brummell, who was one of the few early nineteenth-century dandies to achieve lasting fame and respect. Brummell had a passion for clothes and he was a perfectionist with an infinite capacity for taking pains. His contribution to fashion was to create a new standard of elegance and ideal of perfection in male dress. Contrary to the popular image of the dandy, Brummell was by no means a flamboyant dresser. The whole emphasis of his appear-

70 Beriah Botfield.
T. Phillips, 1828.

In the final flowering of the Romantic period men's clothes boldly and enthusiastically explored the use of line and colour before settling down to a more sober and practical form of dress. Mr Botfield looks suitably Byronic in his loose-collared shirt and voluminous cloak and his hair is worn in the longer curls of the late 1820s. His very loose, long 'moschetto' trousers are shaped at the bottom to completely cover the ankle and top of the shoe, with a strap under the instep.

ance was on refinement and restraint – a simplicity and elegance of cut combined with naturalness and freedom of movement. He stressed the importance of neatness and cleanliness (it was a matter of pride to him that he did not need to use perfume) and although he spent hours each day on his toilette, his aim was to appear as though he had not.

1825–1850

The changes in fashionable men's dress during the second quarter of the nineteenth century were less dramatic than in women's, although the general shape of male clothes quite closely resembled the female silhouette. From 1825 to 1835 coat sleeves were cut in the *gigot* style, less exaggerated than its female counterpart but with an unmistakable fullness at the shoulder tapering towards the wrist; the waist was tightened and curves were created above and below with padded coat fronts, large shawl collars and full coat skirts. During the later 1830s and 1840s the line was modified and tended towards a longer, narrower silhouette: shoulders acquired a softer, more sloping line and the sleeves tightened, much of the front padding disappeared and the waist was lengthened. It was only at the end of this period that men began to lose much of the colour and variety in their dress and adopted the darker, more uniform range of clothes usually associated with the Victorian era.

The form of the suit remained unchanged. A dark blue or black coat was already the convention for full dress but cream breeches were giving way to cream or black pantaloons in the 1820s and by the late 1830s only black pantaloons or trousers were worn with evening dress. For the daytime, coats were tailored in plain woollen cloths in black or subdued shades, but waistcoats were generally brightly coloured and patterned in silk or light wool. Trousers, from the late 1830s, could be checked and striped.[8]

The tail coat with the fronts cut away in a straight line across the waist continued to be worn as a 'dress' coat both during the day and in the evening. An innovation of the 1820s was the 'button stand', a separate band along the front edges to carry the buttons or buttonholes. The large collar, standing high at the back and rolling over at the front, dropped during the 1830s and was lying almost flat by the 1840s with wide, notched lapels. Similarly the sleeves altered in shape from the gigot of the later 1820s and 1830s, with its gathering and padding at the shoulder, to a smoother, tighter fit in the 1840s. The waistline remained a little above the natural level until 1836, when it began to lengthen, but the emphasis was on a close fit and shapely curves.[9] The introduction of a waist seam in the early 1820s solved the problem of an unsightly horizontal crease when the coat was tightly buttoned. Side-bodies,

71 Winter Fashions.
B. Read, 1834–5.

The shape of men's clothes quite closely resembled the female silhouette in the period 1825–35. Sleeves were cut with a little fullness over the shoulder, the waistline was sharply defined and the long coat-skirts swelled out over the hips. In children's clothes there was an increasing tendency towards elaboration and the imitation of fashionable adult styles.

72 The Conversazione.
J. Couts, c. 1843.

By the 1840s the usual form of evening dress for men was a black dress coat, white or black waistcoat and black breeches (right) or pantaloons (left) with black stockings and shoes. The dress shirt was now made like the day shirt, without a frill, and with a pleated front fastened by buttons or studs (although the frill was worn by some men up to the 1850s). The long waist was a feature of both male and female fashions of this date

and these waistcoats dip to sharp 'hussar points' at the centre front.

another innovation of around 1840, ensured a better fit. These were narrow panels, four to five inches wide, let in under each armhole giving the back of the coat five rather than three seams. Until they were adopted the coat had a narrow-backed appearance while the chest was broad and emphasized by front padding.

A similar line was followed by the frock-coat which, after 1825, was becoming the most popular coat for informal daytime wear. It was usually single-breasted with a fitted waist and full, knee-length skirts with straight fronts. In the 1830s there were a number of variations on this style, with names such as the Petersham, Taglioni and Military frock-coat. At the end of this decade the skirts shortened, and this was to be a characteristic feature of the 1840s.

Breeches, pantaloons and trousers were all worn during the second quarter of the

century, but this period saw each garment ascending the scale of formality so that breeches were replaced by pantaloons for evening dress and eventually pantaloons were ousted by trousers for all but the most formal evening wear.[10] The distinction between long pantaloons and the fashionably narrow trousers, both with straps under the instep, was slight, but trousers steadily increased in popularity. In 1825 they were general daytime wear, although many elderly and unfashionable men kept to knee-breeches until the mid-nineteenth century. The fall-front opening was beginning to be replaced by the concealed or 'fly' fastening at the centre front. It was first used around 1823 but was not in common use until the

1840s. In the later 1830s trousers ceased to be made with a waistband; at about the same time men began to stop carrying a watch in the waist pocket of the breeches, pantaloons or trousers and instead used a breast pocket added to the waistcoat for this purpose. Braces were worn to hold up the trousers, and when combined with straps under the foot created a firm, smooth line. Far from being a utilitarian accessory, braces were an object of decorative attention and could be very colourfully embroidered.

Colour and pattern in male dress were now largely concentrated on the waistcoat, and it was given prominence by the fashion for an expansive chest (created by padding and darting at the front and also by wearing one or more waistcoats). When the waist lengthened around 1836 the waistcoat dipped at the centre front to what was called a 'hussar point'. A neat, tight fit was achieved by adjusting the back with a buckle and strap, a method which from 1845 replaced the earlier tapes threaded through tabs.

Pattern and colour also permeated men's neckwear, and the previous discipline and refinement of fine white linen, lightly starched and beautifully tied, gave way to a more imaginative and lively approach in the daytime (although white cravats remained indispensable for evening wear). Black or coloured silk cravats and stocks were adopted, still swathed round the neck but in more stylized arrangements often using buckram stiffeners to keep them upright. In the later 1820s patterned neckcloths were fashionable – bold checks and even floral designs in bright colours were illustrated in the fashion journals. By the early 1840s the spreading 'scarf cravat' of plain silk, covering the whole space above the waistcoat opening, was a popular style, and this was often held in place by long pins with elaborate heads and gold chains. The earlier form of the cravat which passed round the neck with the ends crossing at the back and brought forward to tie at the front, remained a standard style, but during the 1840s its height was reduced and attention was now focused

73 The Marquess of Dalhousie. J. Watson-Gordon, 1847.

The frock-coat was the most popular coat for informal daytime wear and by 1850 had also replaced the dress coat for formal day wear. The shorter length, well above the knees, was characteristic of the 1840s. Most men in Britain were clean-shaven or wore narrow side whiskers, sometimes meeting under the chin, but moustaches were not common in this country until the later 1840s and beards were virtually never worn at this date.

74 Derby Day (detail). W. P. Frith, 1856–58.

Easy-fitting overcoats worn over frock-coats provided additional warmth in winter and protection from the dust in summer. By this date trousers were universal day wear; the fly-front fastening had become general but straps under the instep were beginning to disappear. (Pantaloons were seldom worn after 1850 except for evening dress and knee-breeches were confined to sporting wear.)

on the bow, which in turn grew larger.

The shirt collar remained high until the late 1840s but only the top edge and the points or 'gills' were visible above the prominent neckcloth; on occasion the collar points were turned over at the top. Most shirts were made with a collar attached, but separate collars had appeared in the 1820s and were becoming more usual by the 1840s, especially when the lower collar came into fashion.[11]

The top hat was the common form for daytime wear. The most fashionable style had a narrow curling brim and slightly waisted sides which curved outwards at the top, but other versions were worn including a more cylindrical shape with straight sides and brim. A collapsible top hat with a spring in the crown, known as a *chapeau gibus* (named after the Frenchman who patented it in 1835) was used in the evening; the folding, crescent-shaped opera hat (or *chapeau bras*) fashionable at the beginning of the century was now relegated to the most

formal occasions and Court wear. Other accessories to evening dress included black silk ribbed or patterned stockings and pumps – as dress shoes were called. During the day, boots or shoes with narrow, square or sometimes pointed toes were worn. High boots in the hessian or the Wellington style were worn with pantaloons and breeches but half-boots or shoes were more popular with trousers. A common form of half-boot with lacing at the front was the Blucher, but in 1837 the elastic-sided boot appeared. This was one result of the experiments made with India rubber cloth, and was very fashionable during the 1840s. The Albert, another style of half-boot which appeared in the 1830s, had a cloth top and side-lacing.

1850–1875

Work and Leisure

The second half of the nineteenth century saw an increasing divergence between male and female dress. The dominant element in society was the middle-class businessman, and the clothes he required were sensible, comfortable and practical. Dark colours conveyed a suitably sober and professional air but also answered a need in an industrial age. As Hippolyte Taine remarked in the 1860s, 'the climate is very dirty, things have to be changed and replaced frequently', although he also added that an 'immaculate appearance is obligatory for a gentleman'.[12] The quality of a man's clothes continued to be of great importance as an indication of rank but there was less emphasis on exaggerated shaping. The professional man could not afford to be restricted by his clothes, and during the 1850s and 1860s there was a marked preference for looser shapes. Tight waists, padded chests, full coat skirts and narrow sleeves disappeared and lower shirt collars were worn with smaller neckties. An air of comfort and informality was reinforced by a growing interest in clothes specifically designed for informal wear,

First Elegant Creature. " A—DON'T YOU DANCE, CHARLES ? "
Second ditto, ditto. " A—NO—NOT AT PWESENT ! I ALWAYS LET THE GIRLS LOOK, AND LONG FOR ME FIRST ! "

travelling and holidays. The 1850s and 1860s were to see the introduction of a number of new garments such as loose capes, jackets and overcoats, tweed or flannel lounging suits, knickerbockers and soft hats and caps. On the whole, however, there was a clear division between clothes for work and for leisure as these two spheres of life became more regulated.

In 1850 the fashionable coat for formal day wear was the frock-coat in dark blue or black cloth. It could be single- or double-breasted and fitted close to the body. The waist was long but the separately cut skirts, with overlapping fronts and centre back vent, were relatively short. The day dress coat, cut in across the waist at the front, was now less frequently worn and by 1862 had disappeard from fashion.[13] The other form of tail coat, sloped back at the sides, retained its popularity for day wear and began to rival the frock-coat. The morning coat, or 'cutaway' as it was sometimes called, was usually single-breasted and less fitted at the waist.

The frock-coat and morning coat were usually made in plain dark cloth while the waistcoat and trousers were of contrasting colours and materials, often checked or striped. The fancy waistcoat was still fashionable for day wear and could be brightly coloured in a variety of silk fabrics with woven or embroidered patterns – tartan in particular was popular – but towards the late 1850s a taste for quieter effects was becoming evident. Patterned trousers could have the added ornament of a band of braid or a stripe of contrasting fabric along the outer leg seam, drawing attention to the legs and the fairly tight cut of the trousers fashionable during this decade. For more formal day wear trousers were made in plain light-coloured cloths such as grey and fawn.

The later 1850s saw a marked change in the cut and shape of men's suits. As if responding to the fuller, softer and shorter-waisted style of women's dresses, men's clothes loosened to create a squarer silhouette. As early as 1853, R. S. Surtees was remarking on 'the loose, careless, flowing, sack-like garments' worn by fashionable

76 Woman's Mission:
Companion of
Manhood. *G. E. Hicks,
1863.*

*Although the three
pieces of a formal suit
did not match, it was
now possible for
informal morning and
lounge suits to be made
of a piece – often in a
checked tweed with
braided edges. The
short, loose cut of the
morning coat at this
date makes it almost
indistinguishable from
a lounge coat and even
the tailoring journals
tend to be confusing
about the two forms.*
The Gentleman's
Magazine of Fashion
*wrote in April 1861: 'In
morning or Lounging
suits, the jacket falls
square, having seams
straight, the skirt is not
very long.'*

77 Lord Carlingford.
J. Tissot, 1871. (right)

A narrower line
returned to fashion in
the late 1860s and is
evident in the dark
frock-coat, light
waistcoat and trousers
seen here for formal day
wear. Ankle boots were
the most usual form of
footwear and knee boots
were now only worn for
riding. Buttoned boots
were increasingly
popular in the 1860s
and 1870s.

young men although this was probably an exaggeration as the new line did not become generally noticeable until around 1855.[14] The waistline gradually shortened and coat skirts became longer and straighter, while sleeves were cut fuller at the shoulder in the 'peg top' shape – which was then carried through into trousers in 1857. Peg-top trousers, which were wide at the hips and tapered at the ankles, were a fashionable alternative to the more conventional straight cut, but they were not universally worn and disappeared after about ten years. Well-dressed men avoided extremes in the cut and patterning of their clothes.

Paletots and Baggy Sacks

The loose overcoats and jackets which had appeared for less formal wear in the later 1850s were often referred to as 'baggy sacks'. A number of new styles were invented, each with its own name, but many of them shared the same features and were often known by the general term of 'paletot'. These overgarments were short, usually above the knee or thigh-length, with a wide, almost circular cut and very loose sleeves flaring at the wrist. Large buttons fastening high to the neck and quilted linings were other popular features. Light-weight versions were made for the summer, to protect the frock-coat or morning coat from dust, especially when travelling; others appeared as macintoshes, in waterproofed cloth. In 1859 a caped form of paletot became known as the Inverness, and it was a universal fashion by the early 1860s.[15] Another popular overcoat with a hood and half-belt at the back, known as the Ulster, was to appear ten years later. There were also unwaisted jackets which were short and square in shape, with single- or double-breasted fastenings – the most popular of which were the pilot coat with very large buttons, and the pea or monkey jacket which was a little shorter. 'Pilot' coat may be

a corruption of 'paletot' as many of these coats were also referred to as 'paletot jackets' and 'paletot sacs'.

Another form of jacket, of which there were several versions, was the 'lounge' which was thigh-length and easy fitting, but tailored enough to be worn in place of a coat on informal occasions – literally, for lounging about in. It had a small collar and short lapels, fastening high to the neck; the fashion for closing the top button only and leaving the jacket to hang open at the front contributed to its baggy appearance. By 1857 these coats were becoming fashionable wear for a wide range of leisure activities in the country and at the seaside and during the 1860s the lounge suit became well established in the male wardrobe. The three pieces of the more formal frock-coat or morning coat suit worn in town never matched, but by the early 1850s it became possible to wear an informal coat, waistcoat and trousers of the same material, usually a checked tweed. Illustrations of these appear in Punch as early as 1850.

A liking for both colour and comfort in dress extended to the style of men's shirts. By 1850 day shirts had a centre front fastening with two or three buttons or studs and vertical pleating on either side of the opening. The frill on evening dress shirts was disappearing, but intricate pleating and embroidery on the front gave them a decorative air. Billy Pringle, the engaging 'swell' in R. S. Surtees' novel Ask Mamma, had 'some magnificently embroidered dress shirts, so fine that the fronts almost looked as if you might blow them out', and for day wear in the country, 'several dozen with horses, dogs, birds, and foxes upon them, "suitable for fishing, shooting, boating, etc"', as the advertisements said.'[16] The more conventional fashion was for plain white linen or cotton shirts in town and coloured stripes in the country or for sports. The shirt collar was made and sold separately; set on a straight band, it curved up towards the chin with a gap at the centre front but in general collars were lower and some could be turned down over the cravat.

Neckties and Smoking Jackets

The cravat was now arranged with less emphasis on the swathing round the neck and more on the tie of the bow. The main part of the cravat narrowed into a band and the bow became larger, transforming the neckcloth into a necktie. There was a considerable amount of variety in the styles of

men's neckwear, and a profusion of different names for them. A popular form of the bow tie with fringed ends, for example, was called the Joinville. Very narrow 'shoe-ties' were also fashionable, simply knotted or fastened with a ring at the throat with the long ends left to hang free. A variant of this which appeared around 1857 was a broader tie, called a four-in-hand, similar to the modern man's tie. The scarf or cravat folded in front and fastened with a pin also continued to be worn, but plain white cravats were usually only seen with evening dress. With the high-buttoning style of coats and waistcoats in the later 1850s neckties lost their prominence and during the early 1860s became even narrower, tied in small flat bows.

A habit introduced by the men returning from the Crimean War of 1854–6 was cigarette smoking. Cigars were already smoked (having appeared in Britain in about 1812 with the soldiers returning from the Peninsular War) but cigarettes soon became equally popular and gentlemen withdrew to a room set aside for the purpose where they put on a special jacket and cap to prevent the clothes and hair from smelling of stale smoke. The smoking jacket was cut on the lines of the lounge, although it might be more correct to see it as a short version of the dressing-gown with its easy fit and use of soft materials such as silk or velvet, with cord trimmings and quilted lapels; it was, in any case, a garment to relax in. The smoking cap was usually a pork-pie shape with a tassel and provided scope for embroidered decoration.

The loose cut was a prominent feature of men's fashions until the mid-1860s. The easy fit of men's clothes undoubtedly made them more comfortable to wear but it tended to create a droopy impression and even the most elegant swells of the 1860s were invariably described as 'languid'. A dull uniformity was suggested both by the lack of shaping and the disappearance of colour. The popularity of the lounge suit, with its three pieces made to match, steadily increased and in May 1861 *The Gentleman's*

78 Frock-Coat and Morning Coat. Gazette of Fashion, 1881.

The two main styles of coat for formal day wear were the frock-coat (left) worn with a high silk hat and the morning coat (right) with the less formal hard felt bowler. Both styles of hat had been lower in the crown in the 1870s. A fitted, Chesterfield overcoat is worn over the frock-coat. Also illustrated are the two forms of shirt collar: the single, upright collar worn with a bow tie (left) and the more informal, double or turn-down collar with a four-in-hand knotted tie (right). Spats had appeared by the late 1870s and were fashionable with the frock-coat in the 1880s–90s. A slim walking stick or tightly furled umbrella was another correct accessory and complemented the narrow, elegant line of the late nineteenth century.

Magazine of Fashion reported: 'In Paris the short square jacket, where the entire suit is of one material, is quite the rage; they call it the *Jaquette Anglais* ... In England this kind of jacket will be worn for travelling, for the country, and at the seaside; for very hot weather, the most *recherché* will be of white Jean or coutil.' Nine years later, 'coarse tweed and fancy mixed coatings' were still usual for the country, according the *The Tailor and Cutter*, while 'blue serge is the most fashionable material for those who spend their holidays at the seaside.'[17] The dark blue serge lounge suit for seaside wear often took the form of a short, double-breasted reefer or yachting jacket with matching trousers.

An alternative to the suit all of a piece was a dark velvet lounge jacket (thought to be perfectly suitable for country wear) worn with a light-coloured waistcoat and trousers in small checks called the Shepherd's Plaid pattern. Yet another version of the lounge coat to appear in the early 1860s was the

Norfolk jacket, at first called the Norfolk blouse, cut with box pleats on either side of the centre front and at the centre back, with a belt at the waist. Unlike the reefer which could also be worn informally in town, the Norfolk jacket was strictly country wear and by the end of the decade was often teamed with a new sporting garment: knickerbockers. These appeared at the time of the formation of the Volunteer Movement in 1859–60; they were adopted by many of the Rifle Corps and were subsequently adapted for shooting costume in general.[18] In 1859 knickerbockers also appeared in the dress of little boys.

Plain Style

By 1868 a narrower line was becoming evident. The billowing curves created by the peg-top shape in sleeves and trousers straightened out and disappeared while coats and jackets tightened and shortened to well above the knee. This new line emerged at the same time as women were discarding the crinoline petticoat and beginning to favour a more vertical silhouette. There was an increasing distrust of the effeminate or the ostentatious in male dress by this date, and not only were fancy waistcoats and inessential jewellery on the decline but shirt fronts became quite plain for both day and evening wear. At the same time there was an increased use of starch, which gave a crisper look to collars and cuffs. The tendency towards sobriety and uniformity continued and a typical observation, coming from *The Tailor and Cutter* in 1871, was that 'Gentlemen dress as quietly as it is possible to do and there are no remarkable extremes in dress.'[19]

During the last quarter of the nineteenth century the three principal coats for day wear continued to be the frock-coat, morning coat and the lounge suit, their use depending on the occasion and time of day. The form of these garments altered comparatively little but their roles were to change, especially in the case of the frock-coat and the lounge suit.

1875–1900

In 1875 the frock-coat was still considered correct, if somewhat formal, daytime wear although the morning coat was generally more popular and thought to be smarter. The frock-coat had, in fact, gained the reputation of a rather dull but worthy garment [20] although it changed its shape to keep in line with the narrow silhouette of female dress; during the late 1870s and early 1880s the fit was tighter round the chest and waist, with the coat skirts cut longer and straighter, to the knee. By 1882–3 the exquisite 'mashers', successors to the dandies and the swells of earlier decades, looked pencil-slim in their tight suits and high starched collars. Possibly as a result of this attention to fit and a smart appearance, the frock-coat returned to favour for a period during the 1890s and it became more shaped. The waistline shortened, the silk-faced lapels lengthened and the majority of coats were worn open. Usual materials were thin, smooth worsted or cheviot cloths in shades of grey or black, with silk linings and fancy twist buttons.[21]

In spite of this revival, even the rather conservative *Tailor and Cutter* conceded that the frock-coat was going out of fashion for ordinary wear by the late 1890s. In 1900 it was not even mentioned under 'morning or business wear', but was relegated to the categories of 'weddings, receptions and matinées' and as an alternative to the morning coat for church-going. With the frock-coat it was correct to wear a light-coloured, double-breasted waistcoat, dark striped worsted or cashmere trousers, a white shirt with high collar, a silk or satin necktie, black patent leather boots, a high silk hat and gloves of either grey suede or tan kid or calf.[22] The frock-coat was also falling out of favour in less fashionable society. George Moore's eponymous heroine, Esther Waters (in his novel of 1894), was a servant walking out with a shop assistant, Fred, but she would have liked him better 'if he wore coloured neckties and a short jacket; she wished half of him away – his dowdiness, his sandy-coloured hair, the vague eyes, the black neckties, the long loose frock-coat.' The Dissenting

79 Group at Nunnykirk, photographed in 1891.

The lounge suit was fashionable for informal daytime wear and flannel was a popular material for the summer by the 1890s. The coat and waistcoat still buttoned high on the chest. A soft, peaked cap was often worn with the lounge suit.

80 Young Man with a Dog, photographed c. 1880–90.

The Norfolk suit with its vertically-pleated and belted jacket was worn for country and sporting pursuits – especially cycling and golf. It was usually made of tweed, sometimes with a cap to match. The knickerbockers were tucked into thick woollen hose and worn with ankle boots or shoes. By this date elastic-sided boots were disappearing from fashion and boots or shoes were either buttoned or front-laced. Heels had settled at a height of about one inch.

tradesman for whom Esther worked in Chelsea wore an ill-fitting frock-coat on Sundays but 'on week days he wore a short jacket.'[23]

Throughout this period the morning coat remained the popular garment for day and business wear. It was more versatile than the frock-coat as it could be made in formal or informal versions: the former came in plain black or dark grey cloth worn with a waistcoat and striped grey trousers, while the latter was made of a piece with coat, waistcoat and trousers in matching tweed or woollen cloth. By the late 1890s the distinction was also marked by the cut of the coat: the more formal, for 'semi-dress wear' after lunch, was worn longer in the skirt and sharply cut away; a shorter version with the fronts less cut away and plenty of pockets

was made for businessmen, mornings and less dressy occasions.[24]

The morning coat was usually single-breasted but could be worn with either a single- or double-breasted waistcoat. The high-fastening style of the earlier period continued into the 1880s and, like the frock-coat, the morning coat became tighter and longer. By the 1890s *The Tailor and Cutter* thought the long style had 'a very graceful appearance on a tall figure'.[25] This may also have been the result of using different cloths which were lighter and more pliable. 'The days of broadcloth have long gone by,' observed *Manners for Men* in 1898, 'and coats are now made of vicuna cloth or black twilled worsteds, with a dull finish and of an elastic quality.'[26] Throughout this period the edges of the coat could be bound or

braided. It was not usual to pad the shoulders (a technique which was described as 'American') but the use of wadding increased towards the end of the century. The correct accessories with a black morning coat were black buttoned boots, top hat and grey gloves; but with a tweed suit a felt bowler, brown boots and tan gloves could be worn.

Despite the attention paid to the frock and morning coats, the lounge was steadily gaining in popularity and by the end of the century had become a serious rival to them both.[27] From being a strictly informal suit for sports and country wear it had gradually become a viable alternative to the morning coat for day wear, although in 1900 it was still not thought quite appropriate for the afternoon in London. A book of etiquette advised: 'When you are in town you mustn't appear in a lounge suit and a bowler after lunch, and of course if you had any busi-ness appointment in the morning, you would wear a frock or morning coat suit and silk hat.'[28]

A wide variety of cloths were used for lounge suits. Tweeds, cheviots, worsteds and serges were the most popular and by the 1890s flannels were being used. Very smart lounge suits for town wear were made in striped black cashmere. The general form of the lounge jacket was single-breasted, fastening with three or four buttons, the fronts moderately rounded, flap pockets on the hips and a welt pocket on the left breast. The fit was almost always easy and some jackets with a 'whole back' had no centre back seam; otherwise the 'three-seamer' had one back seam and two side seams (unlike the five seams of the more shaped frock and morning coats).

Another version of the lounge coat was the square-cornered reefer, either single- or double-breasted. In dark navy blue serge, the double-breasted reefer was very fashionable in the 1890s and was also worn as the 'best' suit of working class men. The reefer was a little longer than the lounge and generally made without a back seam – slits were left at the bottom of the side seams and the fronts were cut quite straight. This gave the coat its characteristic boxy appearance. It was a useful coat because it could be worn in both winter and summer. In the winter, apparently, it might serve as a light overcoat and in summer it could be a sports or yachting jacket worn without a waistcoat (and thus not too hot).[29] The twentieth-century version of this coat, in navy blue with brass buttons, worn with flannel trousers, was to be known as a blazer. In the late nineteenth century, however, the blazer usually denoted a brightly coloured or striped flannel jacket. The blazer had become popular for the seaside in the mid-1880s and was worn until the end of the century for summer sports such as tennis, cricket and rowing. The Norfolk jacket remained popular for other sports and was found to be particularly suitable for the new pastime of cycling, especially when worn with knickerbockers.

As in previous decades the cut of the

trousers was an important feature of fashion. With the slender line of the 1880s trousers tended to be rather narrow and straight but they were generally easy-fitting in the 1890s. At the very end of the century the line narrowed again and trousers were looking very elegant by 1900. The most significant change came with the introduction of centre front and back creases in the early 1890s.[30] These resulted from the use of the newly invented trousers press which required the legs to be folded with the insides together instead of pressing them flat with the creases along the side seams. Trousers stretchers and presses helped to prevent the perennial problem of bagging at the knees and they now gave men's legs a smarter appearance. Another change was the increasing practice of turning up the hems. Turned-up trousers had been seen as early as the 1860s in wet and muddy weather or for sports wear, but this practical habit did not become common until the late 1880s. By the later 1890s the trousers of lounge suits were often made to turn up; and although this was not correct for those worn with frock and morning coats, formal trousers could be turned up as a temporary measure in the rain. Braid was no longer applied to the outer side seams of day trousers but a discreet one-inch stripe of mohair or silk braid was usual on the plain black trousers for evening dress.

There was little change in the appearance of the dress coat which remained essential for evening wear until the introduction of the 'dress lounge' or dinner jacket in the late 1880s. This was an evening version of the lounge suit for less formal wear such as dinners at home or 'in houses where one is a familiar guest' and at the theatre (though never when accompanying ladies).[31] For still more informal evening wear at home the smoking jacket could be worn, and by the 1890s it was generally made of dark velvet or silk with quilted silk facings and cord fastenings.

For some years the waistcoat had been obscured by the high-buttoning line of the coat, and it received little serious attention until the 1890s when it had a temporary revival. With lower-cut coats, fancy waistcoats in comparatively bright colours and patterns made a brief return to fashion, but they never really achieved the status they had enjoyed in the 1830s and 1840s. By this time it was the convention to wear only plain white or black waistcoats with evening dress and there was little scope for experiment beyond the use of silk fabrics with self-coloured embroidery or raised patterns. Black waistcoats were a fashionable alternative to white from the 1840s to the end of the century and it appears that either could be worn. Although white was probably considered the more formal of the two there was no clear rule about this, and at some periods, as in the 1870s, it was more correct to wear black. It was not until the beginning of the twentieth century that a pattern was set for wearing only a white tie and waistcoat with the dress coat. In 1893 the cummerbund was introduced as an alternative to the waistcoat in hot weather and was worn informally with both day and evening dress. For smart daytime wear the 'slip' or false under-waistcoat was revived and this provided a narrow contrasting band along the top edge of the waistcoat. The white slip was considered particularly elegant although other colours were worn.[32]

Spotless white linen, of the best quality, was still the badge of a gentleman, and during the later nineteenth century a greater use of starch added to its sparkling appearance and air of stiff propriety. The collar, cuffs and shirt front were all starched for both day and evening wear. Starch had the additional advantage of helping to keep the shirt clean as dirt was less liable to penetrate the smooth and shiny surface. Those who could not afford frequent changes of linen often resorted to paper, rubber or celluloid collars and cuffs which might be scrubbed; there were also disposable shirt and cuff 'protectors'. An alternative for working-class men was to wear a coloured shirt of blue or grey flannel. For gentlemen, striped or patterned shirts were an acceptable part of sports dress, and by the end of the century

these were being worn with informal coats in the country.

The most striking feature of the shirt during this period was the height of the detached collar. This steadily rose, reaching as much as three inches in the 1890s. There was a variety of collar styles, each with its own name, but essentially there were two main forms: the single, upright collar and the double, stand-up, turn-down collar. The single collar was correct with formal dress and could be varied by the shape of its corners which might overlap or turn back in the 'butterfly' shape. The double collar was more suitable for informal daytime wear and was never worn in the evening.

By comparison with the splendour of the collar, neckties were almost insignificant in the 1870s and 1880s but became more colourful and important in the smarter atmosphere of the 1890s. The silk cravat or 'scarf' returned to fashion and in a geometrically folded version was known as the Ascot. The other favourite styles were the bow tie and the four-in-hand knotted tie. Made-up ties were also available.

At the close of the nineteenth century, both men's and women's clothes were changing shape to create a new, slimmer and more sinuous line. It was a tendency in men's tailoring which was to be responsible for much of the elegance now associated with the Edwardian period. In March 1900 *The Tailor and Cutter* noted: 'The fashion for the forthcoming spring, both for ladies and gentlemen, will tend to give the figure an increase of length ... Anything which helps the figure look tall and thin, will be in keeping with the dictates of fashion for 1900.'[33]

-6-
STATUS, TIME AND PLACE
The Etiquette of Dress I

83 For Better, For Worse. *W. P. Frith, 1881.*

The nineteenth century was a highly class-conscious period and there was a great preoccupation with social identity. In Frith's painting of a newly-married couple departing for their honeymoon, clothes are used to distinguish the different spectators of the scene, from the destitute family on the left (married 'For Worse') to the maidservant, crossing sweeper, policeman and young Italian organ grinder on the right. The wedding guests are all fashionably dressed and obviously belong to the wealthy upper-middle class.

In the nineteenth century the appearance of a man's or woman's clothes was regulated not only by fashion but also by the rules of social etiquette. For anyone who wished to stand well in society it was essential for clothing to be appropriate to the person's station in life, to the occasion and to the time of day. These considerations affected the form of garments, their material, colour and decoration. An understanding and observance of such conventions had long been accepted as a social duty among the middle and upper classes, as important as good manners and correct deportment; and while an excessive concern with personal appearance and fashion was considered vulgar, a due respect for the rituals of dress was expected. In 1830 *The Whole Art of Dress* assured gentlemen 'that attention to the exterior is by no means incompatible with the highest order of mental excellence and attainment'[1], and for ladies, *The Workwoman's Guide* of 1838 thought that 'attention to the minutiae of dress adds much to a lady-like and refined appearance, and ... an endeavour to please by an agreeable exterior, does not necessarily involve a disposition to vanity and frivolity.'[2]

With the Victorian period, the etiquette of social behaviour and dress acquired a new significance and complexity, becoming a source of constant preoccupation. A manual on *Etiquette for Ladies and Gentlemen* of the 1840s gave an indication of the reason. 'It may be as well to state that Etiquette is a name given to the code of laws established by the highest class of society for regulating the conduct, words and actions of those admitted within its sphere; and so thoroughly are these rules and regulations based upon the principles of good sense and politeness, that they have become not only absolutely essential to the wellbeing and happiness of society, but even to its very existence. Etiquette is the key-stone in the arch of refinement; and it would be both impolitic and dangerous to remove it: it is an effectual barrier against the innovations of the vulgar ...'[3] Maintaining an appearance of refinement and resisting 'the innovations of the vulgar', though they had always been the objects of social etiquette, were now more important than ever as a result of the swiftly changing social conditions in Britain.

The sense of being caught up in what has been described as 'the vortex of social change'[4] brought with it both feelings of exhilaration about new opportunities and fears of impending disorder and lack of control. The traditional structure of society was being undermined by a number of different factors. There was the rapid expansion of the population and the migration from the countryside to the towns with the change-over from a largely agrarian to an industrial

110

84 The Empty Purse.
J. Collinson, 1857.

Wealth and status could be clearly expressed in nineteenth-century dress. The young woman's fashionable silk gown and decorative accessories point to an affluent background while its impractical nature indicates that she does not need to work for her living. Making and buying fancy articles at church bazaars was a favourite form of charitable endeavour for upper and middle-class ladies.

I Mrs Robert Sherson.

G. Chinnery, 1803

The sitter's one-piece gown of white spotted fabric has a high-waisted bodice with a V-shaped neck opening and short, puffed sleeves set into a deep armband – a fashion of this date. The skirt, with its additional fullness at the back, falls in graceful folds over her legs, clearly outlining the shape of her knees (this and her informal posture, though typical of the period, would have later shocked ladies of the Victorian era). Her straw bonnet tied with silk ribbons and black net or lace shawl for outdoor wear lie beside her.

II   The Reading of the Will Concluded.
E. Bird, 1811

*This dramatic scene includes a variety of people of
different ages, dressed in both indoor and outdoor
wear. On the left, the seated woman wears a straw
bonnet over her indoor cap, a neckerchief and a
shawl; the men to her right and left are dressed in
caped overcoats and riding dress. On the right there is
a boy in a skeleton suit with frilled shirt collar and a
girl with cropped hair, wearing a pelisse and dangling
her bonnet on her arm. Their mother is also in a pelisse
and the neck of her dress is filled in with a habit shirt.
The father, in service uniform, wears a black
neckcloth and a dark dress coat with gilt buttons and
epaulettes.*

III The Bromley Family.

F. M. Brown, 1844

The family are wearing semi-formal dress, possibly for the late afternoon or early evening. The gentlemen are in day clothes with black silk neckties while the three younger women wear long-sleeved dresses with low necks and deep lace collars. The dark dresses suggest that the two women in the foreground are in mourning, although the use of a glossy black velvet (on the left) would indicate a late stage of mourning.

IV Pegwell Bay (detail).
W. Dyce, 1859–60

The 1850s saw the development of more practical forms of dress for outdoor pursuits. The round straw hat was a popular informal fashion for women, especially at the seaside, although the figure on the left wears a bonnet. The crinoline frame, which left the legs free, made walking easier, especially when the skirt was lifted up over a braided petticoat. Voluminous shawls and hooded mantles were the most usual outer garments.

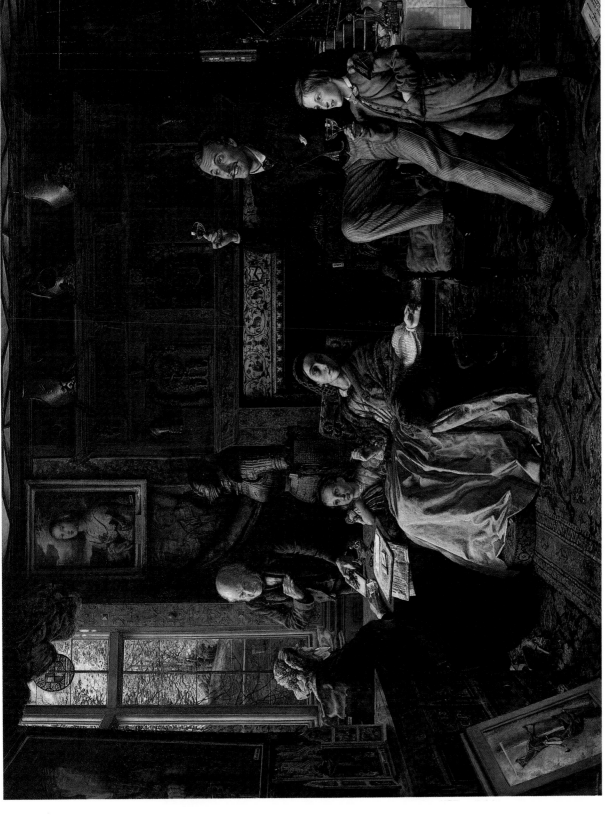

V   The Last Day in the Old Home.

R.B. Martineau, 1862

In this narrative painting of a prosperous middle-class family fallen on hard times through the feckless husband's drinking, the old mother can be seen on the left in an indoor cap and shawl. The harassed wife wears a plain morning dress with white collar and undersleeves and a patterned shawl; her hair is arranged in a fashionable chignon net. The husband's high-fastening morning coat is worn with light, striped trousers and a low-collared shirt, while his son wears a knickerbocker suit trimmed with braid.

VI   The Bridesmaid.
J. Tissot, 1882

*Formal day clothes
were the convention for
weddings at this date
and the bridesmaid
wears a bright blue silk
two-piece dress high to
the neck and with long
sleeves. Her bodice is
flared to accommodate
the bustle projection at
the back of her walking-
length skirt with its
cross drapery and
tiered flounces.
Fashionable accessories
were a small bonnet
trimmed with silk
ribbons, long white kid
gloves and black shoes
with low heels. Amongst
the spectators are two
shop assistants in their
usual uniform of black
dresses.*

VII Joseph Chamberlain.
F. Holl, 1886

The politician Chamberlain was a noted dresser of the later Victorian period. He was described as 'immensely dapper', always wearing a gold-rimmed monocle and an orchid in his buttonhole. His well-tailored frock coat with silk-faced lapels is worn here with a light waistcoat, wing-collared shirt and black necktie knotted through a gold ring. A gold watch chain and white handkerchief in the breast pocket can also be seen.

VIII Mrs Gascoigne and her son Alvary.
E. Hughes, 1897

A more fluid, curving line in dress and the use of soft pastel shades were characteristic of the last three years of the nineteenth century (although this emergent Art Nouveau taste is usually associated with Edwardian fashion). By 1897 the fullness of the leg of mutton sleeves had dropped to the elbow and skirts hung in more natural folds. On formal occasions a small boy could wear a frilled silk shirt and velvet breeches with white socks and patent leather shoes.

economy. Political reforms were extending the franchise and transferring power from landed society to the prospering middle classes, who were benefiting from the great wealth being generated by industrialization. As the political power and wealth of the aristocracy declined, barriers began to be broken down and self-made men were able to ascend the social scale. The impetus for advancement was fuelled by the Victorian passions for hard work and self-help. The affluent middle classes aspired to gentility and strove to adopt the manners and social life of the gentry and aristocracy who, in their turn, tried to repel any such encroachment from below. At a lower social level the goal was respectability, and there was a constant, underlying fear of losing even the slightest of footholds on the social ladder. Any kind of position was to be maintained, if not actively improved, and if a man achieved success he took good care to avoid any exposure of his humble origins.

In these circumstances the unspoken language of social behaviour – manners, deportment and dress – was a useful means of distinguishing one class from another and recognizing outsiders. Attempts to resist intruders might also be made by changing the 'rules' from time to time or by making them more complex. Consequently there was a ready market for the manuals of etiquette which began to be published in increasing numbers from the 1830s onwards, and the advice columns of women's magazines were constantly filled with requests for guidance on various points of etiquette. Although this kind of literature was mainly intended for those who either did not know or were uncertain how to behave and dress correctly (the well-bred having been brought up on such knowledge from their youth) the books and advice columns were extremely popular. One reason was that many readers drew a vicarious pleasure from following the activities of the upper classes and even if, for example, they did not themselves expect to be presented at Court they liked to know what went on and how they should be dressed at these functions. Another factor was that

even those who might be expected to be socially adept could draw reassurance from these publications; social life itself was becoming more complex and there was a bewildering number of choices governing customs and dress. For instance, the popularity of seaside holidays and travel abroad for more than just a leisured élite brought the need for special new clothes; so too did the different sporting activities which began to be taken up. The day and evening became divided into more units requiring their own kind of dress and, in addition, several sets of the same clothes might be required for the four seasons of the year. Every detail was important including the accepted materials, colours and accessories for each occasion. Men needed to consider the appropriate type of shirt, collar, necktie, gloves and shoes. Any kind of lapse would betray the wearer, and Mrs Humphry's *Manners for Men* of 1898 spelt out the consequences: 'If a man does not dress well in society he cannot be a success. If he commits flagrant errors in costume he will not be invited out very much, of that he may be certain. If he goes to a garden party in a frock-coat and straw hat, he is condemned more universally than if he had committed some crime. The evidence of the latter would not be upon him for all men to read, as the evidence of his ignorance on social forms is, in his mistaken notions of dress.'[5]

One of the most important requirements of nineteenth-century dress was that it should accurately reflect the wearer's position in society, and this involved not just social class, occupation or degree of wealth but age and (in the case of women) marital status. This is not to say that in practice everyone dressed as was expected of them – and there were many who transgressed the rules of the etiquette books – but the ideal was a well-regulated society where each person knew his or her place and clothed themselves accordingly.

'Dress tells us first the class to which the wearer belongs' was, in the words of one writer, the nineteenth-century version of Shakespeare's 'the apparel oft proclaims the man'.[6] It was a highly class-conscious period, and there was perhaps a greater preoccupation with social identity than at any other time in history; but while everyone was acutely aware of a class structure its nature was far from simple or clearly defined. The middle classes, for instance, encompassed a very wide range of British society from senior professional men and wealthy manufacturers to small shopkeepers and office workers. The lines of demarcation, dividing them from the upper and lower ends of the scale, were blurred and open to question.

In a rapidly expanding industrial society, income and expenditure were the most significant factors in creating fluid social patterns. Most contemporary observers mention a minimum annual income of £300 as necessary to fulfil the usual middle-class expectations (the upkeep of a house, carriage and servants, food, dress and the education of children). Those in the lower-middle class could earn from £150 to £200 a year, though some had as little as £60. On these sums it was possible to live adequately and even to keep a servant (the middle class was defined essentially as the servant-keeping class[7]) but fewer of the recognized symbols of status could be afforded. Nevertheless, it was extremely important to keep up appearances to retain a position in society, and often items which today might be regarded as luxuries were then considered necessities. Servants and clothes were two obvious examples and were a means of presenting an acceptable front to the world.

Wealth could be indicated in quite obvious ways by dress. The most fashionable styles in the very finest materials, with expensive ornaments and jewellery were, of course, traditional symbols of affluence, as were very elaborate clothes which needed help to put on and to maintain. Extravagant and wasteful dress was a form of 'conspicuous consumption' to express status,[8] and in the nineteenth century this can be seen in the numbers of different clothes required for a variety of social activities and the servants employed in the upkeep of such large wardrobes. Where the nineteenth century differed from earlier periods was that it was largely through women's dress that wealth and status were advertised. As more and more men took up some kind of occupation and the need for practical, working clothes led to an increasing sobriety and uniformity in male clothing, women virtually took over the role of conspicuous consumption in dress, providing the necessary decorative elements and colour. Affluence and the employment of servants freed middle-class women from domestic chores, giving them ample time to devote themselves to fashion. The limited opportunities for any kind of occupation outside the home kept women within a narrow sphere of activity and therefore able to accept highly impractical forms of clothing. Very restricting garments such as tight corsets, voluminous petticoats, cumbersome shawls, deep-brimmed bonnets and narrow, high-heeled shoes also discouraged women from being energetic and thus perpetuated the pattern of idleness which was in itself a status symbol.[9]

The Importance of Gentility

Although wealth and expenditure were important signals in nineteenth-century clothing there was another factor which distinguished superior social class. This was 'gentility', a quality which was valued even more highly than material riches because it was so much harder to acquire. Gentle birth and breeding were the qualifications for membership of the upper class and were consequently the goals of the aspiring middle classes. Throughout the century the ideal was to be accepted as a true 'gentleman' or 'lady' and the belief that one could be immediately recognized as such made dress all the more important. 'The vulgar person is speedily detected by his apparel, even though he should never open his lips in conversation' wrote a tailor's

85 Prince George, Duke of York, 1889.

Prince George epitomizes the clean-cut English gentleman of the later nineteenth century. His clothes are immaculately tailored and his linen is spotlessly white. There is a complete absence of ostentation or untidiness.

guide in the 1840s[10] and an etiquette book of 1898 warned that 'there is no easier method by which to detect the real lady from the sham one than by noticing her style of dress. Vulgarity is readily distinguished, however costly and fashionable the habiliments may be, by the breach of certain rules of harmony and fitness.'[11]

The terms 'gentleman' and 'lady' – like 'class' – were incessantly used but were almost impossible to define. 'How much those words are abused! What various twisted and deformed ideas are connected in different persons' minds with those words!' said Lady Colin Campbell, 'and yet what various meanings are attached to them? Sometimes high birth is denoted; sometimes perfect manners; sometimes merely wealth; the fact of living an idle life, or profuse liberality.'[12] Another writer on etiquette thought that 'Gentility is neither in birth, manner, nor fashion – but in the MIND. A high sense of honour – a determination never to take a mean advantage of another – an adherence to truth, delicacy, and politeness towards those with whom you may have dealings – are the essential and distinguishing characteristics of a GENTLEMAN.'[13] In effect there were both social and moral implications in the term: gentility meant a certain social rank but also a standard of conduct or moral behaviour that was appropriate to it.[14] Although they went together, it was possible to have one without the other, and even quite humble men could aspire to a gentlemanly standard of conduct.

Jane Austen's novels give a clear picture of how the gentleman and lady behaved at the beginning of the nineteenth century and from this can be deduced the principles of dressing well and correctly at that time. In both manners and dress great emphasis was placed on good taste, elegance and fashion. Taste and elegance were to a large extent the outcome of education and the cultivation of the arts which had been the usual upper-class pursuits of the eighteenth century. To be fashionable, without taking it to an extreme, implied an easy familiarity with the capital and a participation in the best social activities. To these could be added more 'moral' qualities in dress, expressive of a gentleman's or lady's natural integrity, courtesy and modesty: affectation was assiduously avoided; neatness and the correct forms of clothing for each occasion were carefully observed, as a part of good manners; and it was important never to be over-dressed or ostentatious. That was the kind of showing-off and drawing attention to oneself that George Brummell deplored and which was identified with vulgarity. These

*86 Evening Dresses.
The Englishwoman's
Domestic Magazine,
1860.*

*Young, unmarried
women were expected
to wear white evening
dresses of thin, gauzy
material, suggestive of
purity and innocence,
whereas richer silks
and darker colours
were thought more
suitable for married
women. These
distinctions in dress
signalled whether or not
a young woman was
'available' in the
marriage market.*

points continued to be made in succeeding decades. As *Hints on Etiquette* in 1836 said: 'It is in bad taste to dress in the extreme of fashion; and, in general, those only do so who have no other claim to distinction.... Men often think when they wear a fashion-ably cut coat, an embroidered waistcoat, with a profusion of chains and other trin-kets, that they are well dressed, entirely overlooking the less obtrusive, but more certain, marks of a refined taste. The grand points are – well-made shoes, clean gloves, a white pocket handkerchief, and, *above all*, an easy and graceful deportment. Do not affect singularity in dress, by wearing out-of-the-way hats, or gaudy waistcoats, etc., and so becoming contemptuously conspicuous; nothing is more easy than to attract attention in such a manner, since it requires neither sense nor taste ...'[15]

As the century progressed it helped, but was not essential, for a man to have been born a gentleman in order to play the part.

Many self-made men gained social accept-ance by following the rules and, with enough money, they could cultivate a genteel appear-ance. George Gissing noticed this in his novel *The Emancipated* (1890) when he de-scribed Mr Bradshaw, a wealthy Lancashire silk manufacturer. 'Prosperity had set its mark on him, that peculiarly English pros-perity which is so intimately associated with spotless linen, with a good cut of clothes, with scant but valuable jewellery, with the absence of any perfume save that which suggests the morning tub.'[16] The reference to cleanliness is significant as this was a par-ticularly nineteenth-century mark of status. Victorian cities were inescapably dirty, but those who had the means and plenty of servants could afford to change their linen more than once a day, keep their clothes in immaculate order and take a daily bath. A tradition of cleanliness, which was first made fashionable by George Brummell at the beginning of the century, came to be

J. David del   AD. GOUBAUD Edr à Paris

associated with British male fashion. 'A very delicate, even exquisite, personal cleanliness is characteristic of the true gentleman,' wrote Mrs Humphry in 1898, 'and more particularly the English gentleman, who is noted all over the world for his devotion to his "tub" and his immaculate propriety in all matters of the toilette. This is not claiming too much for my countrymen.'[17]

For women, a dainty freshness could be conveyed by snowy white collars, cuffs or undersleeves which were fashionable in the middle decades of the century. Another essential refinement and the mark of a lady was to have smooth, soft and white hands. These showed that they carried out no manual labour or even light housework. It was partly for this reason that close-fitting gloves were worn so much, both in and out of doors. The other purpose of the fashionably tight kid leather gloves was to keep the size of the hands as small as possible. In the nineteenth century high breeding was equated with a delicate bone structure, and small, narrow hands and feet were emulated by both men and women.

A lack of money could be excused so long as it was not combined with vulgarity. A vulgar taste in dress was usually associated with flamboyance: clothes which were too fashionable, too loud or too dressy for the occasion. This was especially frowned upon in what were considered to be the lower orders who were expected to know their place and not attempt to ape the manners of their social superiors. It was thought pretentious, for example, at the beginning of the century for maidservants to wear white gowns when a coloured or printed cotton dress was both more practical and the recognized wear for domestics. In the second half of the century *Punch* magazine was full of jokes about servants trying to keep abreast of fashion, and even rivalling their mistresses in dress. One of its favourite themes was of maids being among the first to either adopt or discard the crinoline and the bustle. The other hallmark of vulgarity was slovenliness – anything which might appear dirty or untidy. Respectable dress, on the other hand, was clean, neat, decent, sober and, above all, appropriate to the wearer's means or occupation. These were the virtues constantly commended to the less well-off – and for those in reduced circumstances they must have been a source of hope and comfort. It might not be possible to achieve gentility but it was at least possible to be respectable. Victorian novels were fond of mentioning impoverished gentlemen or ladies who continued to be recognized as such, in spite of their shabby clothes. For many, the loss of respectability was an even more fearful prospect than poverty.

Economic Modesty

The nineteenth-century preoccupation with status extended beyond rank, wealth or occupation to distinctions in age or a woman's marital status. Attempts at deception were viewed with unease, and in the matter of age women were urged to dress according to their years. In the Victorian period a young, unmarried lady's dress was expected to be suitably youthful and innocent. This expressed both the contemporary ideal of young womanhood and her availability in the marriage market. This was especially made clear in evening dress since it was at evening functions that many introductions were made and courtships were carried on. Fashion magazines gave regular guidance on the subject: *La Belle Assemblée* in March 1848 said that 'very young unmarried ladies, whom Fashion will not permit to dress expensively, wear organdy and tarlatane, very simply trimmed; while gauze, crape, satin, tulle and lace, all of the richest description and with splendid garnitures, are adopted by married belles.'[18] Again, in 1862 The *Englishwoman's Domestic Magazine* mentioned that 'tarlatane is one of the favourite materials for young ladies' evening dresses, as it is so simple, elegant and inexpensive.'[19] The lack of expense was repeatedly stressed, for apart from the economical advantages to a girl's parents, modest clothing was thought to be more suitable and attractive to a potential husband. 'The excessive expense of an extravagant toilet intimidates men and prevents them thinking seriously of an establishment which offers nothing for the future but the shameful waste of their means.'[20] Rich silks were for older and married women. 'We certainly think a young lady of eighteen too young to wear moiré antique dresses', advised *The Englishwoman's Domestic Magazine* in 1863. 'wait until you have added fifteen years to your present age, and then it will be quite time enough for you to commence the dowager's fabric, and so you will think in a few years.'[21]

White, with its suggestion of purity and freshness, was considered the most appropriate colour for a débutante's evening dress 'Nothing is so becoming to a young face as attendant clouds of white muslin; there is poetry and modesty in its very appearance.'[22] Similarly, pearls were felt to be more suitable than other precious stones in the matter of jewellery. In 1829 the *Belle Assemblée* complained, 'Diamonds in the hair at grand evening parties are more general than we wish to see them; as pearls are so much more chaste and appropriate to the young'[23] but, ideally, young unmarried women wore no jewellery at all. Age and marital status could also be indicated by subtle variations in the cut of a fashionable dress. At the end of the century, for example, 'all evening dresses for young girls who are "out", should be trained a little, but not so much as for married women's full dress. All that a girl wears should be gay and light-looking, the opposite to the touch of stateliness and the settled air that become her young matron sister.'[24]

Marriage was the most important change in status for a woman in the nineteenth cen-

87 The Only Daughter. *J. Hayllar, 1875.*

It was traditional for married women to wear caps indoors although by this date younger ones were beginning to drop the habit. Elderly ladies often dressed in black, even when not in mourning, as it was economical and was thought to look dignified. A difference in age is also indicated by the dress of the two men.

tury. From being a junior member of the family at home she acquired a home of her own to run and a position in society – and however young she might be, as a married woman she took precedence over any unmarried ladies. For the first few months of her married life she also took precedence over other married women. *Cassell's Family Magazine*, advising newly married couples on accepting invitations to dinner 'or other festivities', wrote in 1876: 'wonderful to relate, the lady has not to consider what she will wear, for the bridal costume is invariably donned on all such occasions, the only difference being that the veil is now used as a shawl. Remember, young matron, that you are the chief personage at all these entertainments. Even if you are still in your teens, you take precedence of older matrons. It is the bride whom the host takes in to dinner; it is she to whom the hostess looks when rising from the dinner-table; it is she with whom the host opens the ball; it is she who must take her departure before the other guests venture to bid their adieux.'[25]

This seniority called for a more mature manner of dressing after marriage and because she was now 'settled' in life a married woman had to signal that she was no longer available. Her new role was to support and promote her husband; she could therefore parade her attractions (as her husband's property) in an approved manner and display his wealth and status by wearing more expensive clothes, materials, furs and jewellery. Darker, richer colours and heavy silks, especially satins and watered silks (such as moiré antique) or velvets, often lavishly trimmed with embroidery, beads or lace were thought suitable for evening wear and the married woman could wear as many diamonds, pearls and other precious stones as she might choose. As she grew older she was expected to dress with a becoming dignity and avoid the frivolities of fashion. The greatest sin, in the words of the popular expression, was to look like mutton dressed as lamb. Etiquette books urged elderly ladies to dress very quietly, frequently recommending them to keep to black and

grey, relieved by delicate touches of lace at the neck and wrists and on their heads. A lack of extravagance looked well in old age (particularly if an elderly woman was financially dependent on relatives) and dressing in black was economical even if not required for mourning. The very long tradition of married women wearing their heads covered indoors was carried on for most of the nineteenth century with the fashion of indoor caps. Generally speaking, the more formal the occasion the smaller the headdress was likely to be and some, around the middle of the century, made of loops of ribbon and lace were hardly caps at all. Distinctions were made between the caps of younger and older married women and by the mid-1880s dress caps were being left off by all but the elderly.

The Society Season

Dress was a reflection of status but it was also required to be appropriate to the time of the day and the occasion. This involved a careful observance of the rules of etiquette as there were an increasing number of different social activities which each had to be marked by a change of clothing. By 1864 *The Englishwoman's Domestic Magazine* felt it must inform its readers that 'the exigencies of the toilette are greater than ever.' Even in the country in August, when a little more informality might be expected, 'to wear a morning dress all day is not permissible; one is obliged to change at least three times a day. One cannot go out in a morning dress, and vice versa. Fancy woollens are still the material worn for walking ... So soon as a lady re-enters the house, she must invest herself in muslin or Chambéry gauze.'[26] A month later the magazine advised: 'There are four kinds of toilette necessary for the country house and its brilliant guest – the in-door morning dress, worn at breakfast time; the walking dress, which is short or looped up; the driving dress, which is such as is worn in town; and, lastly, the evening

88 Hyde Park, London. *T. S. Boys, 1842.*

Hyde Park was a favourite daily meeting place for fashionable Londoners during the Season. The more affluent drove round in carriages while others strolled or sat about in the later afternoon watching the spectacle.

dress, which is cut low.'[27]

Without the requisite number and variety of clothes it was impossible to take part in society or to be accepted as a member of it. Anthony Trollope's novel, *Ayala's Angel* (1881) is one of many which highlight the problem faced by people who did not have enough money to dress correctly for a social occasion or country house visit. The heroine, Ayala, living quietly with an aunt and uncle, was invited to stay at Stalham Park by Lady Albury but 'thoughts as to gloves had disturbed her, and as to some shoes which were wanting, and especially as to a pretty hat for winter wear.' Fortunately the situation was saved by a rich uncle who sent her £20 and she was able to get the hat, shoes and gloves, pay her fare and go with some money in her pocket. The necessary riding clothes were beyond her means but she managed to borrow those on her arrival. In this particular case, Ayala was excused her deficiencies because she was young, very

pretty and about to become engaged to an eligible bachelor.[28] In normal circumstances it would have been very difficult to get by. As a manual of etiquette pointed out, to commit a social solecism 'argues the offender to be unused to society, and consequently not on an equal footing with it. This society resents, and it is not slow in making its disapproval felt by its demeanour towards the intruder.'[29]

The society referred to, often spelt with a capital 'S', had begun to emerge as an organized system with its accompanying calender of events in the 1820s.[30] A kind of Society centred on the Court, had existed before this but following the end of the Napoleonic Wars in 1815 its ranks were swelled by men who had made fortunes or distinguished themselves in the services. As Britain embarked on a long period of peace and prosperity the upper class continued to expand, although access was jealously guarded. 'Good' society followed a recognized pattern of social activities throughout the year. By tradition, the British aristocracy had divided its time between the capital and the country, making an annual pilgrimage to London to attend Parliament and Court functions and returning home to country estates at the height of the summer when London was at its most unpleasant. In time a social 'Season' in London was established.

The Season proper took place during the spring and early summer and was a blend of urban and rural pursuits: occasions such as Court Drawing-Rooms and *Levées*, the preview of the Royal Academy and the sporting events of Ascot, Henley and the Derby. There was also a lesser season between the end of Christmas and the beginning of Lent and some social activities in the late autumn. In August, society left London for yachting at Cowes and grouse shooting in Scotland, to be followed by partridge shooting on country estates in the late autumn

89 Morning Dress, c. 1810.

A loose-fitting gown, high to the neck and with long sleeves was the usual wear for ladies at home during the morning. At the beginning of the century morning gowns were almost always white, trimmed with white embroidery or lace and often had caps to correspond.

and then the hunting season during the winter. For these activities a series of country-house parties were held and were an important feature of entertaining among the leading families in the country. August and September were also the months for travelling abroad and for those a little lower down the social scale to take their holidays at the seaside or in the country. Fashionable weddings usually took place during May and June and the early summer was considered the best time for other popular events such as garden parties, picnics and river excursions. The season for balls was the winter and into the early spring.

In London during the Season there were informal daily gatherings for people to see each other and to be seen: riding on horseback in Rotten Row or Hyde Park in the mornings and driving in carriages through Hyde Park in the later afternoon. Fashionable Londoners could also walk about or sit on chairs in the Park, and this was a favourite meeting place, especially for younger people to see each other informally.[31]

One of the most important social activities, both in town and in the country throughout the year, was paying calls – or 'visiting' as it was also known. This was a very formal arrangement for making short visits of not usually more than fifteen minutes to friends and acquaintances, as a matter of courtesy: for example, following an invitation to dinner or a party, the announcement of an engagement or birth in the family, an illness or bereavement, calling on a bride in her first home or on newcomers to a neighbourhood. 'Visits of form, of which most people complain, and yet to which most people submit, are absolutely necessary – being, in fact, the basis on which that great structure, society, mainly rests', wrote Lady Colin Campbell. 'You cannot invite people to your house, however often you may have met them elsewhere, until you have first called upon them in a formal manner, and they have returned the visit. It is a kind of safeguard against any acquaintances which are thought to be undesirable.'[32] The correct hours for calls were between three

90 Trust Me. J. E. Millais, 1862.

Another form of morning dress was a plain gown of silk or woollen cloth in a solid colour with very little trimming apart from a white collar and cuffs. Gentlemen often came in to breakfast in riding clothes.

and five o'clock (or six o'clock in London where dinner was later). Although they took place in the afternoon they were often referred to as 'morning calls' because they were carried out before dinner. Calls actually made in the morning, before one o'clock, were only permissible between intimate friends.[33] It was very important for calls to be returned, normally within three days. Engraved cards could be left in place of a personal visit or if the lady upon whom one was calling was not at home, but card-leaving was not synonymous with calling. The etiquette for calling, leaving cards and letters of introduction was complex and often merited a chapter of its own in the manuals. These were all upper and middle-class habits which were not followed by the working classes.

Dressing for the Occasion

The times for carrying out social duties, entertainments and having meals became highly regulated during the nineteenth century. Stricter timekeeping had gradually developed with improvements in timepieces and the growth of commercial and mercantile occupations, but it was further encouraged by the establishment of timetables for public coach and railway travel.[34] A new sense of the boundaries and units of time was created and the day began to be more precisely divided up, each part of it being allotted to particular activities such as dressing, meals, visiting and entertaining. Dinner, as in the eighteenth century, was the main meal of the day, but from having been eaten at three or four o'clock in the afternoon it came to be taken later and later, reaching seven-thirty or eight o'clock for fashionable London society by the mid-nineteenth century. Dinner marked the division between day and evening entertainments and consequently the change from 'undress' or 'half-full dress' into 'full dress' wear. As dinner grew later the habits of luncheon (at one-thirty or two

o'clock) and afternoon tea (at five o'clock) were established and distinctions in dress could be made for all four meals of breakfast, luncheon, tea and dinner.

Mornings were the time for the family to gather together to eat breakfast after which gentlemen departed for their place of business or other occupations. Ladies attended to their household duties and passed the time in reading, sewing or practising their musical and artistic accomplishments. Throughout the the century there was a recognized form of morning dress for women – easier, more comfortable and less formal than ordinary day wear but always high to the neck and with long (sometimes loose) sleeves. This was a continuation of the eighteenth-century practice of wearing a loose, wrapping gown and the nineteenth-century morning gown was often described as a 'wrapper'. However, it was more formal than a dressing-gown and it could be elaborately trimmed. At the beginning of the nineteenth century morning dresses were invariably white, decorated with white embroidery or 'appliquéd lace or needlework, in fanciful directions'.[35] Later in the century the loose wrapper was also known as a *peignoir* and it could admit of 'great richness of texture; it may be of Cashmere or of fine Merino; it may be made out of a shawl; of anything but silk, which is more appropriate to gowns. ... The morning coiffure, be it a cap, or be it the dressing of the hair, should be simple, compact, neat.'[36] An alternative to the wrapper was a more fitted but comparatively plain dress, made in a serviceable colour and material simply trimmed. In the mid-1890s ladies were advised: 'Let your style of dress always be appropriate to the hour of the day. To dress too finely in the morning, or to be seen in a morning dress in the evening, is equally vulgar and out of place. Light and inexpensive materials are fittest for morning wear, and low dresses of rich and transparent stuffs for dinner and ball. A young lady cannot dress with too much simplicity in the early part of the day. A morning dress of some simple material, and delicate whole colour,

with collar and cuffs of spotless linen, is, perhaps, the most becoming and elegant of morning toilettes.'[37]

Similarly, it was important to choose appropriate accessories. 'There is as much propriety to be observed in the wearing of jewellery as in the wearing of dresses. Diamonds, pearls, rubies, and all transparent precious stones belong to evening dress, and should on no account be worn before dinner. In the morning let your rings be of the more simple and massive kind, wear no bracelets, and, in fact, very little jewellery of any description. Your diamonds and pearls would be as much out of place during the morning as an evening dress.'[38]

For men, the choice of dress for the morning depended on the type of activity followed and the appropriate coat would be selected for riding or other outdoor pursuits, business or town wear. The dress coat was not usually worn before the afternoon or evening. 'In the morning, during work hours, whatever be a man's employment, and wherever,' advised one manual, 'his outside garb should be suited to ease and convenience,

its only distinctive marks are the most scrupulous cleanliness and the invariable accompaniment of fresh linen.'[39] In his own house and in the morning, another writer saw no reason why a gentleman 'should not wear out his old clothes. Some men take to the delightful ease of a dressing-gown and slippers; and if bachelors, they do well. If family men, it will probably depend on whether the lady or the gentleman wears the pantaloons.'[40]

On going out of doors either before or after luncheon, women were obliged to make an alteration in their dress. Their two most usual pursuits, carried out on foot or riding in a carriage, were shopping and paying calls. Walking dress, of necessity, had to be practical and for most of the century it was a shorter length than indoor skirts, without a train. The material depended on the time of year, but for cooler weather it was obviously important to provide something warm which was not likely to spoil in the rain. Bright colours, fancy silks or elaborate trimmings were out of place, and it was advised: 'Never dress very richly or showily in the street. It attracts attention of no enviable kind, and is looked upon as a want of good breeding.'[41] Walking dress 'should be quiet in colour, simple, substantial' but at the same time, 'the very dowdy and common-looking style of dress should be avoided; there should always be visible, through every change, the lady. Some of our ladies of rank, it must be allowed, though maintaining well the characteristics of *grandes dames* in society, are negligent in their walking dress, and seem to consider it is only necessary to put on their dignity when they dress for dinner.'[42] Probably the most satisfactory walking dress was a plain, well-cut costume tailored from woollen cloth, and at the beginning of the century the riding habit was often used for this purpose (as it had been in the eighteenth century). Later, practical jackets and matching skirts were adopted and the 'tailored costume' for smart day wear was perfected in the 1880s and 1890s. A summer equivalent could be made from neutral-coloured linen.

91 Riding Habit, 1806.

Well-tailored riding habits, of woollen cloth in winter and neutral-coloured linen in the summer, were also worn for walking and travelling during the nineteenth century. A later development was the tailored costume which became fashionable for daytime wear in the 1880s and 1890s.

92 Mrs Hamilton.
H. J. Stewart, c. 1845.
Carriage or visiting dresses were more formal than walking costume and in the mid-nineteenth century would have looked similar to this Scottish lady's. She wears a silk gown with a matching three-quarter length mantle trimmed with lace, a bonnet, gloves, shawl and small carriage parasol.

With carriage and visiting dresses, that is for calls not made on foot, there was no need to be practical since the carriage afforded all the necessary protection; also a degree of formality was required for morning calls. Dresses, in fact, 'should be exceedingly handsome; gayer in colour, richer in texture than the morning dress at home ... A really good shawl, or a mantle trimmed with lace, are the concomitants of the carriage, or a visiting dress in winter. In summer all should be light, cool, agreeable to think of, pleasant to look at.'[43] A parasol was necessary in summer to shield the face from the sun in an open carriage and, in order not to take up too much space, carriage parasols were smaller in size, often with jointed handles which allowed them to

be folded away.

Although gentlemen participated far less in the ritual of morning calls they were obliged to make visits from time to time and to dress for them accordingly. This called for formal day dress: a frock-coat or morning coat with top hat, gloves and cane. On arrival, the gentleman was expected to proceed directly into the drawing-room without leaving any garments or accessories in the hall. On such a short visit it was felt unnecessary to do otherwise and 'would be to make himself too much at home.'[44] For this reason it was recommended that 'if you have visits to make you should do away with the great-coat, if the weather allows you to do so. On the Continent it is always removed before entering a drawing-room, but not so in England.'[45] Umbrellas had to be left in the hall, but the hat, gloves and stick were taken into the drawing-room. 'The hat, however, must never be laid on a table, piano, or any article of furniture; it should be held gracefully in the hand. If you are compelled to lay it aside, put it on the floor.'[46]

In addition to short formal calls there were other social activities to be carried out in the afternoon during the second half of the nineteenth century. Friends and acquaintances could be invited to afternoon tea – or 'five o'clock tea' as it was usually called – and this might range from a small, informal gathering to a large party with musical entertainment. Afternoon parties began at about half past three or four and ended around six-thirty or seven o'clock. Elegant day dress, as for visiting, was the usual wear.

Something a little more decorative and elaborate was expected for garden parties, bazaars and flower shows, and by the 1890s these could afford 'the display of much taste and elegance. Young women attire themselves in delicately tinted fine materials – materials which have a refinement, beauty, and softness characteristic of those whom they are designed to embellish, but quite distinctive from those worn in the ball-room. These costumes are made as effective and

93 'A Philological Poser'. G. du Maurier, Punch, 1873.

The lady on the left and the gentleman are paying a formal 'morning call'. The other two girls are obviously the hostesses as they are in indoor clothes. The correct dress for gentlemen when making a call was a frock-coat; the top hat, gloves and cane were all carried into the drawing room and could be laid on the floor beside the chair.

coquettish as possible – everything that will add to the gaiety, without passing the limits of morning attire, is permissible, and the whole is crowned by a bonnet or hat of like description. The elder ladies should wear silks or some handsome material, richly trimmed with lace, a foreign shawl or lace mantle, and bonnets, not hats, whether in town or country.'[47] There were also after-noon dances which, though not usual in London, were a popular form of entertainment in the suburbs, garrison towns and watering places. Dances were also given by naval officers on board their vessels at various naval stations. As they generally took place from four to seven o'clock day clothes were worn: 'any simple summery-looking or bright autumn costume being equally appropriate to the occasion.'[48]

For men and women of every social class, Sunday church-going was a formal occasion which required suitable clothes. Except for the really poor and destitute, most people possessed one set of 'Sunday best' clothes and in losing these felt that they also lost their hold on respectability. A German visitor to London in 1851 noted that 'the most instructive drama is provided by the pawn-shops … Many a wife pawns her bridal gown or the baptismal gift of her firstborn in order just once to eat enough to feel full, or with the earnings of the previous week she redeems her Sunday clothes – only to pawn them on Monday morning.'[49] The middle and upper classes wore formal day dress to church. By the last quarter of the nineteenth century this meant a dark grey or black frock-coat for gentlemen, with a dark silk necktie, top hat and gloves. It was not correct to carry a stick when going to church.[50] The frock-coat and silk hat lingered on for church wear although

94 The Ball on Shipboard. *J. Tissot. c. 1874.*

Afternoon dances were often given by naval officers on board their vessels at naval stations although this scene is of a grander society event, on board a yacht during Cowes week. Day clothes were worn – 'any simple summery-looking or bright autumn costume being equally appropriate to the occasion.'

they were passing out of fashion in the 1890s. In 1898 Mrs Humphry remarked that 'frequently a silk hat is never seen between Sunday and Sunday. Churchgoers still, to a certain extent, affect it, but in these days of outdoor life, bicycling, and so on, the costume worn by men in church is experiencing the same modifications that characterize it in other departments.'[51] Evening dress was never worn on Sundays 'as there are, of course, no dinner parties given on that day'.[52]

The distinction between 'dress' and 'undress' was clearly marked throughout the nineteenth century. From an early date the irony of the language was noted in that for women, the fuller the dress the less was actually worn. As Ackermann's *Repository* remarked in 1812: 'the *undress* of the present day consists of a comfortable kind of habiliment closed round the neck and covering the arms; the *half-dress* is rather more open and exposed; and the *full-dress* scarcely admits of any covering at all, but in common language would be called complete nakedness.'[53] It was a general rule that full or evening dresses were made with a low-cut neckline and short sleeves although there were exceptions. From time to time long sleeves (of a thin material or lace) were fashionable and less formal evening dresses, for example for dinners rather than balls, were generally more covered up. There were also differences in the degree of

95 The Concert.
J. Tissot, c. 1875.
Music was frequently
provided at evening
parties and receptions.
Full dress wa expected
and for women this
meant a low-necked
bodice and short
sleeves; the hair was
carefully dressed with
the addition of a dress
cap or flowers and
jewelled ornaments.
Gentlemen wore black
dress suits.

décolleté sanctioned in France and Britain. In the 1820s several writers noted that the neckline was much lower for full dress in England than was permitted in France[54] and in the 1870s it was the case that 'in France, the high dress is still worn at dinners, even those of full dress. In England, that custom, often introduced, never becomes general.'[55] By this date a woman moving in society needed several different types of evening dress, from the 'ordinary evening costume at home' to something more elaborate for a dinner party, which in turn was distinct from the correct attire for an evening reception, the theatre, opera or a concert; and lastly, the most decorative dresses of all were required for balls and dances. Very often the distinction lay in the amount of jewellery and ornaments that were worn or how elaborately the hair was dressed. Dinner dress was intended to be stately and even splendid whereas 'for a ball, everything even in married women may be light, somewhat fanciful and airy. What are called good dresses seldom look well. The heavy, richly-trimmed silk, is only appropriate to those who do not dance; even for such, as much effect should be given to those dresses as can be devised.'[56] Apart from the visual effect of thin, gauzy materials it was important for ball dresses to be as light as possible because it became very hot dancing in crowded and badly ventilated rooms.

(It was equally necessary to have a warm evening cloak or wrap to put on when going out into the cold night air – many illnesses were attributed to young women becoming overheated in the ballroom and then catching a chill returning home.)

One of the features of nineteenth-century fashion was the development of a distinctive form of evening dress for men. The restricted palette of black and white, however, belongs mainly to the second half of the century and before the 1850s there was a certain amount of colour in male evening costume. The dress coat remained essential for all occasions of a formal nature but a significant innovation was the introduction of an evening version of the lounge coat for less formal wear. When it first appeared in 1888 it was called the 'dress lounge' but from 1896 it was known as a dinner jacket. By the 1890s the etiquette books were of the opinion that the dinner jacket had 'very largely superseded the dress-coat for home wear and at dinners in houses where one is a familiar guest. It is occasionally seen at the play, too, but it would be incorrect to wear it when accompanying ladies.'[57]

–7–
LUXURIOUS PROFUSION
Making and Buying Clothes

The Sewing Machine and Mass-Production

Like so many areas of nineteenth-century life, the ways in which clothes were produced and sold underwent some dramatic changes between 1800 and 1900. Inevitably the textile and clothing industries were affected by technological developments, the prosperity of an industrialized society and an increasing demand for fashionable goods. Improved systems of communication brought greater mobility and awareness of what was happening in other parts of the country or even elsewhere in the world. Shopping patterns altered and the concept of fashion widened. Whereas in the past only those in the top levels of society had enough wealth and leisure to devote to the pursuit of fashion, in the nineteenth century a wider range of goods at affordable prices became available. Mass-produced clothing made no pretence to exclusivity but offered the less well-to-do the opportunity to buy new and stylish garments instead of second-hand ones which were usually out of date and rarely fitted properly. The introduction of paper patterns and the domestic sewing machine enlarged the scope of home dressmaking so that quite complex and up-to-date fashions could be attempted without recourse to the professional.

Many of these effects were not apparent until the later decades of the nineteenth century and, in fact, it is tempting to make a neat division of the century into two halves. Up to the 1850s there was a virtual continuation of the traditional methods of tailoring and dressmaking. The majority of clothes were individually made to measure, by hand. Throughout the century only natural fibres were used (wool, silk, linen or cotton) and after 1856 chemical or aniline dyes extended the range of natural dyes. The first man-made fibre, artificial silk, was not developed until the 1890s. Dress materials, trimmings and fashion accessories were bought from specialist tradesmen and a new garment might involve separate visits to the silk mercer, woollen draper or linen draper, haberdasher and milliner before the fabric was made up – either by a professional tailor or dressmaker, or at home by a lady's maid, servant or the wearer herself. The two operations of purchasing materials and having them made up into garments did not necessarily take place on the same premises but in Paris the English-born couturier, Charles Frederick Worth, saw the sense in combining the two – first persuading his employers to try the experiment and then setting up his own business in 1858. In Britain, some enterprising provincial shopkeepers

96 St James's Fair, Bristol. *S. Colman, 1824.*

At the beginning of the nineteenth century many dress fabrics and costume accessories were bought at country fairs, market stalls or from travelling salesmen. These supplemented the goods available from village shops and stores in larger towns which were not always very accessible to those who lived in country areas.

began to extend their businesses in the 1830s and 1840s, and by the second half of the century the departmental stores were successfully setting up in London and the larger towns throughout the country. The idea of being able to buy a variety of goods under one roof was rapidly developed and as part of the service shops offered made-to-measure, partly-made and ready-to-wear items.

The sewing machine was the most significant factor in the development of ready-made clothing, although other inventions such as the band knife for cutting several layers of cloth and steam pressing equipment played an important part. Attempts at producing a sewing machine

had been made since the late eighteenth century but it was not until the 1850s, after Elias Howe had patented his lock-stitch machine in 1846, that it came into general use. By the 1860s almost all dresses were partly machine-sewn, but until the end of the century they were usually finished by hand. Ready-to-wear clothing for women proved slow to develop because of the difficulty in achieving the correct fit of fashionable styles, but the men's trade was well established in the East End of London by the 1840s and continued to expand.

By tradition, Britain looked to France for the lead in fashion and was willing to acknowledge 'the superior taste and elegance in dress of our fair neighbours on the sunny

131

97 Advertisement for Arthur Cambell's Dainty Dresses, 1899. This plate and the preceding one illustrate the dramatic changes which took place in making and buying clothes between 1800 and 1900.

side of the Channel',[1] although French influence was less dominant during the first half of the nineteenth century. Contact with France and with French fashion had been cut off at the time of the Napoleonic Wars and until 1826 there was a ban on luxury goods imported from there. This did little to diminish the prestige of French fashion (and silks continued to be smuggled in) but it brought a realization that it was possible

to exist without French direction, un-comfortable though this might be. With the resumption of trade and normal exchanges, however, France often failed to offer the inspiration and leadership usually expected from her fashions. The quality of French materials and the standards of workman-ship remained high but the French Court was dull. Louis-Philippe of Orléans (1830–48) in particular was thought to be hopelessly bourgeois. The British Court offered little challenge to France but the death of William IV in 1837 brought a new young Queen to the throne and, though not geatly interested in fashion, Victoria was pre-tty and lively, making the sovereign an object of interest once again. The Queen, in fact, appeared to be a thoroughly contemporary figure, and when she and her husband paid a state visit to France in 1845 the French were impressed by her looks and clothes. It was not until the establishment of the Second Empire that the French Court regained its magnificence and sparkle. The Empress Eugénie was Spanish by birth but had the serious interest in clothes and the natural chic associated with French women. She immediately became the focus of attention and set a new standard of elegance, assisted to some extent by the talents of Charles Worth (although he was never her sole dress-maker). Worth's own *maison de couture* took the business of dressmaking from the sphere of the craftsman into a clothing industry. When he opened his business in Paris in 1858 he employed fifty hands; by 1894 he had about twelve hundred and he was turning out six or seven thousand dresses and three to four thousand cloaks a year, supplying customers throughout Europe and America.[2]

At the beginning of the nineteenth cen-tury the most usual method of relaying news about changing styles in fashion was by word of mouth and by letter. For centuries it had been common practice to discuss details of new clothes and seek advice on points of etiquette (such as the correct wear for mourning) when corresponding with rela-tives or friends. Those who lived in the

Fashion magazines and illustrations were not produced on a regular basis until the late eighteenth century and were still quite expensive in the early decades of the nineteenth century. Many people could not afford to subscribe to the early fashion periodicals and Jane Austen, for example, never mentions them in either her novels or letters. Le Beau Monde *was a short-lived English magazine published by John Bell from 1806 to 1808.*

country relied particularly on such news from London or the larger provincial towns and often gave their correspondents commissions to purchase items for them. This is well illustrated by the letters written by Jane Austen to her sister Cassandra and others from 1769 until her death in 1817.[3] The sisters were very close and corresponded regularly when either was absent from home. Living for a good part of their time in the country, they were interested in the fashions seen in Bath, London or the large country houses they sometimes visited. Clothes were carefully observed and reported, the information being used for guidance when they came to ordering new garments or altering existing ones. The lengthy descriptions and precise details about dress are typical of letters of this period as these often took the place of illustrations. Fashion plates and magazines had only recently begun to be published on a regular basis and were expensive to buy.

Niklaus von Heideloff's *Gallery of Fashion*, for example, – the first English magazine to be devoted entirely to fashion and the first to be issued with all its plates in colour, cost three guineas a year. It was issued in monthly parts from 1794 to 1803, each having two engraved plates – aquatints coloured by hand, with touches of metallic paint. This was an advance on the earlier magazines which were generally illustrated with smaller, black and white engravings.

After Heideloff began the practice of issuing regular plates month by month, other publications followed suit, and an increasing number of ladies' magazines were published in the early decades of the nineteenth century. Later, the Victorian enthusiasm for periodical literature, improved printing processes and the spread of literacy (following the Education Bills of the 1870s) also stimulated the publishing industry. In the second half of the century the scope of women's magazines widened to include articles on cookery and other domestic matters, advice on etiquette and dress and the issue of regular needlework and dressmaking patterns. The invention of photography in the 1840s did not have a significant effect on fashion illustration and the magazines continued to use engraved plates, mostly coloured by hand, until the end of the century; but the popularity of portrait photography indirectly helped to spread news of changing fashions by providing many more images of what was being worn in London and other parts of the country.

Purchase of Materials

Although Jane Austen had mentioned ready-made cloaks for sale in Hampshire in 1812[4] there were very few ready-to-wear clothes available at that date. Outer garments such as gowns, spencers or pelisses which required fitting were made individually, to measure. It was usual for at least one or two items to be professionally made – generally evening dresses or best clothes where the fit and finished appearance were important – but most women were skilled enough to make some of their own clothes or to carry out alterations and vary the trimmings. Similarly, the various accessories to dress were supplied by milliners and shoemakers but caps, hats, bonnets and other items were frequently trimmed and altered at home. In more prosperous households this kind of work could be carried out by a well-trained lady's maid. Even when a garment was professionally made the customer was closely involved in its production. She would usually make the choice of material and trimmings and instruct the dressmaker on the style that was required. As the illustrated fashion magazines became more widely available in the nineteenth century they gave women the suggestions and directions they needed and were, perhaps, a more reliable source of inspiration than relatives or friends.

A term often used by Jane Austen was a 'gown', in the sense of meaning not the finished garment but the length of material required to make it. In a similar way, other

nineteenth-century writers mention sending for 'patterns' when they mean sample pieces of fabrics rather than the paper patterns for cutting out a garment. This underlines the distinction between buying dress materials and taking them to the tailor or dressmaker to be made up. Choosing the fabric was an important initial step in the process of ordering new clothes; most materials were expensive and often they could cost more than the labour of making them. It was expected that the garment would be altered or remodelled during its life and it could be taken to pieces several times for cleaning or 'turning', when the more worn parts were reversed to bring the fresh side to the front. (One of the reasons why both bodices and skirts were lined was to preserve the freshness of the material on the inside for this purpose.) Clothes were made to last and were carefully looked after, therefore the material had to be carefully selected and mistakes avoided whenever possible.

Dress fabrics could be bought from a range of tradesmen to suit every pocket. In the more remote country areas families relied on the travelling salesmen – itinerant drapers who carried their wares in a pack on their backs. Even those who had access to the shops in nearby towns usually bought some items from these salesmen and women. Alternatively there were itinerant weavers who could set up their looms in a customer's house or barn to weave the wool and linen already spun by the ladies of the family.[5] Elizabeth Grant, recalling her childhood in Scotland in 1812, said that her mother 'was a beautiful needlewoman, and taught us to sew and cut out, and repair all our own, our father's, brothers' and family linen. She had become Highland wife enough to have her spinnings and dyeings, and weavings of wool and yarn, and flax and hanks, and she busied herself at this time in all the stirring economy of a household "remote from cities", and consequently forced to provide its own necessities.'[6] In country towns, cloth could be bought from market stalls and from

100 Messrs. Williams and Company's Premises, Oxford Street, London, 1856.

In London and the larger provincial towns dress materials were bought from specialist tradesmen. Very few ready-to-wear garments were available at this date although a number of shawls and mantles already made up could be bought from silk mercers like Williams of Oxford Street. Examples in black net or lace can be seen in the right-hand illustration.

INTERIOR OF A PORTION OF

MESSRS. WILLIAMS AND COMPANY'S PREMISES,

61, OXFORD-STREET.

shops of varying sizes. Most villages had a shop which stocked necessary items, combining the functions of grocer, draper and haberdasher. In London and the larger provincial towns, on the other hand, there were the specialist shops which dealt in only one type of merchandise.

There was a great variety in the weight, texture and patterning of dress fabrics. Although there were only four natural fibres, they could be mixed to create different effects and woven in a number of weights to suit each season of the year. A wool and silk mixture, for example (woven with a silk warp and woollen weft), could provide both lightness and warmth between seasons and exploit the soft and lustrous qualities of the two fibres. Advances in the technology of weaving and printing expanded the range of decoration. Technological progress did not extend to the creation of any new fibres until the first artificial silk was produced in 1892, but a major achievement was the successful application of rubber to the development of elastic and waterproof materials. Charles Macintosh patented his method of sandwiching rubber, sofened by naptha, between

two layers of cloth in 1823, and the following year the cotton and rubber material began to be manufactured in Manchester. In 1843 Thomas Hancock patented the vulcanization or hardening process which made rubber less sensitive to changes in temperature and it became possible to use a single-coated fabric for waterproofed garments. Elastic, which was well established by the 1830s, was also a more viable proposition once the rubber could be prevented from growing hard when cold and sticky when warm.[7]

Home Dressmaking

In general, nineteenth-century women had a sound understanding of textiles and were experienced in handling them from an early age through learning their needlework skills. Needlework was the one accomplishment considered necessary to women of every social class and was usually referred to as their 'work'. For the least well-off it was important for women to be able to clothe

135

101 Frontispiece. The Workwoman's Guide, *1838.*

Nineteenth-century women of all social classes were skilled in needlework from an early age. 'Few ladies, except quite in the higher ranks, can wholly dispense with some degree of attention to their own wardrobe and to that of their husbands', said the author of The English Matron *(1861). In this somewhat idealized scene of a village school in the late 1830s, little girls are being taught to cut out and sew.*

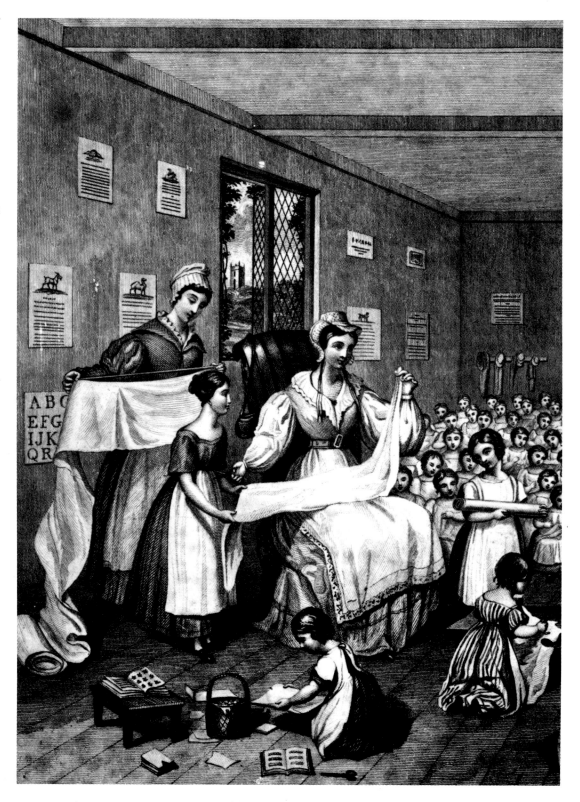

themselves and their families; needlework was also a means of livelihood for many poor women. In the middle classes too, impoverished women looked to needlework as one of the few areas of employment open to them and for which they had some training; but even if they were well-to-do it was thought becoming and prudent for ladies to be always occupied with some kind of sewing – either for their own families or for those of the poor. However, although women had centuries of experience in needlework it was mainly in fine sewing on light materials, especially linen, and the clothes they were most skilled in making were babies' and children's garments, men's shirts, women's shifts and other items of underwear. Until the late seventeenth century it had been usual for the male tailors to make women's outer garments and even in the eighteenth century when the female dressmaker – or mantua-maker as she was then called – was well established, men continued to deal with heavier-weight materials. These were for the most part the woollen cloths in which their superior skill was recognized; they were used for women's riding habits and, later in the nineteenth century, the fashionable tailored costumes. Tailors also produced some of the corsets, which were made of stout linen or cotton fabric which required heavy stitching.

For the home dressmaker sewing itself posed little problem, but some skill was required in cutting out clothes and fitting them correctly. If the garment was not cut out in the right way it hung badly, a fault which was virtually impossible to disguise or rectify later. There was also an art in cutting out as economically as possible to save any wastage of material. Throughout the nineteenth century fit was an important element of fashion, especially in bodices, coats and jackets which were generally tight to the figure. Some styles involved exaggerated shaping and a complex construction which were beyond the capabilities of an amateur. Even the enterprising *Workwoman's Guide* of 1838 'strongly recom-

mended to all those who can afford it, to have their best dresses invariably made by a mantua-maker, as those which are cut out at home seldom fit so comfortably, or look so well, as when made by persons in constant practice.'[8]

Success at home dressmaking depended largely on the use of good patterns. At the beginning of the century paper patterns were generally unavailable although professional tailors and dressmakers were able to buy sets from firms which specialized in supplying 'models made up in paper'. It was in response to this need that instruction manuals such as *The Workwoman's Guide* were published, although their patterns needed to be drafted out from scaled diagrams, which many women found difficult. A more familiar and therefore easier method was to use an existing garment as a pattern. The item was unpicked and the pieces traced out on thin paper or the lining fabric of the new garment. Children's clothes were often made in this way, and adult fashions were also copied by borrowing a new garment from a friend or relation. Not surprisingly, a professionally made garment was particularly desirable to copy.

By the mid-nineteenth century paper patterns had begun to be issued with women's magazines or could be obtained on request, following the publication of an illustration and detailed description of the garment in a journal. Pattern supplements first appeared in the mid-1840s and in 1850 *The World of Fashion* began to include full-size patterns for bodices, mantles, underwear and other items in its monthly magazine. The pattern pieces were all printed on one large sheet of paper which was folded up and enclosed in the publication. The home dressmaker had then to trace off the relevant parts and adjust them for size. Other magazines followed suit, and as the sewing machine came into widespread use the demand for patterns increased. Individual paper patterns could be purchased when the commercial pattern companies were founded. These first started in America: Ebenezer Butterick of Sterling, Massa-

HEPPLE'S CONDENSED SYSTEM
OF CUTTING COATS, VESTS, &c.

CUTTING ROOM MANIPULATIONS.

102 Tailor's cutting Room. The Tailor and Cutter, *1873.*

Tailors used 'scientific' methods for measuring customers and cutting out garments. The introduction of the tape measure in the early years of the nineteenth century made this easier and a number of tailors' manuals were published.

chusetts, opened his paper pattern service in 1863 and the McCall's Pattern Company appeared in 1870. By 1876 Butterick had branches in London as well as in Paris, Berlin and Vienna. The pattern pieces were cut out in white tissue paper with notches and perforations for directions (there were no printed markings until a later date).

The recommended way to make a dress was firstly to cut out and fit the lining. This meant that any mistakes could be rectified before cutting out the more expensive material, and it ensured a better finish. It was a method that was also used by professional dressmakers for making their own patterns. The lining was cut out against the body

and when a satisfactory fit was achieved the pieces were used for cutting out the garment itself. *The Book of Trades* of 1804 included an illustration of the mantua-maker 'taking the pattern off from a lady by means of a piece of paper or of cloth. The pattern, if taken in cloth, becomes afterwards the lining of the dress.'[9] The alternative way to make a pattern and one favoured by tailors was to use a 'scientific' method or series of measurements based on the natural proportions of the body and arithmetical calculations. The introduction of the tape measure in the early years of the century made this easier and a number of these new methods were devised. Benjamin Read, for example, offered his 'Patent measures' to other tailors and was advertising his arithmetical system as early as 1819.[10] Tailors took this mathematical approach when making ladies' riding habits but it was not commonly used by dressmakers for other female garments until the last quarter of the nineteenth century.

There was a very wide range of dressmaking establishments, catering for every kind of customer. At the lower end of the scale there was the small, private dressmaker working on her own from her home, sometimes in partnership with a sister or a friend. There were also freelance sewing women or seamstresses who would undertake work for other dressmakers or carry out sewing and mending in the customer's house. The court dressmakers represented the top end of the business and were the most fashionable establishments. specializing in the grandest clothes, especially court dresses and trains, wedding dresses and trousseaux. The first-rate houses had the nobility for their clientèle; the term 'court dressmaker', however, did not imply court patronage but rather that the firm was of sufficiently high standing to be able to make court dresses and to cater for the needs of those eligible to be presented at Court. Henry Mayhew described 'a first rate house of business, conducted by a dressmaker and milliner of the highest fashion' as 'always a very large house, more like a mansion for a nobleman than a milliner's establishment. In some there is nothing to indicate that they are places of business, except a plate on the door with the names of the proprietors engraved thereon; while others have two or three splendid plate-glass windows – each window consisting of one pane – with a brass bar outside, across which a lace vest or an embroidered collar or handkerchief is hung, to show the business carried on within.'[11] These establishments were large enough to house one or more showrooms where the customers were received and could look at the goods, workrooms where the clothes were cut out and made up, and accommodation for the staff who lived in. Some of the London firms were very big and Madame Elise of Regent Street, for instance, housed seventy to eighty girls in season and kept twenty-five day workers.[12]

Charles Worth – the 'Man-Milliner'

The milliners with whom dressmakers were often associated did not deal exclusively in hats until the end of the nineteenth century. They sold haberdashery, trimmings and small luxury goods (many of which had originally come from Milan, hence the derivation of the term 'milliner'). By the late eighteenth century the milliners were making dresses and hats as well as providing the trimmings for them, and they gradually began to specialize in the hats, bonnets and caps. Charles Frederick Worth, who was unusual in being a male dressmaker, was often referred to as the 'man-milliner'.

Worth's couture house in Paris and others like it (such as E. Pingat, Laferrière, Madame Paquin, M. Felix and Morin Blossier) were organized in a similar way to the leading London court dressmakers. Worth's premises at 7 rue de la Paix were described in an article in *The Strand Magazine* in 1894: 'The rooms where clients are received are many in number, but plainly furnished, with counters for measuring material, and the floor is covered with carpet in imitation of tiger skin, in grey and black, with scarlet bordering. Several young ladies are dressed in the latest style of morning, visiting, dinner, and reception toilettes, and are paraded in turn, this way and that, before clients, to enable them to judge of the effect of the garments when worn. ... A stranger would be specially struck with the constant, attentive supervision over all departments by M. Worth and his two sons.... Above all, all the workrooms that I was freely permitted to visit, as well as the kitchen, where the food is cooked for the many employés, show the care and forethought of the master for those who work for him. At the top of the house is a studio, where all the models are photographed.'[13]

Made-to-measure model clothes from one of the great houses in Paris were the ultimate symbol of social and financial success; but even if few women were able to afford such luxury it became possible for many more to buy copies of Parisian models from British dressmakers. Worth and other couturiers developed a profitable side to their businesses in selling models and one such example was advertised in *The Queen* in November 1871, not long after Worth had re-opened at the end of the Franco-Prussian War. Entitled 'Worth's Last Creation' there was a long description in French of 'a new design received by Mrs C. E. Brown on the 15th inst. It is exceedingly unique. Ladies desirous of dressing *à Worth* have an opportunity presented. It is a polonaise costume.... The petticoat is made in coloured satin, the remainder in black velveteen; or the costume can be more economically made in two shades of satin cloth, but the materials and trimmings must be correct in colour to produce the real French effect. Mrs Brown will supply patterns (by post only, for the benefit of her country customers) of the proper shades in both. Three or four yards of material are always saved to ladies who work from Mrs Brown's models; this is an

103 *Lucy in the Dressmaker's Workroom at the West End of London, 1858.*

Dressmakers' workrooms were generally overcrowded, poorly lit and badly ventilated. The hours were long and the pay was very low. The Belle Assemblée *magazine* noted in December 1847, 'the extreme trouble and anxiety we of the gentle sex occasion to the hard-working Milliners and Dressmakers, in not allowing necessary time to complete their orders . . . dressmakers often receive but twelve hours' notice to begin and finish a dress.'

established and well-known fact. Price of the new model, with flat pattern, 6s 6d.'[14]

It is doubtful whether Mrs Brown's country customers were able to achieve anything like the fit and finished effect of a Worth original. The skills of a professional tailor or dressmaker depended on a long apprenticeship and years of experience in making clothes. Apprenticeship could begin as early as twelve years old but was usually at fourteen or fifteen. The first two years were spent carrying out miscellaneous tasks in the workroom, popularly known as 'picking up the pins'. In the following five years the apprentice gradually rose in status, acquiring experience in stitching and making up the garments, then in cutting and fitting. The work varied according to the time of year and the social season so that during the busiest times the hours were extremely long. Before the Court Drawing-Rooms, when a number of dresses and trains were required, or on the death of a monarch or public figure when mourning was in great demand, the workrooms might be operating for eighteen or even twenty hours a day. On average, out of season, twelve hours a day was usual. the working conditions were generally bad, the workrooms being overcrowded, badly ventilated and poorly lit – and the pay was low. Those who worked on their own at home could be even worse off, having to work very long hours and for very little pay with no security of employment. Poverty, disease and misery were the lot of many seamstresses, a fact which was to become a cause for widespread concern. The plight of the seamstress was highlighted by Thomas Hood's poem, 'The Song of the Shirt' which was published in *Punch* in December 1843. Hood's poem made an enormous impact and did much to inspire other attempts to alleviate the problems.'[15]

Although most employers recognized

104 The Sempstress. *R. Redgrave, 1846.*

The freelance needlewoman was often worse off than the seamstress in a dressmaking establishment. Several charitable organisations were founded in the 1840s to help distressed needlewomen.

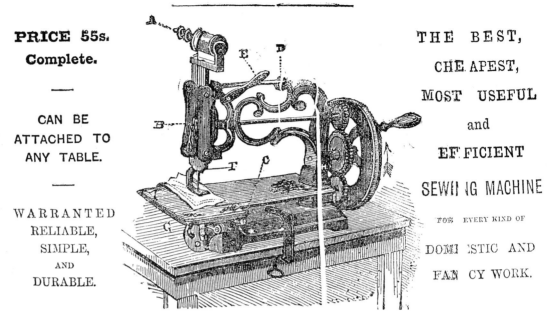

WEIR'S IMPROVED FAMILY SEWING MACHINE.

PRICE 55s. Complete.

CAN BE ATTACHED TO ANY TABLE.

WARRANTED RELIABLE, SIMPLE, AND DURABLE.

THE BEST, CHEAPEST, MOST USEFUL and EFFICIENT SEWING MACHINE FOR EVERY KIND OF DOMESTIC AND FANCY WORK.

ELEGANT, COMPACT, NOISELESS, AND RAPID.

Guaranteed suitable for finest Book-Muslins, Cambrics, and Silks, to the coarsest materials. Uses the ordinary reels of sewing cotton, thread, and silk, thus avoiding all re-winding. For Fine Stitching this Machine is unsurpassed by any ever sold in this country.

JAMES WEIR, 23, Featherstone Buildings, High Holborn, London, W.C. ONE DOOR FROM 64, HIGH HOLBORN.

that the hours were too long and the pay was low, there was immense pressure to respond to the demand for clothes. Because so few garments were available ready-made and customers were obliged to wait for new clothes, those dressmakers who could fulfil their orders quickly were the most successful in business. The sewing machine, rather surprisingly, neither made life much easier for the seamstress nor posed a real threat to her livelihood. By the 1850s the sewing machine was coming into general use and when it was employed in running up long seams or yards of trimming it took much of the drudgery out of needlework; but instead of simplifying the art of dressmaking, it tended to make it more complex. It encouraged the use of more stitching and elaborate decoration because this could now be more easily and cheaply done. Plain seams

and darts, however, were often done by hand since most outworkers could not afford to buy machines. Skilled needlewomen also remained in demand to deal with the complicated construction and trimming of fashionable dresses, and it was usual for these to be finished off by hand.

Nevertheless, the sewing machine had a profound effect on the tailoring and dressmaking trades which in the long term adapted themselves to mechanization. The complex history of the sewing machine makes it impossible to attribute its invention to one particular name or date, although Elias Howe's patent of 1846 is usually regarded as a milestone. The earliest attempt at creating a machine was the one designed by Thomas Saint for sewing leather and patented in London in 1790. In 1830 a French tailor, Barthélemy Thimonnier, patented a chain-stitch machine with a hooked needle which he later exhibited at the Great Exhibition in 1851; and in America in 1834 Walter Hunt invented (but did not patent) a lock-stitch machine. Attempts continued to be made to perfect the sewing machine, and by defending his patent rights in court the American Elias Howe brought his own version of the lock-stitch machine to public notice. The earlier chain-stitch machine used only one thread whereas the lock-stitch machine used the two threads familiar in domestic machines today. A seam was sewn by passing the lower thread through loops made by the upper thread. An important element in this technique was the use of a needle with the eye and the point at the same end, a principle patented by Howe. A further development was the introduction of a disc-shaped bobbin onto which the under-thread was wonld – perfected by Allen B. Wilson in 1852. But the name with which the sewing machine has become virtually synonymous was that of Isaac Merritt Singer, another American who was more successful than Howe in marketing and distributing his machine. In 1851 Singer patented a lock-stitch machine with improvements on Howe's. In 1856 he opened a sewing-machine agency in Glasgow, making the machines easily available to professional and home dressmakers through retail shops, but he did not have the right to market his machine throughout Britain until the English patent on Howe's original machine expired in 1860. The Jones Company made machines under the Howe patent and opened retail shops in England although these were to be outnumbered by the Singer shops. By the 1860s there were many other makes available and *The Englishwoman's Domestic Magazine* reviewed about twenty different machines in an article of 1867. The prices generally ranged from £10 to £15 but some cost less and it was also possible to acquire machines on the hire purchase system. Both hand and treadle machines were bought by home dressmakers but the

hand machines had the advantage of being easily portable from room to room.

Ready-Made Clothes

In Britain, machines were not introduced into clothing factories until the 1850s. John Barran of Leeds was one of the first, with the installation of twenty to thirty machines in about 1856. At first the treadle machines used in factories were driven by steam power; later gas or gasoline engines were introduced and finally, individual electric motors appeared around 1900.[16] By speeding up the sewing of plain seams, the need for a quicker method of cutting out became apparent and by 1860 John Barran had also led the way in using the band knife to cut through several layers of cloth at one time. This was described by *The Tailor and Cutter* in 1898 as 'a wonderful and valuable invention, and does its work correctly and well'. Another invention, said the journal, 'which is a great time and labour saver, and is now at work in all the leading clothing factories in the country is the Marsden Process Marker, which absolutely prevents any waste of materials, and, by the use of which the longest and most intricate lay can be marked out in about a minute, and that, too, without the slightest chance of an error or the omission of any part of the garments, a thing that often occurs when lays are marked out by the old-fashioned hand method.'[17] These technical advances made it possible to produce garments on a large scale for the first time, although a ready-to-wear service for men had become well-established by the 1840s.

It had been usual for men's tailors to make up a few clothes for immediate wear when business was slack but this had never been a significant part of their work, as it tended to lock up capital if done in quantity. In any case, for fashionable and well-dressed people, the only acceptable ready-made garments were those which required no particular fit, such as cloaks and mantles.

Among the less well-to-do, however, fit was a luxury that few could afford and many people were obliged to make do with second-hand clothes. The flourishing second-hand market was not always able to keep up with demand and there was a trade in cheap, ready-to-wear clothes for working people. These basic garments, many of which were for men, were known by the general term 'slopwork', originating from the 'slops' or loose clothes made for sailors; much of the trade, in fact, was carried on in the dock areas of London and around some of the large ports. Other customers were the many travellers arriving in or leaving the country, who required inexpensive clothes at short notice. Complete 'outfits' were often advertised for sale to emigrants and all the items would have been ready to wear at once. There was also a brisk export trade in ready-made clothing for the colonies.

Enterprising clothiers in the early decades of the nineteenth century began to build up the slopwork business, making better-class clothes and expanding and improving the service they offered. In particular, Elias Moses and Son and H. J. and D. Nicoll were successful London firms which took a lead in this market, and E. Moses advertised his business widely.[18] They were able to provide both made-to-measure and ready-made clothes and although they catered mainly for the middle and lower classes they set themselves up in competition with the West End tailors. The clothes were made in tailoring workshops and by using a number of out-workers or 'sweaters'. With machinery it became possible to develop the factory system to produce clothing on a more ambitious scale. John Barran of Leeds was one of a number of wholesale manufacturers who were able to supply small shops with ready-made goods.[19]

By the end of the century *The Tailor and Cutter* was commenting on the development of the ready-made trade during the previous forty years as 'undoubtedly one of the most phenomenal features of the Record Reign'.[20] Rather than fearing this development the

107 Eight o'clock a.m. Opening Shop. Twice Round the Clock, *1859.*

A typical London shop in the mid-nineteenth century. The shutters are being taken down to reveal windows filled with an extensive range of fashionable goods, This shop is referred to as a 'warehouse', a common term during the first half of the century, meaning a large retail (or wholesale) establishment stocking and selling goods which had not been made on its own premises.

journal appears to have welcomed it. In another issue in 1898 it noted that: 'The most extraordinary feature in connection with this new industry of tailoring by steam, as it has been called, is that whilst it increases and extends it has not in any wise injured the ordinary bespoke tailoring trade.'[21] This confidence was no doubt based on the fact that ready-to-wear men's clothes could not rival the cut and fit of bespoke tailoring and, if anything, served to enhance that skills of the tailor rather than to detract from them. It was to be a long time before off-the-peg suits for men became socially acceptable in middle and upper-class circles.

The comparative uniformity and conservative styling of men's clothes in the later nineteenth century lent themselves to the development of mass production. Women's clothes, on the other hand, were considerably less utilitarian in construction and there was more emphasis on individuality of appearance. Most women had time to

devote to dress and the ability to make some, if not all, of their clothes. There was no shortage of professional dressmakers and their charges varied to suit most types of customer. As a result there was less impetus to develop the female ready-to-wear market although some steps were taken in this direction. The shawl and ready-made mantle businesses were highly successful in the middle years of the century when these loose-fitting outer garments were in fashion, and a number of designs for mantles were registered from the late 1840s onwards.[22] With other clothes, the perennial problem of fit was tackled by the provision of partly-made garments. There is evidence that London firms sold half-made bodices on a wholesale basis to country drapers and dressmakers in the 1830s and it was also possible at this time to buy partly-made clothes which could be finished off by the customer or her dressmaker. Later in the century a popular compromise between ready-to-wear and made-to-measure was to

108 Applicants for
Admission to a Casual
Ward. L. Fildes, 1874.

*The poor had to rely on
second-hand clothes
and these were often ill-
fitting and impractical
garments. Those who
were really badly off
might be obliged to
pawn their Sunday-
best clothes in order to
eat. In spite of their
extreme poverty, these
applicants for a night's
lodging in the
workhouse preserve
their respectability by*
*observing the
nineteenth-century
convention of wearing a
hat or bonnet.*

purchase a dress with the skirt ready-made
and the material for making the bodice to
match.

There were some occasions when clothes
were needed at very short notice, and in the
case of mourning it was not possible to wait
long for new garments. The mourning
warehouses which supplied all the necessary
clothes and accessories were aware of this
problem and by the 1860s the leading firm,
Jay's was advertising ready-made mourning
dresses. Theses probably required a little
alteration to fit properly and may have had
partly-made bodices for the purpose. The
example of the mourning establishments
helped to promote the idea of ready-made
clothing for women and they were also to

play a role in the development of large shops in the second half of the century. The idea of being able to buy a variety of different goods from one large firm instead of visiting several small specialist shops steadily gained ground, leading to the emergence of the departmental stores. The idea itself was not entirely new because the early nineteenth-century warehouses, bazaars and many provincial shops sold a range of goods under one roof; but in the second half of the century the idea was taken further by creating a number of departments in one shop and offering various services to the customers.[23] Inexpensive railway travel, the London underground (opened in 1863) and horse omnibuses made it possible for customers to travel up to London for a day to shop and for Londoners themselves to move about the city more easily. Not only did these shops satisfy the demand for goods generated by the new middle-class prosperity but they also provided a kind of entertainment for their customers. Shopping had always been a pleasurable activity for those with the means, leisure and interest to devote to it but the later nineteenth-century department stores added a new dimension. A visit to a large shop could be an end in itself, providing several hours' diversion, particularly when customers took adantage of such facilities as rest rooms and restaurants.

For those much less fortunate, second-hand clothes and the pawn shops were a more familiar experience. Not all second-hand clothes were undesirable. It was a prerequisite of some domestic servants to receive the cast-off clothes of their employers, and this privilege was jealously guarded. In particular, ladies' maids would keep a proprietorial eye over their mistresses' new clothes, and a well-to-do employer might pass on several dresses each year, hardly worn or out of date. Ladies' maids had a reputation for dressing well, but no doubt some preferred to sell their acquisitions to the second-hand dealers. There was a ready market for cast-off clothing of all kinds, and advertisements frequently appeared in the press offering to buy these.

The pawnbrokers were another standby for the poor. George Augustus Sala noted, 'On a Saturday night the customers were deliriously anxious to redeem their poor little remnants of wearing apparel for that blessed Sunday that comes tomorrow, to be followed, however, by a Black Monday, when father's coat, and Polly's merino frock, nay the extra petticoat, nay the Lilliputian boots of the toddling child, will have to be pawned again ... But the poor are *so* poor, they have at the best of times so very little money, that pawning with them is an absolute necessity; and the pawnbroker's shop, that equitable mortgage on a small scale, is to them rather a blessing than a curse. Without that fourpence on the flat-iron, there would be very frequently no bread in the cupboard.'[24]

-8-
OCCASIONS, LEISURE AND PLEASURE
The Etiquette of Dress II

Festive Occasions

The nineteenth-century liking for regulating every aspect of life extended to the adoption of appropriate forms of dress for different occasions and occupations. Apart from the day-to-day social activities of visiting, afternoon tea, garden parties, evening entertainments or Sunday church-going there were the more infrequent and important events which marked a significant phase in human life, such as a christening, confirmation, marriage, presentation at Court and mourning. The ritual surrounding these ceremonies included special clothing for the participants, with often a great deal

of attention being devoted to this aspect. Mourning dress, in particular, became an expensive and complex element in most people's wardrobes as the rules of mourning etiquette grew more elaborate during the Victorian period. On the other hand, an exaggerated sense of modesty about bodily functions made pregnancy a topic of some secrecy and maternity clothes were very rarely discussed or illustrated in print.

There were many occasions for leisure and pleasure in the nineteenth century, and in some cases the clothes worn for them actually contributed to the enjoyment of the

109 Changing Homes.
G. E. Hicks, 1862.

Marriage was an important change in status for a woman in the nineteenth century although, greater attention was focused on the bride's trousseau than on her wedding dress. The trousseau was intended to provide enough clothes for the first two or three years of her married life and a measure of her social success depended on its splendour.

110 Wedding Dress.
Le Petit Modiste, *1820.*

At the beginning of the century the wedding dress was made in the 'full dress' style with a low neck and short sleeves. Orange blossom trimming was already fashionable in France in 1820 (the date of this plate from a French magazine) and was popular in Britain by the 1830s.

event. Fancy dress balls and parties were extremely popular throughout the period and both men and women adopted the costumes with enthusiasm. In less formal circumstances there were new opportunities to wear comfortable and practical clothes – for example, when on holiday, in the country or at the seaside and for the numerous sports which were being taken up. Although to twentieth-century eyes many of the garments appear restricting, it was a matter of degree; an increased measure of ease and a temporary relaxation from conventional routine made them an attractive alternative to everyday dress.

One of the most festive social occasions was the wedding, although the ceremony and its accompanying celebration were, in general, much smaller and quieter family affairs than they were to become in the following century. By 1800 it had become usual for brides to be dressed in white or cream but as a symbol of virginity it was a comparatively recent tradition, dating back to the mid-eighteenth century. More practical coloured gowns, though not so popular, were also worn and were preferred by widows, older brides and the less well-off. The dress always conformed to the current fashion but it changed from being 'full dress' (with a low neck and short sleeves) in the earlier decades of the century to semi-formal wear, high to the neck and with long sleeves, by the late 1830s. Until 1886, when there was a change in the rules for conducting church weddings, services always took place before noon and the day-dress form was clearly more suitable.

Lace was an important trimming both on the wedding dress itself and for the veil. The finest laces were used, and the most fashionable were Mechlin, Brussels and Honiton. Sometimes the whole dress was of lace over a white silk foundation, or there were deep flounces on the skirt. The long veil came into fashion for bridal wear at the beginning of the nineteenth century and the earliest ones hung down from the head at the back, but subsequently shorter veils were worn over the face before the wedding ceremony. Queen Victoria was probably the first British royal bride to wear a veil, although hers did not conceal her face at her wedding in 1840. It was made of Honiton lace, and her dress of white silk satin, woven at Spitalfields, was also trimmed with Honiton lace at the neck and sleeves, with a deep flounce on the skirt. Like many other nineteenth-century brides Queen Victoria treasured her wedding lace and she wore it throughout her life on important family occasions.[1] With her veil the Queen wore a wreath of orange blossom, a wedding fashion which appears to have originated in France and was popular in this

149

111 Till Death Do Us Part. *E. B. Leighton, 1879.*

The elderly gentleman on the bride's arm is not her father but the bridegroom and he is correctly dressed in a dark frock-coat and grey trousers with a high silk hat, light gloves and a flower in his buttonhole. The bride's satin dress is in the fashionable Princess style and by this date wedding dresses were made high to the neck with long sleeves. Wedding guests were attired in formal daytime clothes, much the same as those worn for afternoon visiting.

country by the 1830s. Not all brides wore veils and the bonnet was an acceptable alternative, especially with a coloured wedding dress. Two other bridal accessories were the bouquet of fresh flowers and a court train. Queen Victoria had worn a court train with her wedding dress in place of robes of state, but it became customary for other brides to do the same if they expected to be presented at Court following their marriage. Most brides made good use of their wedding dresses, altering them for evening and formal afternoon wear in the months after their marriage (often until the birth of the first child).[2] Poorer brides who did not marry in white were able to wear a coloured gown as a best dress for a long time afterwards.

The bridegroom's clothes were expected to be smart, fashionable and to conform to the prevailing rules of etiquette. At the beginning of the century 'full' dress was correct for weddings and the bridegroom was attired in a dark blue dress coat, white or light-coloured waistcoat, knee breeches, stockings and gloves. From the 1830s formal day dress rather than full or evening dress was worn, and by the mid-nineteenth century the day dress coat was being replaced by the frock-coat – but the coat was usually dark blue rather than black, which was thought to be unsuitable for a wedding. For most of the century the suit was distinguished from ordinary wear by a wedding waistcoat, generally made of white or cream figured silk or white silk with embroidery. A buttonhole, first added to the left lapel of the coat in the 1840s, allowed the bridegroom to wear a white flower for the wedding ceremony. Gentlemen in the armed services were married in full dress uniform, as were royal bridegrooms.

It was not until the nineteenth century that particular care was taken over the dress of the bridesmaids, who could number as many as six, eight or even twelve – often dressed as pairs or with three in one colour and three in another. It was not unusual for bridesmaids to wear white or cream but by the second half of the century light blue

and pink had become popular shades, accompanied by a bouquet of mixed flowers. At some very fashionable London weddings bridesmaids wore veils of net or tulle[3], but it was more usual for them to wear a bonnet or hat to match the dress.

When the bride left for her honeymoon she changed into a travelling dress. At the beginning of the century this was often a tailored cloth riding habit which, since the previous century, had also been worn for travelling and walking. By the beginning of the Victorian period the going-away clothes were usually a smart day dress, a mantle or shawl, bonnet and gloves. *The Habits of Good Society* (c. 1875) advised that a bride's travelling costume 'should be *good* in quality, but plain, like a handsome dress for morning calls. An elegant bonnet, not too plain, a handsome shawl or mantle, and coloured gloves ... the style should be of the very best, so that the impression left may be suitable, agreeable and elegant.'[4]

The bride's trousseau was, in effect, a part of her dowry, as she came to her husband with enough clothes and household linen to last her several years, if not a lifetime in the case of some items. It was considered extremely important to send a bride off in as much style as possible, and the trousseau was a status symbol in itself, proudly displayed to relatives and friends before the wedding. Huge sums could be spent on the trousseaux of fashionable people, who would order clothes by the dozen, in the latest styles and most luxurious fabrics. Even the more modest trousseaux were extensive and *The English-woman's Domestic Magazine*'s recommendation in 1862 for a wedding trousseau sufficient for a bride 'in the middle-class of society; that is to say, of those who may soon have command of incomes ranging from £400 to £600 a year' ran to several column-inches of items, under the headings of 'Under-linen', 'Etceteras', 'Dresses, Mantles etc' and 'House-linen'. Many items were listed in dozens and half-dozens, while at least eighteen dresses were thought necessary, not counting evening dresses which were to

*112 Morning Gowns.
Enquire Within, 1896.*

*Loose morning gowns,
wrappers and peignoirs
could be adapted for
maternity wear but
would only have been
worn at home, in the
morning and early
afternoon. For more
formal wear, pregnant
women continued to
wear tightly laced
corsets although lighter,
more elastic stays and
'accouchement belts'
were frequently
recommended by the
medical profession.*

be 'according to requirement'.[5] By the 1870s it was thought that 'a trousseau may, in quiet life, be formed upon so low a sum as £60 or £70; it seldom costs, however, less that £100, and often mounts up to £500.'[6]

If a bride was wise she included in her trousseau a number of garments which could be adapted for maternity wear, such as easy-fitting morning gowns, wrappers or peignoirs, loose indoor jackets, shawls, mantles and – later in the century tea gowns or tea jackets. Women's magazines were reticent on the subject and when references were, in fact, made to maternity clothing ladies were usually described as being 'in a delicate state of health', 'invalids' or simply, 'young matrons'. Young matrons were expected to be as discreet and dignified as possible. It was not always possible to disguise the condition but it could be camouflaged so as not to attract the attention of the opposite sex or young, unmarried girls who were ignorant of the facts of life. However, contemporary evidence suggests that Victorian women were more active during

pregnancy than might be supposed and many carried on their social engagements until a few weeks before the confinement.[7]

In order to avoid notice, ladies were generally recommended to keep in line with current fashion and alter existing garments rather than adopt ones which were too obviously designed and made for the specific purpose of pregnancy. This was also more economical as the clothes could often be altered back to their original state when the pregnancy was over (and it may account for the comparatively small number of maternity dresses to survive in museum collections). During the first two decades of the century the fashion for a high waistline and very light stays favoured the pregnant woman but problems arose when the waistline began to lengthen and tighten in the 1830s, making it difficult for a woman to hide her changing shape. For informal, indoor and morning wear she could manage with a loose-fitting, plain gown or type of wrapper and by the 1850s and 1860s it was also possible to wear unshaped indoor jackets over a blouse and skirt. Afternoon and evening dress was less easy to adapt and usually required the camouflage of a shawl.[8] When large, square shawls went out of fashion in the 1870s lace shawls and mantles were accepted as an alternative. Outer wear presented very little problem as shawls, mantles and cloaks were fashionable for most of the period.

Although the line of dress became very narrow in the late 1870s and 1880s the last quarter of the nineteenth century allowed more latitude in maternity wear. The Princess line and polonaise dresses without a break at the waist were less restricting and a thickening waist could be lost beneath the layered effect of skirt drapery and apron fronts. Dresses with separate bodices were often adapted for maternity wear by using false waistcoat fronts and plastron effects. Jeannette Marshall who married and was pregnant in 1892 added jabots of lace, chiffon and ribbon bows with long streamers to the bodices of some of her dresses.[9] With the advent of the tea gown in the late 1870s semi-formal and formal evening wear for pregnant women became easier and by the early 1890s the tea gown could be worn for dinner at home. The loose fit and highly trimmed nature of the tea gown and tea jacket made them particularly suitable for maternity wear and no doubt their very decorative, even seductive image did much for the morale of the wearer.

While the birth of an infant was a very private event its christening in church marked its first public appearance and was an occasion to be celebrated. From an early date the Church decreed that a child should be baptised in a white garment (signifying its innocence and purity) and by the beginning of the nineteenth century this was a long, white or cream robe as splendid as the parents could afford. In the eighteenth century the finest christening robes had been made of silk or satin amply trimmed and embroidered; some nineteenth-century gowns were made entirely of lace over a silk foundation, but the most usual form of christening dress in the nineteenth century was a very fine white cotton or linen with white embroidery. In many cases the dress was made by the baby's mother who lavished all her needlework skills on it; the one dress might then do duty for all the children in the family and be handed down to following generations. A very popular type of decoration in the mid-nineteenth century was 'Ayrshire work', a very fine white embroidery with cutwork and needlework fillings. In later decades the centre front panels of the bodice and skirt were ornamented with ordinary white embroidery, pintucks and lace insertion. With the long dress the baby always wore a close-fitting white cap and might also be carried to church in a mantle. The guests at a christening were smartly dressed, as for a joyful social occasion. This generally meant formal day wear, of the kind worn for church on Sunday, but not as elaborate as for a wedding. The less fashionable or well-off would wear their 'Sunday best' clothes.

Confirmation at the age of about fourteen was another essentially religious occasion which required a suitable form of dress. In the predominantly Roman Catholic countries on the Continent 'First Communion' dresses were often featured in fashion plates, but these were not so popular in British magazines with their more Protestant readership. However, it was customary for young girls to wear a white dress, a cap or veil and white gloves for the ceremony and boys wore 'black suits, black ties and gloves'.[10]

Apart from marriage, presentation at Court was the most important milestone in the life of a young woman in upper-class British society. The custom had evolved from the seventeenth- and eighteenth-century practice of leading members of society attending Court to pay their respects to the monarch. As this circle increased in number the arrangements began to be organized on

113 A Couple, photographed c. 1892.

It is possible that this lady was pregnant when she was photographed. The loose fit of fashionable mantles and capes in the second half of the nineteenth century helped to disguise the condition.

114 Morning Dress. La Belle Assemblée, *1814.*

This nursing gown with its practical front flap opening is discreetly referred to as a 'Morning Dress'. Two decades later, The Workwoman's Guide *of 1838 described nursing stays, petticoats and gowns with instructions on how to make them. On nursing stays the author wrote: 'It is essential to open the front of nursing stays, so as to give the mother the greatest ease while feeding her infant.'*

a more formal basis and by the nineteenth century ladies were presented at one of several 'Drawing Rooms' held each year. This was essentially a passport of admittance to the very best society since 'Society' in its most precise sense was understood to mean those people eligible for access to the Court.[11] Aristocratic families took this as a matter of course but there were many others who aspired to membership of this exclusive circle – too many, in fact, for comfort – and it became necessary to put a strict limit on eligibility. George IV began a process of tightening up the regulations and these continued to multiply and grow more complex during Queen Victoria's reign. Only certain categories of people could be presented and those connected with trade were debarred. By the 1880s, for example, those entitled to attend included the families of the aristocracy and country gentry, military or naval professions, the bar, clerical, medical and other professions. The families of merchants, bankers and members of the Stock Exchange were also eligible, 'and persons engaged in commerce on a large scale; but at trade, known as retail trade, however extensive its operations, the line is drawn and very strictly so.'[12] At the same time it

was absolutely necessary to 'bear a good character in society' and it 'would be in vain for any lady to sue for admittance into the courtly circle, however high her rank, if there were the least stain upon her reputation.'[13] Applicants for this privilege had to be sponsored by someone who had already been presented at Court, and only married women could act as sponsors.

The strict regulations included the correct dress to be worn at Court which, by its nature, demanded great formality. Clothes which are highly regulated and very formal tend to lag behind fashion, and in the eighteenth century, for example, wide hoop petticoats were retained for court wear long after they disappeared from ordinary dress. They were still being worn at the beginning of the nineteenth century even though hoops were quite incongruous with highwaisted dresses made of thin fabrics. Long, narrow trains and plumed head-dresses were also required. Hoops were at last discarded for the coronation of George IV in 1820 and during the remainder of the century court dresses followed the line of fashionable evening dress, that is, with a low bodice and short sleeves. Although presentations took place in the aftenoon, full evening dress was essential and the rule on low necklines was very strict. No lady could appear in a high dress without special permission and this could only be obtained by presenting a medical certificate to the Lord Chamberlain's office.[14]

By the late nineteenth century it was usual for débutantes to wear white for presentations while newly married women adapted their wedding dresses for the occasion. Other married women could dress in colours and the materials were of the richest kind, handsomely trimmed with embroidery and lace. Ladies in mourning were permitted to wear black, as did the Queen during her widowhood. Two other essential components of female court dress were the train and the head-dress. The train was very important and could be even more opulent than the dress itself. It was a separate item, made of rich silk, satin or velvet lined with white silk and trimmed with lace or flowers; until the 1870s it was usually attached at the waist, but by the last quarter of the nineteenth century there were alternative methods of attaching it and in the 1890s the train generally hung from the shoulders. The length of the train was considerable and was not permitted to be less than three and a half yards long from the ankles. It had grown to seven or eight yards by the 1870s and was wide in proportion.

The head-dress consisted of feathers and either lace lappets or a tulle veil. Plumes were worn by both married and unmarried ladies but by the late nineteenth century it was customary for married women to wear three feathers and the unmarried to wear two. The correct colour was white, but black feathers were worn for mourning. Lappets – a survival of the eighteenth century – were bands of lace hanging down on either side of the head. The later nineteenth-century

115 HRH The Princess of Wales in her Court Dress. La Belle Assemblée, 1807.

Elizabeth Grant remembered as a young girl in 1810, visiting a London dressmaker with her mother, 'the three or four rooms full of hoops before the court days, machines of whalebone, very large, covered with silk, and then with lace or net, and hung about with festoons of lace and beads, garlands of flowers, puffings of ribbon, furbelows of all sorts . . .'

alternative was a long veil of white silk net or tulle fixed on the crown of the head to hang down at the back. Diamonds, pearls or jewelled ornaments could also be worn in the hair and other necessary accessories were long white kid gloves, a large bouquet or dress fan and white satin shoes.

Gentlemen's court dress also retained close links with the eighteenth century, and the suit consisted of a tail coat, waistcoat and knee-breeches worn with silk stockings, buckled shoes, a sword with a cut-steel hilt and a bicorne hat. The coat, cut in the style of the 1780s–90s, was tailored in a fine dark woollen cloth (often plum-coloured or brown) lined with silk and with cut steel buttons; from the 1840s it could be made of velvet. The waistcoat was made of white silk with floral embroidery in coloured silk threads, again in the style fashionable at the end of the previous century. A change came in 1869 when new regulations were issued for gentlemen's court dress. The cut and form of the new-style suit were similar but the coat and breeches were of black velvet and the waistcoat was of plain white silk or black velvet.

The Complexities of Mourning

One form of dress which involved some of the strictest and most complicated rules of etiquette in the nineteenth century was mourning. The wearing of mourning, to mark the death of a member of the royal family or of a person's own relatives, had long been usual, but the custom became even more widespread during the Victorian period. Viscountess Harberton, a critic of this practice, pointed out in 1889, 'let no one solace themselves by imagining that the poor are less slaves to customs than the rich. On the contrary, they are even more bound by them.'[15] At every level of society there was an anxiety to avoid censure for failing to observe the conventions surrounding death and bereavement. Even a working man, it was reported, could experience 'extraordinary

155

116 At the Queen's Drawing Room. *E. Hopkins, 1890.*

A young woman's presentation marked her début into society at the age of about seventeen or eighteen. When she married (having entered a new family) she was presented again, usually by her mother-in-law. She might be presented on a third occasion, to mark yet another change in status, such as her husband succeeding to a title. Having once been presented, a lady or gentleman could attend the annual Drawing Rooms and Levées but it was not usual to go to more than one in a season.

117 The Widow's Mite. *J. E. Millais, 1870.*

The distinctive dress of the widow set her apart from the rest of society and she was often portrayed as a romantically tragic figure. However, many people considered the clothes, and especially the cap, to be rather becoming to young and pretty widows.

ill-will and anger excited in a neighbourhood' when his family decided not to go into mourning for fear of running into debt. 'As a consequence, they were insulted in every possible way, and jeered at by their neighbours for a long time after.'[16]

There seems little doubt that the cult of mourning was stimulated by Queen Victoria, following the death of her husband the Prince Consort in 1861. Women's magazines also heightened an awareness of the rules and regulations by printing articles and advice on the subject. Men wore mourning, but to a lesser extent, and by the second half of the century their clothes had in any case become very sombre. Henry Mayhew made his well-known remark in 1865 that 'a

gentleman of the present nineteenth century, attired for the gayest evening party, would, apart from his jewellery, be equally presentable at the most sorrowful funeral.'[17] Children and even babies were also required to adopt some form of mourning dress but this was often limited to white dresses trimmed with black ribbons and crape sashes. Women, however, had to put aside all their ordinary clothes and wear nothing but black, in the appropriate materials and with particular accessories, for the first stages of mourning. A death in the family, Lady Harberton said, 'obliges all the women of that family to at once provide themselves with a sort of trousseau.' The closer the relative the more pronounced the mourning was expected to be, reaching a climax with the dress of a widow which in Lady Harberton's words 'positively amounts to a mild form of *Suttee*.'[18]

In a sense, women were obliged to carry out the principle of conspicuous consumption. Mourning was expensive and extravagant besides being a symbol of conformity and respectability. It was wasteful mainly because it was not divorced from fashion; mourning garments were exactly the same as others in respect of shape and style but differed from them in colour and materials. They could not be put away and re-used at a later date without being remodelled and often it was easier to buy new clothes when the need arose. Periods of mourning could sometimes last several years if there were consecutive deaths in a family and ordinary clothes had to be put aside for the duration; they too needed to be remodelled when they were taken out again and if this was impracticable they might have to be discarded.

Black was the principal mourning colour and for deepest mourning, during the first days or months after a death in the family, it was at its most intense. A lifeless, lustreless quality was required and glossy materials such as satin, velvet or furs were forbidden. A suitably matt effect was created by the use of wool or cotton fibres and by weaving techniques which broke up the smooth surface of the cloth, as with twilled, ribbed or crimped fabrics. Consequently the most favoured mourning materials were bombazine, paramatta and crape. Bombazine, which had first appeared in the late sixteenth century, was woven from a silk warp and a worsted weft with a twilled effect. Cheaper versions were made from a mixture of cotton and wool and one form, called bombazet, was used for servants' mourning.[19] Paramatta was a less expensive alternative to bombazine, having a cotton warp and worsted weft, and was much worn by widows in the later nineteenth century. All-wool fabrics like cashmere and merino were also used. For lesser mourning, poplin, alpaca and dull, ribbed or twilled silks were acceptable.

Of all the materials for mourning, crape was probably the most distinctive and it was used in enormous quantities. Crape (always spelt in this way) was a black silk gauzelike fabric with a characteristic crimped surface and stiff texture. The weave was plain but a high twist yarn was used and it was crimped by heat; the material was also treated to give it a dull, hard finish. This was very effective when new but it tended to wear off in time and was particularly susceptible to spoiling in the rain. The principal manufacturer of mourning crape was Courtauld's, whose fortunes were made by the almost insatiable demand for the material until the last decade of the nineteenth century.[20] Crape was used to trim mourning garments and almost covered the dress of a widow in the first phase of mourning. For example, the skirt was overlaid with a deep flounce which reached up from the hem to within six or seven inches of the waist. The bodice, sleeves and outer garments had applied bands, panels or facings of crape and crape was used for bonnet veils. As the wearer moved into stages of lesser mourning in the following months or years, the crape was diminished and finally discarded. It was then possible to wear black silks and velvets with jet ornaments. In the final stages of mourning, before returning to ordinary clothes, the lighter mourning colours could be worn: white, grey and shades of purple. Since white was a traditional mourning colour it was an acceptable alternative to black on formal occasions and it was also used for accessories to the widow's dress. A widow in deepest mourning wore a closefitting white cap with long streamers and plain white collars and cuffs. The cap of white muslin or crape, often made in the 'Marie Stuart' shape dipping to a point at the centre front, was worn for a year and a day after the death of a husband; but some widows, including the Queen, kept them for the rest of their lives.

Mourning accessories included black jewellery, made of jet, bog oak or enamel and memorial pieces set with the hair of the deceased relative or friend; black-bordered handkerchiefs and black crape fans. No detail was too small to be overlooked. *The Young Ladies' Journal* in 1890 suggested that: 'All the ribbons with which a lady of refinement loves to adorn every trifle – her lingerie, her scent-bottles, looking-glass, scent-cushions, and so on, should be mauve or purple. Slippers, sunshades, umbrellas, card-cases, purse, blotting-book, paper-borders, must be strictly black. The gold watch must disappear in a case of ebony inlaid with silver, unless it is exchanged for a steel one. The prayer book should be of black morocco, the book-mark embroidered in black silk and silver; the book-cover of ancient damask, in multi-coloured designs, is now exchanged for one of black or purple, embroidered with silver. All this may appear very trifling, but real feeling shows itself even in the most trivial circumstances.'[21]

The complexities of mourning etiquette lay in the correct combination of materials, trimmings and colours worn for the right periods of time. The total length of mourning depended on the nearness of the relative and ranged from two and a half years for a widow mourning her husband, to six weeks for a mother mourning the parents-in-law of her married children; but within that period there were changes from first or deepest mourning to second mourning, then to ordinary mourning and finally half-mourning.

Mourning. Cassell's Family Magazine, *1878.*

Mourning was far less oppressive for men and the usual dress was a black suit, necktie, gloves and silk hat with a deep band of crape. 'Some gentlemen also have black bordered handkerchiefs'. Any departures from the accepted rules were quickly noticed and deplored.

Thus, during the last quarter of the nineteenth century, it was usual for a widow to wear plain black bombazine and crape for a year and a day, followed by a further nine months of second mourning in less crape; the next three months of ordinary mourning permitted her to wear black silk with ribbon and jet trimming, without crape; and then she could spend six months (at least) in half-mourning colours. For more distant relatives the first and second phases were omitted and mourning was observed for several weeks or months by wearing black or half-mourning colours. Servants were put

into mourning on the death of an employer's relative and they followed all the same rules except that they wore cheaper, stronger materials and only black or white (not half-mourning colours).

For men, mourning was less oppressive and they were able to take up their work and social activities after a shorter length of time. By the end of the century the usual dress was an ordinary black suit, necktie, gloves and hat with the addition of a deep band of black crape on the hat and 'some gentlemen also have black bordered handkerchiefs', while in the Army and Navy mourning was indicated 'by a band of crape on the left arm, placed above the elbow' and bright metal buttons were replaced with black.[22] The long black cloaks and 'weepers' (long bands of crape hanging from the hat) formerly worn by mourners were now only seen on the undertaker and his staff. Children's mourning was also lessened in the last two decades of the century and it was generally felt that 'the little children do not understand it and it is absurd to invest them with the signs of grief they cannot feel.'[23]

This was one of several voices to be raised against extreme forms of mourning in the mid-1870s. In 1875 the National Funeral and Mourning Reform Association was founded and by the 1880s other societies had appeared.[24] They were concerned about the senseless display and extravagance involved in funerals and mourning, especially when they impoverished needy families. Lady Harberton, a promoter of rational dress, also objected to the way in which mourning pressed far more heavily on women than on men. Whether or not it was as a result of these opinions, the mourning regulations were beginning to relax in the 1890s and the use of crape was declining. In 1897 *The Tailor and Cutter*, in an article on mourning said, 'it must be acknowledged it is a custom that is on the wane, and we think this well, for there is no disputing the fact that this custom has often developed into strange absurdities, and especially amongst the fair sex...'[25]

159

119 Costumes for a Bal Masqué. The Englishwoman's Domestic Magazine, *1864.*

Fancy dress balls were a very popular diversion throughout the nineteenth century and the costumes were often researched with great thoroughness. Historical themes were amongst the most frequently chosen and were stimulated by contemporary literature and history paintings. The ladies in the foreground of this illustration are dressed in a variety of styles inspired (from the left) by sixteenth-, eighteenth- and seventeenth-century dress.

Bal Masqué

Mourning, with its monotonous colouring and rigid etiquette, was a restricting form of dress. The return to ordinary clothes and colours must have been greeted with relief by most wearers (although some widows preferred to retain their distinctive garments). Similarly, the opportunity to escape, from time to time, from the restraints of everyday formal clothes was welcomed and this encouraged the development of dress for sporting and leisure pursuits. True escapism, however, was to be found in the fancy dress costumes for which there was such a passion throughout the nineteenth century. Fancy dress balls and parties were enjoyed at every level of society, including the royal family, and both men and women liked dressing up. The costumes could be extremely fanciful and elaborate; many of them were beautifully and expensively

made, and were a lucrative side of even the most exclusive dressmaking establishments.

To some extent the fancy dress ball was a continuation of the eighteenth-century masquerade, which had been a popular social diversion; but in the nineteenth century there was less of the element of disguise and masks were rarely worn. In general, nineteenth-century fancy balls were rather more sedate affairs with quite serious and often academic attention being paid to the costumes. Nevertheless, it could be an opportunity to dispense with the usual standards of modesty and good taste in dress. For many people fancy dress was simply the enjoyable experience of being able to change their identity or status for a short period of time – anyone might be a king or queen, prince or nobleman for an evening. Dressing up as a character from history or as an exotic foreigner created an aura of glamour and romance which modern dress could never impart. Much of contemporary life was seen as ugly, materialistic and insecure; there was a nostalgic yearning for a better world in the past or in another country – happier, more beautiful and with higher ideals than the present. Modern dress, especially men's, was felt to be uniform and dull but fancy dress allowed scope for creativity and invention. Favourite themes were historical costumes of various kinds (revivals of earlier fashions, dressing up as a famous character in history or copying an 'Old Master' painting); pastoral dress (shepherds and shepherdesses, milkmaids, fisherfolk, peasants); and foreign costume, particularly Turkish, Greek and oriental garments whose rich colours and flowing lines had an enduring appeal.

Holiday Attire

The fancy dress party provided a brief excursion into a world of fantasy, far from the humdrum nature of everyday existence, but this was not the only means of relaxation from the pressures of modern life. The nineteenth century saw a marked development in the holiday and the creation of leisure time as a break from work. With the growth of an urban-industrial society the need was increasingly felt for periods of rest and for a change of air. At the height of the summer large towns seemed unbearably hot, crowded and dirty, and there was a general exodus (amongst those who could afford it) to the more healthy countryside or seaside. The most affluent were able to travel abroad and spend long periods at fashionable resorts on the Continent; many

120 Pegwell Bay, Kent. *W. Dyce, 1858–9.*

At the height of the summer when large towns were hot, crowded and dirty there was a general exodus to the more healthy countryside and the seaside. The seaside, in particular, became extremely popular and its health-giving properties were preferred to the inland spas and watering places favoured during the eighteenth century. Holidays required comfortable, practical clothes such as the shorter walking skirt, stout boots with low heels, plain gloves and a dark hat.

121 The Fashions. The Englishwoman's Domestic Magazine, *1862.*

Fashion journals advised the purchase of specially designed travelling wear and condemned the practice of wearing out old clothes on a journey. Walking skirts with loose-fitting, matching jackets came into fashion in the 1850s and were ideal for holiday and seaside wear. The practical, masculine inspiration is evident in this plate, not only in the suit but in the shirt collar, bow tie and straw hat worn by the lady on the left.

middle-class families took a fortnight's holiday in lodgings out of town; but even the less well-to-do had the opportunity to take short breaks or day excursions, made possible by inexpensive and efficient railway travel. During the second half of the century women's magazines had regular features on holiday and travelling clothes, and etiquette books began to include chapters on how to behave and dress in hotels or when away from home.

Clothes for these purposes followed the lines of current fashion but were adapted to the circumstances. Holidays were a time for informality, relaxation, a certain amount of physical exercise and, very often, an opportunity for romance. Dress was therefore expected to be comfortable, practical and attractive. Travelling garments needed to take account of dust, dirt and creasing. Facilities for laundering were limited *en route* to destinations, and space for hand-luggage was restricted. Having arrived at a resort, however, a number of different clothes

were needed for the daytime leisure activities and evening entertainments.

For both travelling and general holiday wear skirts were made in the shorter, walking length, without trains. The late 1850s saw the advent of the looped-up skirt worn over a coloured petticoat and bright stockings – a form of dress Queen Victoria adopted for walking in Scotland. The 'Balmoral petticoat' which she made respectable was of white or grey horsehair worn instead of a crinoline frame. The Queen also wore 'Balybriggan stockings' of knitted cotton which were recommended for country wear.

Sports Dress

Fresh air and sunshine were enjoyed in the country and at the seaside but sunburn or freckles were not admired (being associated with manual labour out of doors). Heads and faces were protected by bonnets, hats or parasols at all times. Two particular seaside fashions were 'uglies' and broad-brimmed straw hats. In the 1840s and 1850s a kind of extension to the bonnet brim was made by the addition of half-hoops of cane covered in silk. This projected over the face almost like a carriage hood and – presumably because it was not considered very attractive – was called an 'ugly'. Much more popular were the large straw hats with ribbon streamers which became fashionable seaside wear in the 1850s. Many illustrations from the mid-nineteenth century also show young women wearing their hair long and loose at the seaside and this was a permitted informality there. The hair invariably got wet during morning bathes and was allowed to dry over the shoulders before more formal clothes were put on in the afternoon.

Fashions in bathing clothes changed and the long, loose shift of dark serge or flannel worn in the earlier part of the century was replaced by a two-piece costume of a belted jacket and trousers in the early 1860s. The new form of costume was considered much more comfortable and alluring. Men and boys bathed nude for much of the nineteenth century, and although drawers were recommended they were not always used or liked. By the late 1870s an alternative style of bathing dress was available for men: a one-piece costume with top and drawers combined. The style was probably derived from the combinations which had come into fashion in underwear. In the last decade of the century the one-piece costume was very generally worn and was often boldly striped.

The many social diversions at holiday resorts called for frequent changes of clothing. In 1885 *The Lady* advised that 'at some of the most fashionable watering-places costumes are changed at least five times a day'. The outfits required included the breakfast toilette, the dress for listening to the band, the dress for excursions, the dinner toilette and the evening dress for the casino, not to mention all the petticoats, lingerie and a 'complete bathing arsenal'.[26] Ten years later *The Lady* was still of the opinion that a large amount of luggage was necessary for 'the up-to-date woman who goes to some smart seaside hotel where there are dances, concerts, and picnics, and where the table d'hôte is really a dinner party to all intents and purposes. ... Everything must be fresh and fashionable, and smart demi-toilettes, afternoon gowns, a serge for boating parties, a dust-cloak for drives and picnics, and a pretty bathing costume, are only a few of the indispensable items.'[27] By the mid-1890s dark serge skirts and light blouses, with short jackets and straw sailor hats were a particularly fashionable and practical form of dress for holidays and the seaside.

Holiday and travelling clothes shared several characteristics with sports dress, which needed to be serviceable and provide freedom of movement. In the informal atmosphere of holiday and sporting occasions new ideas could be tried out and liberties were allowed which might be unthinkable in ordinary dress. An example of this was the adoption of trousers for women in some types of sportswear. Bloomers had caused a scandal in the early 1850s, but only ten years later trousers were thought acceptable and even attractive as part of bathing costume. Similar tunics and trousers or combination garments (sometimes with the addition of a knee-length overskirt) were also worn for gymnastics. However, attempts to introduce the divided skirt for tricycling in the 1880s and knickerbockers for cycling in the 1890s met with a considerable amount of hostility, possibly because the trousers were being worn openly in mixed company, as part of normal day dress.

Trousers for women were permissible if suitably disguised and confined to specific and secluded activities. They had, for example, been an 'invisible' part of female riding dress since the early decades of the nineteenth century. Long, cotton drawers began to be worn instead of petticoats with the narrower skirts of that period, and were a modest precaution if the rider should be

122 Bathing Dress. The Englishwoman's Domestic Magazine, 1863.

A new style of bathing dress for women had appeared by 1860 and consisted of a belted tunic and long trousers, usually of dark serge. This was felt to be much more attractive than the shapeless bathing shifts worn earlier in the century. In July 1864, for instance, The Englishwoman's Domestic Magazine *described a coquettish 'sailor' style in which 'a young woman looks like a pretty boy'. Oiled silk caps and shoes were also worn for bathing.*

163

123 Riding Habits by Nicoll & Co. The Englishwoman's Domestic Magazine, 1863.

Women's riding habits were made by tailors and the tightly-fitting bodice incorporated features of the fashionable male coat. Long trousers were worn beneath the matching skirt which was cut with extra length to fall gracefully from the side saddle.

thrown from her horse or have her skirts lifted by the wind. By the mid-nineteenth century the trousers were made of stouter cloth or chamois leather to the knees with the lower part of the legs in material to match the skirt. These long, straight, dark trousers were worn beneath the riding habit until the 1890s when they began to be replaced by breeches under the skirt. By the 1890s long tweed trousers were also worn under matching skirts for following a shoot, walking on the moors or fishing. Masculine inspiration had long been a feature of women's riding clothes and for most of the nineteenth century two-piece riding habits were severely tailored in plain, dark woollen cloth, and from the 1840s an alternative to the short jacket bodice was a longer-skirted coat with a collar and lapels, similar to a man's coat. By the 1890s this could be worn with a waistcoat. The female riding hat was also borrowed from the male wardrobe: the beaver top hat (with a flowing veil) was

a favourite style but it was joined in the early 1870s by the hard felt bowler.

By the mid-1890s women were taking an increasingly active part in sports and other aspects of daily life. Perhaps not surprisingly many men and some ladies were alarmed at the independence and masculine appearance of the New Woman. Mannish features had begun to appear in fashionable dress in the 1880s, but it was in sports clothing that some of the more advanced ideas were tried out. Trousers, jerseys and tailored jackets all looked towards the easier clothes women were to adopt in the following century, although not all women's sportswear was so comfortable or practical. Some clothes made virtually no concessions to the sport. Archery was one of the few outdoor activities open to women in the early part of the century and it was very popular. The dress was chosen with care and was usually considered attractive, but it appears not to have been adapted in any significant way to allow the

124 A Summer
Shower. *E. Hayllar,
1883.*

*Lawn tennis became a
popular sport in the
1870s. By the 1880s
special aprons with
pockets to hold the
tennis balls were
fashionable wear for
women but their clothes
made few other
concessions to the sport.
Lawn tennis was
played in dresses with
high-necked bodices,
long tight sleeves and
cumbersome skirts.
Men's clothes were
more adaptable and the
young man on the left
has obviously been
playing in his shirt
sleeves; he wears
knickerbockers, knitted
hose and sports shoes.
In the background
another young man has
the hems of his white
flannel trousers turned
up well above his
ankles.*

arms to move freely. Croquet, which became popular in the 1850s and 1860s required no special dress but benefited from the fashion for looping up the skirt to a walking length. Another new pastime was roller-skating, a craze popularly known as 'rinking', in the mid-1870s, but again, ladies were able to manage in spite of wearing hats or bonnets, full-length skirts and several layers of petticoats.

More to be wondered at, perhaps, is the way in which lawn tennis was played from the late 1870s in tightly laced corsets, close-fitting, high-necked bodices and long skirts encumbered with drapery, bustles and underpetticoats. The usual materials for tennis dresses were fine woollen serges or flannels, even in hot weather. In the 1880s special aprons for holding the tennis balls were also worn. The use of jersey-weave fabrics for tennis costumes offered some freedom of movement and in the mid-1880s, as *The Lady* reported, for tennis or boating,

'underskirts are very much given up in favour of pants or a scanty "divided-skirt" which should be of the same material as the costume, and be unseen, or at least unnoticeable.'[28] Supporters of rational dress thought that trousers would be sensible wear for tennis, but this found little favour. Tennis was a social sport and women wished to look attractive, especially to the opposite sex. The rules of etiquette hardly relaxed for tennis dress before the end of the century. *The Illustrated London News* in September 1897, for instance, described 'a particularly successful example' consisting of a skirt of black and white striped flannel, a shirt of white pongee with a turned-down collar and necktie to match, a belt of black suede fastened in front with an enamelled buckle set with diamonds (or their equivalent) and a French sailor hat with a scarf of white chiffon dotted with black chenille spots.[29]

CONCLUSION

As the nineteenth century drew to a close a style of dress had evolved which was to set the pattern for the next dozen years. Women were to enter the twentieth century still wearing the full-length skirt, tightly laced corset and boned bodice, high-heeled shoes, fanciful hats, and their hair long and elaborately dressed. Female fashions in the Edwardian era were to be as restricting and impractical as any worn during the nineteenth century but, at the same time, dramatic changes were about to take place. By the time the First World War had ended in 1918 tight lacing had been universally abandoned, the hemline had risen well above the ankles, women had begun to crop their hair short and could wear trousers for certain occupations. Although the War was to act as a catalyst for many of these changes their roots lay, in fact, in the nineteenth century and it was in the Victorian period that the foundations of what might be called 'modern' fashion were laid.

It has been seen, for example, that more practical forms of dress had begun to emerge, often by the way of sports and leisure wear. The tailored cloth costume, the blouse and skirt and the jersey all looked forward to the more functional styles of the twentieth century. For men, the three-piece suit in dark cloth was established for business wear and has endured, with comparatively little alteration, to the present day, but the less formal and more comfortable tweed suits and lounge jackets appeared as an alternative for activities outside working hours. Although male dress was often condemned for being ugly and dull most men found it satisfactory and had little real urge to change it.

Women had more cause for complaint, and a campaign during the second half of the nineteenth century for more rational styles of clothing was bound up with the wider issues of women's rights and the fight for female emancipation. Unlike men, it could be argued that their clothes actively curtailed their freedom and some garments, such as tight corsets, were injurious to their health. It was concern about these issues which was to have a profound effect, not so much on later nineteenth-century dress but on fashion in the early decades of the twentieth century.

Attitudes to dress underwent a transition during the nineteenth century. At the very end of the eighteenth century Jane Austen had dismissed dress as 'at all times a frivolous distinction, and excessive solicitude about it often destroys its one aim'[1] – a decided and commonsense view typical of the Regency period which followed shortly afterwards. During the second half of the nineteenth century the subject was seen in a different light, becoming a matter of important social concern. Artists, writers and

125 Woman in Walking Dress, photographed in 1893.

This young woman in her smart tailored costume cut on masculine lines, with a waistcoat, stiff-collared shirt, tie and straw boater, is typical of the 'New Woman' of the mid-1890s. Her confident pose and mannish clothes reflect the challenge she posed to accepted roles for women and the desire for more practical forms of dress.

126 Amelia Bloomer, originator of the new dress. The Illustrated London News, *1851.*

Mrs Bloomer did not, in fact, invent her famous costume but the knee-length dress and Turkish trousers became completely associated with her and she campaigned actively for their adoption during the early 1850s. Her objection was to the hampering nature of many layers of floor-length petticoats then in fashion for women and she advocated the comfort and practicality of trousers. The knee-length overskirt was a gesture towards feminine modesty but did little, at that time, to mitigate the shock of seeing women wearing trousers in public.

intellectuals began to apply themselves to the problems posed by contemporary fashion and with an earnestness and reforming zeal that were characteristic of the later Victorian period. When the need for reform became apparent, the harms of modern clothing were tackled as conscientiously as other political, social and economic problems. This body of thought has come to be known as the Dress Reform movement, but although 'Dress Reform' was a term which was in common use in the 1880s and 1890s

the movement itself was not cohesively organized with any kind of formal structure or manifesto. Rather, it was a climate of opinion drawn from several different strands of thought which were being argued at the time.[2]

Health, for example, was a matter of interest in the nineteenth century and, apart from concerns about disease, sanitation and poor living conditions among the less well-off, there was some awareness of the need to improve the diet, exercise and clothing of the more affluent. This culminated in the immensely popular International Health Exhibition held in London in 1884. It was the most comprehensive if not the first exhibition devoted to the subject and included most aspects of healthy living, including vegetarianism. There were two sections dealing with dress, one of which concentrated on 'sanitary' and 'rational' clothing (the most notable being Dr Gustav Jaeger's Sanitary Woollen System which had recently become available in London and was to attract a devoted following).

The issue of health and dress, however, had been raised at least fifty years earlier when medical writers began to attack tight lacing and the hampering clothes which prevented women and young girls from taking adequate exercise.[3] By 1844 *Punch* was drawing attention to the practice of tight lacing, by making the obvious comparison with such barbaric customs as Chinese foot-binding. Criticism was directed not so much at the corsets themselves, since they had been usual for well over a century, but at the way in which they were worn. It was the adjustment of the back lacing, so that the corset (which actually fastened at the centre front) could pull in the waist as firmly as possible, which caused the damage. Extreme compression could lead to giddiness, headaches, indigestion and poor circulation, resulting in unsightly red noses and swollen hands and feet. On the other hand, it was difficult to prove that really serious or even fatal consequences might follow and this made it difficult for reformers to persuade women against tight lacing.[4] A small waist

169

was a focal point of fashion for most of the century and as long as it was thought beautiful women were prepared to suffer for it.

Also to be criticized were the long, full and often heavy skirts that women were obliged to wear. The most famous attack on petticoats came from the young American, Amelia Bloomer, who adopted a novel form of dress in the early 1850s. This consisted of an easy-fitting, knee-length dress worn over Turkish-style trousers.[5] The idea of women wearing trousers in public was considered very shocking and was generally ridiculed but did not disappear. By the early 1860s trousers had been adopted for a new style of bathing costume for women and, also by the 1860s, women working at the colliery pit brow in Wigan had begun to wear trousers under tucked-up skirts (in spite of much

adverse comment).[6] Trousers continued to be recommended for women's sportswear and, though they aroused controversy until the end of the century, opinion gradually changed. In 1895, *Punch*'s obituary of Mrs Bloomer mentioned that her costume would 'scarce provoke criticism' now that lady cyclists in knickerbockers were an accustomed sight.[7]

Mrs Bloomer herself stopped wearing the costume in about 1857 when she found the new cage crinoline was light and comfortable and eliminated the need for numerous heavy petticoats. The weight of women's clothes was a recurring problem which was exacerbated by the revival of the train in the later 1870s and by the heavy, elaborately draped skirts fashionable in the 1880s. Ada Ballin in her *Science of Dress* (1885) stressed how exhausting it was for women to walk in long skirts and bulky petticoats – even men complained of fatigue 'if they walk in those long ulsters which flap against the legs'.

The crinoline frame may have freed women from their cumbersome petticoats for a while but this and other methods of distending the skirt were deplored by a number of artists and those who considered themselves to be aesthetically knowledgeable. Tightly laced corsets, crinolines and bustles all distorted the natural lines of the female figure and were therefore felt to be ugly and artificial (as also were the false chignons of the 1870s, tight hairstyles and sleeves of the 1880s, and narrow, high-heeled shoes of the last quarter of the nineteenth century). Among the first to object to contemporary fashion on aesthetic grounds were the members of the Pre-Raphaelite Brotherhood and their circle, in the late 1840s and 1850s. William Holman Hunt, Dante Gabriel Rossetti and John Everett Millais in particular, became interested in and admired the dress of the Middle Ages. Male and female styles of around the mid-fourteenth century, during the reign of Edward III (1327–77) appeared to be perfectly conceived, with their carefully fitted garments cut on the cross grain of the fabric to gently indicate

127 *A Fashionable Lady, photographed in the early 1880s.*

Artists and dress reformers disliked the unnatural aspects of contemporary fashion especially tightly laced corsets which distorted the lines of the female figure. The very rigid boning and extremely tight fit of women's clothes in the early 1880s can be appreciated in this photograph. It is interesting to note the strong resemblance the bodice bears to a low-cut corset (giving it a disconcerting, but evidently unconscious erotic appearance).

128 Dress in striped Indian silk, c, 1881.

This aesthetic dress designed by the sculptor, Sir Hamo Thorneycroft, for his wife is the complete antithesis of the costume in the previous plate. It is made in a soft, light material, gently draped about the figure and worn without the support of either corset or bustle. The absence of a tightly laced corset resulted in a suitably 'antique' waist, though fashionable ladies would have thought this unattractively thick.

tellectuals. A dislike of the meaningless decoration, crude aniline dyes and stiff fabrics favoured by contemporary fashion led to the adoption of soft, thin materials in subtle shades created by natural dyestuffs. If surface decoration was needed, 'art embroidery' might be added, but this was usually in a free style, specifically designed for the dress and quite unlike the stereotyped needlework patterns generally used at the time. Antique and exotic effects were frequently sought after and the ideal colours were described as 'old'-looking, 'strange' or 'indescribable tints'. Many of the best fabrics and, from the mid-1880s, artistic clothes themselves, could be purchased from the shop opened by Arthur Lasenby Liberty in Regent Street in 1875. So-called 'aesthetic' dresses were intended to be worn without a corset or bustle (although some surviving examples have lightly boned bodices).

Artistic garments were also proposed for men but met with only limited success. The idea of wearing knee-breeches – considered more picturesque than shapeless, tube-like trousers – though well established for sportswear by the 1870s was not accepted for more formal day or evening dress. It would be a long time before the easier-fitting, more colourful and informal clothes worn by some nineteenth-century artists found their way into the conventional man's wardrobe, although the proposals for more comfortable and interesting styles for men no longer seem out of place a hundred years later.

Aestheticism was in part a reaction against the perceived ugliness and monotony of mid-Victorian industrialized society. There was a genuine interest in raising standards of design which went hand in hand with an appreciation of the art and craft of earlier periods; and there was a keenly felt need to reconcile beauty with utility. Fashion, as a concept, was seen by many as an irrational and despotic force which ought to be modified and kept within reasonable bounds, if not dispensed with altogether. It was believed that if a form of

and enhance the shape of the body. No corsets or padding contradicted this line and the skirt fell in soft folds. William Morris, another admirer of mediaeval dress, was to remark: 'No dress can be beautiful that is stiff; drapery is essential.'[8] Later in the 1860s a revival of interest in classical art led other artists to propose Ancient Greek and Roman costume as an ideal.

An alternative style of dress which incorporated some of these features began to be adopted by women in artistic circles and by the later 1870s had spread to a much wider audience, mainly of middle-class in-

129 Algernon Charles Swinburne. *G. F. Watts, 1865.*

The poet, Swinburne, was one of several aesthetic men who were parodied by Punch *cartoons and Gilbert and Sullivan's comic opera,* Patience, *in the late 1870s and early 1880s. In this portrait, Swinburne's intense expression, long bushy hair, very informal turn-down collar and loose necktie would have appeared excessively 'artistic' to conventional men. Dress reformers felt that modern male fashion was uniformly ugly and dull and wished to introduce more colour, variety and informality.*

dress could be devised which answered the requirements of comfort, utility and beauty then it need not be changed, or at least not with the frequency of existing fashion. It was a noble and ambitious aim which was destined to failure but it was significant as a challenge to accepted ideas and conventions.

130 Advertisement for Elliman's Embrocation, 1897.

Although rational dress in the form of the knickerbocker costume for cycling became an accustomed sight in the 1890s a comparatively small number of British women were brave enough to wear it. However, much of the fury and venom first aroused by the Bloomer costume in the early 1850s had disappeared by the end of the nineteenth century and trousers for women were now accepted in sports dress. It is perhaps significant that the artist has portrayed the lady cyclist as a confident New Woman casting a scornful, backward glance at the prostrate and inferior male. Women were already looking forward to greater freedom and emancipation in the new century.

Emergence of the 'New Woman'

An important and ultimately more successful element in the Dress Reform movement was the issue of women's rights. This had begun to be discussed in the 1840s when a type of 'strong-minded' woman who espoused the cause was identified. Strong-minded women were thought to 'despise dress and all such appurtenances',[9] signalling their views by wearing mannish accessories. Miss Jenkyns in Elizabeth Gaskell's *Cranford* (set in the 1840s) 'wore a cravat, and a little bonnet like a jockey-cap, and altogether had the appearance of a strong-minded woman; although she would have despised the modern idea of women being equal to men. Equal indeed! she knew they were superior.'[10] During the 1850s the feminist movement, though derided, began to take a hold and by the 1870s there were signs of a new climate of opinion on the 'woman question.' Many people still clung to the belief that a woman's sphere was in the home but it was realized that a number of middle-class women were unable to marry through no fault of their own as there was an increasing surplus of women over men in the population. Some bold women were even choosing not to marry and to carry out work of their choice, although the classic example of Florence Nightingale and her nursing work during the Crimean War remained unusual. However, many more women became interested in educating themselves and from the 1870s they began to be admitted to the universities. New opportunities for work were also opening up in the 1870s, for example with the commercial manufacture of the newly invented typewriting machines. Central to the women's movement was the demand for the vote, and John Stuart Mill raised the possibility of equal enfranchisement in a speech to the House of Commons in May 1867.

It was against this background that the Rational Dress movement developed, many women feeling it important to give the appearance of being both sensible and attractive. A series of societies or organizations were set up to promote better sense and more practical features in women's clothing. By 1881 the Rational Dress Society had been formed under the presidency of Florence, Viscountess Harberton. 'Health, comfort and beauty' were the guiding principles and one of its aims was the adoption of the divided skirt for women. With the invention of the 'safety' bicycle in the late 1880s women were able to take up the popular new sport of cycling and this was an added incentive to adopt the divided skirt or, as an alternative, the knickerbocker costume (which was already worn in Paris and appeared in Britain in 1893[11]). Those who were brave enough to wear knickerbockers were often jeered at in the street and in 1899 a discouraged Lady Harberton felt that it was 'very certain that women will never ordinarily wear knickerbockers, or even the far more becoming and almost as convenient Turkish trousers, without covering skirts'. With more accurate foresight, she added that 'quite short skirts for walking would be a boon that ought to be easily attained'[12] and, indeed, the hemline had begun to rise just over a decade later, in 1913. A change in the fashionable line of women's dress was to give the final blow to tight lacing by 1910. It was clear at the end of the nineteenth century that it would not be possible to dispense with fashion but reforms were ultimately possible through persistent effort and patient waiting.

Notes

Introduction

1 See, for example, T. S. R. Boase, *English Art 1800–1870*, Clarendon Press, 1959 and 'The Regency Period 1810–1830', *The Connoisseur Period Guides*, ed. R. Edwards and L. G. G. Ramsey, London, 1968

2 G. Kitson Clark, *The Making of Victorian England*, Methuen, 1962, p. 63

3 For a recent, scholarly discussion of this aspect see V. Steele, *Fashion and Eroticism: Ideals of Feminine Beauty from the Victorian Era to the Jazz Age*, Oxford University Press, 1985. A. Ribeiro's *Dress and Morality*, Batsford, 1986 is also of interest

1 Classical Inspiration

1 E. Grant, *Memoirs of a Highland Lady 1797–1827*, John Murray, 1950, p. 8

2 *Elizabeth Ham by Herself*, ed. E. Gillett, Faber, 1945, p. 109

3 *The Memoirs of Susan Sibbald (1783–1812)*, ed. F. Paget Hett, London, 1926, p. 138

4 *Elizabeth Ham by Herself*, op. cit.

5 J. Austen, *Mansfield Park* (1814), ed. R. W. Chapman, Oxford, 1926, p. 222

6 S. Ferrier, *Marriage*, 1810, vol. 1, ch. 26

7 *Barbara Johnson's Album of Fashions and Fabrics*, ed. N. Rothstein, Thames & Hudson, 1987

8 J. Austen, *Letters to her Sister Cassandra and Others*, ed. R. W. Chapman, Oxford University Press, 1932, 30 June 1808, p. 204

9 See M. Ginsburg, 'Barbara Johnson and Fashion', in *Barbara Johnson's Album*, op. cit., p. 26. Barbara Johnson acquired her first pelisse in 1803

10 *The Repository of Arts, Literature, Commerce, Manufactures, Fashions and Politics*, published by Rudolph Ackermann, May 1810, p. 327; November 1810, p. 304

11 Ibid., June 1809, p. 397

12 Grant, op. cit., p. 69

13 Ackermann's *Repository*, op. cit., June 1809, p. 397

14 Ibid., November 1811, p. 303

15 *The Memoirs of Susan Sibbald*, op. cit., p. 192

16 *Lady's Monthly Museum*, January 1809, p. 48

17 Ibid., December 1811, p. 340

18 Grant, op. cit., p. 214

19 Austen, *Letters*, op. cit., 17 January 1809, p. 64

20 Ibid., 14 October 1813, p. 348

21 Ibid., 2 September 1814, p. 507

22 Grant, op. cit., pp. 192–3 and 204–5

23 See A. Ribeiro, *Fashion and the French Revolution*, Batsford, 1988, p. 34

24 *Barbara Johnson's Album*, op. cit., p. 26; Austen, *Letters*, op. cit., 5 May 1801, p. 125

25 M. Edgeworth, *Letters From England 1813–1844*, ed. C. Colvin, Oxford, 1971, 19 December 1821, p. 299

26 Ackermann's *Repository*, op. cit., January 1810, p. 49

27 Edgeworth, *Letters From England*, op. cit., ?10 March 1819, p. 181

28 Ibid., 19 September 1818, p. 103

29 Ibid., ?10 March 1819, p. 181

2 The Romantic Spirit

1 *The Ladies' Pocket Magazine*, March 1825, p. 108

2 Ibid., April 1831, p. 143

3 'Modes de Paris' in *Townsend's Monthly Selection of Parisian Costumes*, December 1827, p. 4

4 M. Edgeworth, *Letters from England 1813–1844*, ed. C. Colvin, Oxford, 1971, 6 January 1831, p. 469

5 *The Workwoman's Guide*, by A Lady, 1838, 2nd rev. ed., London, 1840, p. 82

6 Ibid., p. 83

7 *Ladies' Pocket Magazine*, May 1825, p. 177

8 E. Eden, *The Semi–Attached Couple*, 1860, ch. XXVIII

9 Ibid., ch. VI

10 *Ladies' Pocket Magazine*, April 1831, p. 144

11 M. Russell Mitford, *Our Village, 1824–1832*, selected ed., Harrap, 1947, p. 25

12 G. Eliot, *Scenes of Clerical Life*, 1857, ch. I

13 *Modes de Paris*, October and November 1837, no pagination

14 *Workwoman's Guide*, p. 50

15 Lady Eastlake (Elizabeth Rigby), 'The Art of Dress' in the *Quarterly Review*, March 1847. Reprinted in *Music and the Art of Dress*, John Murray, 1854, p. 73

16 *La Belle Assemblée*, November 1838, p. 289

17 Mrs Merrifield, *Dress as a Fine Art*, Arthur Hall, Virtue and Co., 1854, Part V, p. 65

3 Prosperity and Expansion

1 Mrs Merrifield, *Dress as a Fine Art*, Arthur Hall, Virtue and Co., 1854, part IX, p. 127

2 *Illustrated London News*, 7 September 1850, p. 219; 3 May 1851, p. 355

3 Ibid., 27 November 1852, p. 461; 30 July 1853, p. 63

4 Ibid., 26 September 1857, p. 316

5 *Journals and Correspondence of Lady Eastlake*, ed C. Eastlake Smith, 2 vols, John Murray, 1895, vol. I. p. 314

6 *Illustrated London News*, 1 January 1853, p. 5

7 Ibid., 28 January 1854, p. 77

8 Merrifield, op. cit., pp. 62–4

9 See S. Levitt, *Victorians Unbuttoned: Registered Designs for Clothing, their Makers and Wearers*, George Allen & Unwin, 1986, p. 38; and *Punch*, vol. 15, 1848, p. 200

10 *The Englishwoman's Domestic Magazine*, March 1862, p. 237

11 See D. Langley Moore, *Fashion Through Fashion Plates*, Ward Lock, 1971, p. 96

12 *The Worktable*, Supplement to *The Lady's Newspaper*, 8 March 1856, p. 3

13 *Illustrated London News*, 2 October 1858, p. 301

14 Ibid., 26 January 1850, p. 61

15 M. Lutyens (ed.). *Effie in Venice*, unpublished letters of Mrs John Ruskin written from Venice 1849–1852, John Murray, 1965, p. 275

16 Sir William James (ed.), *The Order of Release*, John Murray, 1948, p. 185

17 *Illustrated London News*, 26 June 1852, p. 504; *The Lady's Newspaper*, 1 March 1856, p. 136

18 H. Taine, *Notes on England 1860–1870*, Thames and Hudson, 1970, pp. 19, 20, 46, 57, 263

19 *E. D. M. Supplemental Fashion and Needlework*, August 1860, p. 189; May 1860, p. 47

20 *Illustrated London News*, 30 April 1864, p. 433; *Punch*, 25 March 1865, p. 124

21 Ibid., 2 June 1866, p. 546; *Punch*, 14 July 1866, p. 16

22 *The Ladies' Treasury*, 1 March 1867, p. 138

23 *E. D. M. Supplemental Fashion and Needlework*, March 1868, p. 146

24 *The Queen*, 14 October 1871, p. 250

25 *E. D. M. Supplemental Fashion and Needlework*, May 1862, p. 3

26 Ibid., August 1864, p. 354

27 A. Trollope, *The Eustace Diamonds*, 1873, ch. 35

4 Fin de Siècle

1 W. Graham Robertson, *Time Was*, Hamish Hamilton, 1931, p. 68

2 G. Gissing, *The Odd Women*, 1893, vol. I, ch. 3 and 4

3 W. Wimble, 'Incomes for Ladies', in *The Lady's Realm*, vol. I, November 1896, p. 104

4 *Cassell's Family Magazine*, February 1876, p. 175

5 *The Ladies' Treasury*, January 1876, p. 61

6 *Cassell's Family Magazine*, July 1876, p. 499

7 Ibid., December 1876, p. 60

8 Ibid., July 1878, p. 511

9 Ibid., April 1878, p. 295

10 *Punch* magazine published two items referring to 'five o'clock tea' on 2 January and 10 April 1875 which suggests that the custom had already become fashionable in the mid-1870s

11 *The Lady*, 28 May 1885, p. 447

12 *The Ladies' Treasury*, January 1882, pp. 44–5

13 See, for example, Z. Shonfield, *The Precariously Privileged*, Oxford University Press, 1986, p. 107, in which Jeannette Marshall made herself two or three brown dresses

14 *The Lady*, 8 October 1885, p. 871

15 *The Ladies' Treasury*, January 1882, p. 44

16 *The Lady*, 19 February 1885, p. 45

17 Ibid., p. 46

18 *The Woman's World*, May 1889, p. 355

19 *Lady's Realm*, November 1896, pp. 92–3

20 *The Lady*, 10 October 1889, p. 370

21 Ibid., 31 December 1885, p. 1111

22 *The Young Ladies' Journal*, March 1890, p. 170

23 *The Lady*, 25 July 1889, p. 90

24 *The Lady*, 4 April 1895, p. 409; 14 March 1895, p. 315

25 Advertisements for the sanitary towel appeared for example in *The Lady*, 17 January 1889, p. 74 and 14 February 1889, p. 180. See also N. Tarrant, *Great Grandmother's clothes*, National Museums of Scotland, 1986 and S. Levitt, *Victorians Unbuttoned: Registered Designs for Clothing, their Makers and Wearers 1839–1900*, George Allen & Unwin, 1986. Sarah Levitt has found registered designs for sanitary belts or 'ladies' belts' from as early as 1849 but they were not widely available or openly advertised until the close of the century. The disposable towel did not replace the linen or cotton 'napkins' generally used for this purpose but they made life easier for women when travelling.

26 *The Lady*, 21 March 1895, p. 346 and *Illustrated London News*, 18 September 1897, p. 394

27 *Illustrated London News*, 12 August 1899, p. 222

28 M. Lutyens (ed.), *Lady Lytton's Court Diary*, Rupert Hart-Davis, 1961, pp. 89 and 70

29 *The Graphic*, 27 March 1897, p. 379

30 Ibid., 10 April 1897, p. 443 and *Illustrated London News*, 28 October 1899, p. 624

31 *The Graphic*, 5 June 1897, p. 692

32 Ibid., 26 March 1898, p. 390

33 *Illustrated London News*, 18 September 1897, p. 394

5 Sense and Sobriety

1 *The Tailor and Cutter*, 9 January 1874, p. 176

2 See R. Ellmann, *Oscar Wilde*, Penguin, 1988, p. 157. For a detailed discussion of the Dress Reform movement, see S. M. Newton, *Health, Art and Reason: Dress Reformers of the Nineteenth Century*, John Murray, 1974

3 M. Beerbohm, 'Dandies and Dandies', *Works* (1896), Bodley Head, 1952, p. 22

4 A black coat for the evening was correct during periods of mourning; also, as *Le Beau Monde* commented in March 1808 (p. 183), 'the approach of Lent will, in its usual course, introduce the wearing of black suits, as the most genteel and most proper Evening dress, in all polite parties.'

5 Ackermann's *Repository of Arts* in February 1810 (p. 122) described the fashionable style: 'Great-coats are in general worn of olive, olive brown, dark bottle green superfine cloth, or superfine Bath coating; single breasted, with three or four straps in the front ... The waist is worn long, three inches below the hip-bone, and the skirts must reach to the bottom of the calf.'

6 'The bosom of the shirt now presents an air of peculiar neatness; the shirt itself is plaited, and is without a frill, the opening being united with three or four linen buttons. This improvement for a morning dress promises to be very generally adopted', said *Le Beau Monde* in December 1806 (p. 122).

7 A satirical work, *Neckclothitania or Tietania* was published in London in 1818. Starch, it said, gave the wearer 'a look of hauteur and greatness ... the air of being puffed up with pride, vanity, and conceit ... indispensable qualifications for a man of fashion,' Quoted by A. Ribeiro in *Dress and Morality*, Batsford, 1986, p. 125

8 Care was needed in their selection. Albert Smith in *The Natural History of the Gent* (David Bogue, 1847, p. 6) spoke of the vulgar 'gent' met in the street: 'He wore large check trowsers of the true light comedian pattern.'

9 'To be in the mode, the dress coat must be long waisted, broad across the shoulders, and about two and a half inches in breadth between the waist buttons. The side-seams should be very slightly curved . . . the lapels, which are necessarily long, because of the length of the waist, should be broad and square at the top to correspond with the front of the collar . . . The skirts of this dress coat have no flaps (pocket covers); but they should be broad and full on the hips.' J. Couts, *A Practical Guide for the Tailor's Cutting Room*, Blackie & Son, *c.* 1843, p. 58

10 Black trousers are mentioned as possible wear with evening dress as early as 1816 (Captain Gronow, *Reminiscences*, quoted by N. Waugh, *The Cut of Men's Clothes*, Faber, 1964, pp. 151–2) but did not, in fact, become usual until the 1830s.

11 Patterns and instructions for making separate collars which fastened to the shirt with a button and string ties are given in *The Workwoman's Guide*, by A Lady, 1838, 2nd ed. 1840, p. 142

12 H. Taine, *Notes on England 1860–1870*, Thames & Hudson, 1970, p. 19

13 The dress coat of 'rich blue cloth' was still being featured for 'Visiting Costume' by *The Gentleman's Magazine of Fashion* in October 1861 but by 1862 it was no longer mentioned for formal day wear. In May 1862 the journal reported that 'the frock-coat, either double or single breasted, still continues in favour in fashionable society as a morning visiting costume.'

14 R. S. Surtees, *Mr Sponge's Sporting Tour*, 1853, ch. XXXI

15 See *The Gentleman's Magazine of Fashion and Costumes de Paris*, ed. Louis Devere, London, September 1859 and November 1861.

16 R. S. Surtees, *Ask Mamma*, 1858, ch. XVIII

17 *The Tailor and Cutter*, 16 July 1870

18 Knickerbockers were later described as 'merely short, rather wide Trowsers, the legs, in fact, being cut of the same width from the top to the bottom, where they are gathered or pleated into a garter, which is fastened by a strap and buckle just below the knee. As the length of the knickerbockers is ruled at about 4¼ inches below the garter length, the bottoms of course droop, or fall over the garter in graceful folds.' C. Compaign and L. Devere, *Complete Manual of Trowsers Cutting*, Simpkin, Marshall & Co, 1881, p. 36

19 Quoted by C. W. and P. Cunnington, *Handbook of English Costume in the Nineteenth Century*, Faber, rev. ed. 1970, p. 254

20 Norah Waugh in *The Cut of Men's Clothes 1600–1900*. Faber, 1964 (p. 114) has described the late-nineteenth century frock-coat as 'the badge of middle-class respectability'.

21 *The Tailor and Cutter* on 15 July 1897 (p. 354) admired a 'particularly appropriate' fabric for a frock-coat worn by the Prince of Wales: 'being a dull finished stockinette, with not a loose particle of material anywhere'.

22 Ibid., 6 December 1900, p. 608

23 G. Moore, *Esther Waters*, 1894, ch. XXIX and XX

24 *The Tailor and Cutter*, 11 March 1897, p. 129 and 18 March 1897, p. 138

25 Ibid., 1 April 1897, p. 159

26 Mrs Humphry, *Manners for Men*, James Bowden, 1898, p. 114

27 In 1897 *The Tailor and Cutter* estimated that one in three coats ordered from tailors were lounges, and when a representative from the paper stationed himself midway between Charing Cross and the Law Courts in London he noticed nearly two lounges to every morning coat and three lounges to one frock coat going past (20 May 1897, p. 244)

28 *Clothes and the Man* by The 'Major of Today', Grant Richards, 1900, p. 192

29 *The Tailor and Cutter*, 26 July 1900, p. 378

30 In 1895 *The Tailor and Cutter* remarked: 'Trousers have not varied much in shape or material, but we all must have noticed the revival of the crease down the centre of the leg'. Quoted by C. Walkley and V. Foster, *Crinolines and Crimping Irons*, Peter own, 1978, p. 129

31 Humphry, op. cit., p. 114

32 The Prince of Wales was commended by *The Tailor and Cutter* for wearing with his favourite frock-coat a white slip, white spats and his linen shirt cuffs showing at the wrists. 'The white being placed at the extremities of his figure has the effect of giving him all the advantage of every inch of height he possesses, and thus helps to counteract the excess of width which is often found in gentlemen getting beyond the prime of life.' (7 July 1898, p. 253)

33 Ibid., 8 March 1900, p. 130

6 Status, Time and Place

1 *The Whole Art of Dress, or, The Road to Elegance and Fashion*, by A Cavalry Officer, Effingham Wilson, London, 1830, p. 4

2 *The Workwoman's Guide*, by A Lady, Simpkin, Marshall & Co., 1st ed. 1838, 2nd ed. 1840, p. 107

3 *Etiquette for Ladies and Gentlemen or The Principles of True Politeness: to which is added The Ball-Room Manual*, Milner & Co., *c.* 1840s, p. 7

4 J. F. C. Harrison in *Eminently Victorian: Aspects of an Age*, British Broadcasting Corporation, 1974, p. 13

5 Mrs Hymphry, *Manners for Men*, James Bowden, 1898, p. 113

6 M. Bateson, 'Dressing in Character', *The Woman's World*, 1889, p. 482

7 J. F. C. Harrison, *Early Victorian Britain 1832–1851*, Fontana, 1979, p. 136

8 The theory of 'Conspicuous Consumption' was first described by Thorstein Veblen in *The Theory of the Leisure Class*, George Allen & Unwin, 1925. Quentin Bell has explored Veblen's ideas with regard to clothing in his book *On Human Finery*, The Hogarth Press, rev. ed. 1976

9 See S. Levitt, 'Fashion and Etiquette', *Feminist Art News*, no. 9, 1983, pp. 9–11

10 J. Couts, *A Practical Guide for the Tailor's Cutting Room*, Blackie & Son, *c.* 1843, p. 74

11 Lady Colin Campbell (ed.), *Etiquette of Good Society*, Cassell, 1898, p. 77

12 Ibid., p. 14

13 C. W. Day, *Hints on Etiquette and the Usages of Good Society*, Longman, 1834, 3rd ed. 1836, reprinted by Turnstile Press, 1947

14 See P. Mason, *The English Gentleman: The Rise and Fall of an Ideal*, André Deutsch, 1982. As Mason points out, the 'gentleman' was not a Victorian invention but has a long pedigree running back to Chaucer, if not earlier.

15 Day, op. cit.

16 G. Gissing, *The Emancipated*, 1890, ch. II

17 Humphry, op. cit., p. 33

18 *La Belle Assemblée*, March 1848, p. 191

19 *The Englishwoman's Domestic Magazine*, February 1862, p. 188

20 Mrs A. Walker, *Female Beauty as Preserved and Improved by Regimen, Cleanliness and Dress*, Thomas Hurst, 1837, p. 382. Quoted by S. Levitt, op. cit.

21 *E. D. M. Supplemental Fashion and Needlework*, November 1863, p. 215

22 Ibid., November 1864, p. 402

23 Quoted in *Regency Costume*, Exeter Museum, publication no. 89, 1977

24 *Illustrated London News*, 25 November 1899, p. 768

25 *Cassell's Family Magazine*, February 1876, pp. 154–5. However, *Manners and Tone of Good Society* by A Member of the Aristocracy, (Warne, 1888, p. 61), says: 'No precedence is accorded to brides in society, though occasionally in the country old-fashioned people consider it due to a bride to send her down to dinner with the host, on the occasion of her first dining at a house within three months of her marriage.'

26 *The Englishwoman's Domestic Magazine*, Needlework supplement, August 1864, p. 354

27 Ibid., September 1864, p. 370

28 A. Trollope, *Ayala's Angel*, 1881, ch. XXIII

29 *Manners and Tone of Good Society*, op. cit.

30 See L. Davidoff, *The Best Circles: Society, Etiquette and the Season*, Croom Helm, 1973, p. 14

31 Z. Shonfield, *The Precariously Privileged*, Oxford University Press, 1987, pp. 50–51

32 Campbell, op. cit., p. 62

33 *Party-Giving on Every Scale*, Frederick Warne, 2nd ed. 1882, p. 32

34 Davidoff, op. cit., p. 35

35 Ackermann's *Repository of Arts*, July 1812, p. 44

36 *The Habits of Good Society: A Handbook of Etiquette for Ladies and Gentlemen*, Virtue & Co, *c.* 1875, p. 176

37 *M. H. E., A Manual of Etiquette for Ladies and Gentlemen*, George Routledge & Sons, *c.* mid-1890s, p. 14

38 Ibid., p. 15

39 *The Manners of Polite Society or Etiquette for Ladies and Gentleman*, Ward, Lock & Co., *c.* 1870s, vol. II, p. 25

40 *Habits of Good Society*, op. cit., p. 147

41 *Manual of Etiquette*, op. cit., p. 14

42 *Habits of Good Society*, op. cit., p. 177

43 Ibid., p. 178

44 *Manual of Etiquette*, op. cit., p. 44

45 *Habits of Good Society*, op. cit., p. 148

46 *Manual of Etiquette*, op. cit., p. 44

47 Campbell, op. cit., pp. 79–80

48 *Party-Giving on Every Scale*, op. cit., p. 26

49 W. L. Arnstein, 'A German View of English Society: 1851', *Victorian Studies*, XVI, no. 2 (1972–3), p. 201

50 *Manual of Etiquette*, op. cit., p. 53

51 Humphry, op. cit., p. 120

52 *Manners of Polite Society*, op. cit., p. 25

53 Ackermann's *Repository*, March 1812, p. 180

54 Fanny Kemble noted in her memoirs that in the period *c.* 1820–25 'the French fashion for full dress, of that day, did not sanction the uncovering of the person usual in English evening attire.' F. A. Kemble, *Record of a Girlhood*, Richard Bentley, 1879, vol. I, p. 100

55 *Habits of Good Society*, op. cit., p. 178

56 Ibid., pp. 181–2

57 Humphry, op. cit., p. 112

7 Luxurious Profusion

1 *The Englishwoman's Domestic Magazine*, needlework supplement, June 1863, p. 127

2 M. Griffith, 'Paris Dressmakers', *The Strand Magazine* vol. VIII, July–December 1894, p. 745

3 *Jane Austen's Letters to her Sister Cassandra and Others*, ed. R. W. Chapman, Oxford University Press, 1932

4 Austen, op. cit., letter dated 29 November 1812

5 A. Adburgham, 'Shopping for clothes in the nineteenth century', *Costume*, vol. 1, no. 2 (winter 1965–6)

6 E. Grant, *Memoirs of a Highland Lady 1797–1827*, John Murrary, 1950, p. 126

7 S. Levitt, 'Manchester Mackintoshes: A History of the Rubberized Garment Trade in Manchester', *Textile History* 17 (1), 1986, pp. 51–70

8 *The Workwoman's Guide*, by A Lady, 1838, 2nd ed. 1840, p. 107

9 J. Arnold, 'The Dressmaker's Craft', *Strata of Society*, Proceedings of the 7th Annual Conference of the Costume Society, 1973, pp. 32–3

10 See A. Buck, *Benjamin Read's Splendid Views 1829–1839*, Guildhall Library and the Costume Society, London, 1984, p. 2

11 Quoted by C. Walkley, in *The Ghost in the Looking Glass: The Victorian Seamstress*, Peter Owen, 1981, p. 14

12 M. Ginsburg, 'Clothing Manufacture 1860–1890', *High Victorian*, Proceedings of the 2nd Annual Conference of the Costume Society, 1968, p. 4

13 Griffith, op. cit.

14 *The Queen*, 18 November 1871, p. 327

15 *Punch*, vol. V, July–December 1843, p. 260. The problems of the Victorian seamstress are dealt with at length by Christina Walkley in *The Ghost in the Looking Glass*, op. cit.

16 H. Schramm, 'Evolution of the Men's Ready-Made Clothing Industry', *Men's Dress*, CIBA Review No. 124, January 1958, p. 28

17 *The Tailor and Cutter*, 8 September 1898, p. 488

18 See S. Levitt, *Victorians Unbuttoned: Registered Designs for Clothing their Makers and Wearers 1839–1900*, George Allen & Unwin, 1986, pp. 11–12

19 Ibid.

20 *The Tailor and Cutter*, 12 May 1898, p. 241

21 Ibid., 1 September 1898, p. 474

22 S. Levitt, 'Registered Designs: New Source Material for the Study of the Mid-Nineteenth Century Fashion Industry', *Costume*, 15, 1981, p. 55

23 For a detailed study of the department stores and other shops see A. Adburgham, *Shops and Shopping 1800–1914*, George Allen & Unwin, 1964

24 G. A. Sala, *Twice Round the Clock or the Hours of the Day and Night in London*, Houlston & Wright, 1859, pp. 266–7

8 Occasions, Leisure and Pleasure

1 See K. Staniland and S. M. Levey, 'Queen Victoria's Wedding Dress and Lace', *Costume*, 17, 1983, pp. 1–32

2 See, for example, Z. Shonfield, 'The Expectant Victorian', *Costume*, 6, 1972, p. 39. Jeannette Marshall wore her wedding dress (made and subsequently altered by Allison's of Regent Street, London) until the twenty-fifth week of her pregnancy in 1892.

3 *The Habits of Good Society*, Virtue & Co., *c.* 1875, p. 367

4 Ibid., p. 373

5 *The Englishwoman's Domestic Magazine*, March 1862, p. 238

6 *Habits of Good Society*, op. cit., p. 367

7 See Shonfield, op. cit. Jeannette Marshall, who was carrying a child in 1892 remained

active up to the day of her baby's birth, going shopping in central London, making afternoon calls and visiting the theatre.

8 See N. E. Tarrant, 'A Maternity Dress of about 1845–50', *Costume*, 14, 1980, pp. 117–120, for a discussion and pattern of a silk maternity dress probably used as a best dress for a not too wealthy middle-class woman.

9 Shonfield, op. cit.

10 *Manners of Modern Society*, Cassell, Petter & Galpin, 3rd ed. 1880s, p. 33

11 See N. Arch and J. Marschner, *Splendour at Court: Dressing for Royal Occasions since 1700*, Unwin Hyman, 1987, p. 7

12 *Manners and Tone of Good Society* by A Member of the Aristocracy, F. Warne, 4th ed. 1888, p. 63

13 *Manners of Modern Society*, p. 201

14 *The Queen*, 30 March 1878, p. 234

15 F. W. Harberton, 'Mourning Clothes and Customs', *The Woman's World*, 1889, p. 418

16 Ibid.

17 H. Mayhew (ed), *The Shops and Companies of London and Manufactories of Great Britain*, 1865. Quoted by J. Morley in *Death, Heaven and the Victorians*, Studio Vista, 1971, p. 63

18 Harberton, op. cit.

19 See L. Taylor, *Mourning Dress: A Costume and Social History*, George Allen & Unwin, 1983, pp. 202–3

20 For the history of crape, see D. C. Coleman, *Courtaulds – An Economic and Social History*, Oxford University Press, 1969, vols. I and II

21 *The Young Ladies' Journal*, February 1890, p. 90

22 *The Tailor and Cutter*, 4 November 1897, p. 557

23 *How to Dress on a Shilling a Day*, c. 1875, quoted by A. Buck, 'The Trap Re-Baited: Mourning Dress 1860–1890', *High Victorian*, The Costume Society, 1968, p. 35

24 Harberton, op. cit. Lady Harberton herself directed in her will that no one should wear mourning for her when she died in 1911. (*The Complete Peerage* by G. E. C., St Catherine Press, 1926, p. 295)

25 *The Tailor and Cutter*, op. cit.

26 *The Lady*, 2 July 1885, p. 575 and 3 September 1885, p. 769

27 Ibid., 20 June 1895, p. 835

28 *The Lady*, 3 September 1885, pp. 770–71

29 *Illustrated London News*, 11 September 1897, p. 362

Conclusion

1 J. Austen, *Northanger Abbey*, 1818, ch. 10 (Although published in 1818 the novel was actually written in 1798–9.)

2 These lines of thought have been clarified by Stella Mary Newton in her book *Health, Art and Reason: Dress Reformers of the Nineteenth Century*, John Murray, 1974 – the standard reference work on this subject

3 Dr Andrew Combe was one of the first to write about the problem in his *Principles of Physiology Applied to the Preservation of Health and to the Development of Physical Education*, published in 1834. See Newton, op. cit., ch. 1

4 As *Punch* remarked on 18 September 1869, p. 113: 'If you were to take a woman, put a strap or a girdle round her neck, and pull it in several inches, you would seriously inconvenience her . . . But lacing has evidently no consequences which prevent women from wearing stays as tight as they think pretty.'

5 Amelia Bloomer was always quick to point out that she did not invent the Bloomer costume and had only followed the lead of her two friends, Elizabeth Cady Stanton and Elizabeth Smith Miller, who was given the idea for the costume by some clothes seen being worn by women convalescing in a Swiss sanitorium. See for example, C. N. Gattey, *The Bloomer Girls*, Femina Books, 1967 and S. Foote, 'Bloomers', in *Dress*, 5, 1980

6 J. Tozer and S. Levitt, *Fabric of Society*, Laura Ashley, 1983, pp. 124–5

7 *Punch*, 19 January 1895, p. 36

8 Quoted by A. Gernsheim, *Fashion and Reality 1840–1914*, Faber, 1963, p. 65

9 *La Belle Assemblée*, January 1847, p. 47

10 E. Gaskell, *Cranford*, 1851–3, ch. 2

11 D. Rubinstein, 'Cycling in the 1890s', *Victorian Studies*, vol. 21, no. 1, 1977–8, p. 63

12 *Illustrated London News*, 9 September 1899, p. 366

Glossary

A guide to terms not fully explained or discussed in the text. It should be noted that only their nineteenth-century meanings are referred to.

ALPACA   A shiny, springy fabric woven with the silky, wool yarn from the fleece of the alpaca goat.

BASQUE   A short extension of the bodice, to flare over the hips.

BEAVER   A fabric made of felted fur fibres, used for men's and women's hats. Also a type of woollen overcoating.

BLONDE   A silk bobbin lace with a creamy, lustrous texture.

BOMBAZET   A cheaper version of BOMBAZINE, made from a mixture of cotton and worsted.

BOMBAZINE   A twilled fabric usually woven with a silk warp and a worsted weft, much used for mourning.

BROADCLOTH   A fine-quality woollen cloth, closely woven and with a raised nap. By the nineteenth century it was made from merino wool.

BROCADE   A woven fabric, usually silk, with a slightly raised pattern created by the introduction of additional threads in different colours.

BRODERIE ANGLAISE   White cutwork embroidery on a cotton or linen fabric, consisting of overcast eyelet holes interspersed with satin stitch and stem stitch motifs.

BUCKRAM   A very stiff fabric made from a coarse linen impregnated with gum or size.

CALICO   General term for plain cotton fabrics which were heavier than muslin. Originally produced in Calicut, east India.

CAMBRIC/CAMBRIC MUSLIN Fine, plain-weave linen fabric originally made at Cambray in Flanders. Cambric muslin was probably a muslin which resembled cambric through the appearance of its yarn and weave.

CASHMERE   A very fine, soft wool from the Kashmir goat.

CHALLIS   A thin, soft dress fabric with a silk warp and woollen weft.

CHEVIOT   A hard-wearing and rough-surfaced woollen cloth similar to tweed, named after the wool from sheep reared on the Cheviot Hills.

CHIFFON   A light, thin, almost transparent silk fabric.

CHINE SILK   A warp-printed silk giving the pattern a blurred effect, as if it had 'run'.

CHINTZ   Cotton cloth printed in various colours and with a glazed surface. It was originally imported from India but by the late eighteenth century was also being produced in Europe (Britain included).

CHIP   A fine straw or woody fibre in thin strips, used for bonnets and hats.

CLOCK   Decorative patterning or embroidery on stockings, covering the ankle area.

CLOTH   Although the term is used to describe any type of fabric it generally refers to a closely woven material of fine-quality wool.

CORSAGE   The upper part or bodice of a woman's dress.

COUTIL   A strong, cotton fabric in a twill weave. Often used for corsets.

CRAPE   A silk gauze fabric with a crimped surface (created by the use of a high twist yarn). A special variant of black crape for mouring was prepared from gummed yarn and had an embossed 'figure' which produced a duller, denser texture.

CUIRASS/CUIRASS BODICE The breast plate piece of body armour. The term was used to describe the fashionably tight, rigidly boned bodice of the late 1870s.

DRAB A woollen cloth of a dull, grey-brown colour.

DRILL A strong, twilled cloth, either cotton or linen.

ECRU The name given to the natural creamy colour of undyed linen or silk thread.

EPAULETTE An ornamental shoulder-piece.

FICHU A light scarf worn round the neck or shoulders. A nineteenth-century term for the earlier handkerchief or neck-handkerchief.

FLANNEL Soft, woollen fabric with a loose weave.

GAUGE/GAUGING A method of containing fullness by means of small gathers (rather than flat pleats). A series of running stitches are made in the material and the threads are then drawn up to the requisite length.

GAUZE A very thin, almost transparent fabric of silk, wool, cotton or linen yarn distinguished by the twisted thread of its weave.

GINGHAM A yarn-dyed, plain-weave, firm cotton fabric.

GLACE/GLACE SILK A light, plain-weave silk with a shiny surface.

GRENADINE A fine, gauze-like fabric of silk or a silk and wool mixture.

GUIPURE A rich, heavy lace with a raised thread and large motifs joined by bars or brides.

HOLLAND A medium-weight, plain-weave linen cloth.

JABOT An ornamental frill on the front of a woman's bodice.

JACONET/JACKONET A thin, soft variety of muslin.

JEAN A strong, twilled cotton cloth, similar to drill.

JERSEY A knitted fabric, made by hand or machine, from a silk, wool or cotton yarn. A bodice or top made of this material.

JUPON An underskirt or petticoat.

KERSEYMERE Fine woollen cloth with a twill weave.

LAWN A fine, smooth fabric in a plain weave. Originally made from linen yarn but later also made of cotton.

MANCHERON A small oversleeve like an epaulette.

MERINO A fine, soft wool from the merino sheep, used for high-quality cloth.

MOIRE/MOIRE ANTIQUE Also known as watered silk. A finish giving the effect of a wavy watermark. Most often used on plain silk fabrics which were passed through heated, engraved rollers to create the effect. Moiré antique was a grosgrain or heavy, ribbed silk treated in this way.

MUSLIN A general term for the lightest, most delicately woven cotton fabrics, but can also refer to similar, thin materials with an open weave in silk or wool.

NAINSOOK A fine, soft cotton fabric.

NANKEEN/NANKIN A twilled cotton cloth with a yellowish-brown tint, originally produced in Nankin, China.

NET A meshed fabric of which the threads may be twisted, plaited, looped or knotted.

ORGANDIE/ORGANDY A thin, gauze-like cotton fabric with a stiff finish.

PARAMATTA A mourning fabric made with either a silk or cotton warp and a worsted weft.

PEIGNOIR A dressing-gown or loose wrapper.

PELUCHE French term for PLUSH.

PIQUE White cotton fabric with a raised rib or a self-coloured surface pattern.

PLAIT/PLEAT The term 'plait' was used throughout the nineteenth century to refer to the technique of pleating or folding material.

PLASTRON A panel at the centre front of the bodice, usually made in a contrasting fabric or colour.

PLUSH A type of cotton velvet with a long, shaggy pile.

POLONAISE A long bodice, extending into an overskirt which could be looped up or draped over the hips.

PONGEE A light silk fabric.

POPLIN Fabric of silk and worsted with a corded surface. Later made of cotton.

SARCENET/SARSENET/SARSNET A fine, soft silk fabric in a plain or twilled weave.

SATIN Silk with a diagonal weave to create a glossy surface on one side.

SEAMSTRESS/SEMPSTRESS A woman who sews by profession (although plain sewing rather than embroidery is implied by this term).

SELF-COVERED As in self-covered buttons. Covered in the same fabric as the garment, as opposed to being made of some other material such as metal, wood, etc.

SERGE A strong, twilled woollen or worsted cloth.

SHIRR/SHIRRING A technique similar to GAUGING but employing several parallel rows of very small gathers.

STOCKINETTE A fine, pliable, machine-knitted fabric.

STOMACHER A panel in the shape of an inverted triangle at the centre front of the bodice. A nineteenth-century imitation of seventeenth- and eighteenth-century fashion.

SUPERFINE A high-quality broadcloth made from merino wool.

TABLIER French term for apron, used to denote a manner of trimming the skirt.

TARLATAN/TARLATANE An open, plain-woven cotton fabric, similar to muslin but much stiffened.

TOILENETTE/TOILINET/TOILINETTE A fine woollen cloth or a silk, wool and cotton mixture. Much used for men's waistcoats during the first half of the nineteenth century.

TOURNURE Genteel name for a bustle.

TULLE A fine bobbin net made from silk yarn.

TUSSORE Also known as wild silk. A natural-coloured silk with an uneven, slubbed texture.

TWEED A woollen cloth with an open weave, originating in Scotland. Produced in a variety of textures, the most common of which was rather coarse and hairy.

TWILL A type of weave producing parallel, diagonal lines. A hard-wearing textile fabric woven in this way.

VELVET Silk fabric with a short, dense and smooth piled surface.

VELVETEEN A cheaper version of velvet made with a cotton back.

VEST A term commonly used to denote a waistcoat.

VICUNA A fine, silky wool from the South American animal of this name, related to the llama.

WATERED SILK See MOIRE.

WORSTED A fine, smooth yarn spun from long staple fibres. A woollen fabric woven from this yarn.

Bibliography

Adburgham, A. *A Punch History of Manners and Modes 1841–1940*, Hutchinson, 1961
Shops and Shopping 1800–1914, George Allen & Unwin, 1964, 2nd ed. 1981
Victorian Shopping (Introduction), David & Charles, 1972
Liberty's: A Biography of a Shop, George Allen & Unwin, 1975

Alexander, H. *Fans*, The Costume Accessories Series, Batsford, 1984

Arnold, J. *Patterns of Fashion: Englishwomen's Dresses and their Construction*, vol. 1, *c.* 1660–1860, vol. 2, *c.* 1860–1940, Wace, 1964, Macmillan, 1972

Baines, B. *Fashion Revivals from the Elizabethan Age to the Present Day*, Batsford, 1981

Blum, S. *Ackermann's Costume Plates: Women's Fashions in England 1818–1828*, Dover, New York, 1978

Buck, A. *Victorian Costume and Costume Accessories*, Herbert Jenkins, 1961, 2nd ed., Ruth Bean, Bedford, 1984

Buxton, A. *Discovering Nineteenth-Century Fashion: A Look at the Changes in Fashion through the Victoria and Albert Museum's Dress Collection*, Hobsons Publishing plc, Cambridge, 1989

Byrde, P. *A Frivolous Distinction: Fashion and Needlework in the Works of Jane Austen*, Bath City Council, 1979

The Male Image: Men's Fashions in Britain 1300–1970, Batsford, 1979

Clabburn, P. *Shawls in Imitation of the Indian*, Shire Publications, 1981

Clark, F. *Hats*, The Costume Accessories Series, Batsford, 1982

Cumming, V. *Gloves*, The Costume Accessories Series, Batsford, 1982

Cunnington, C. W. and P. *Handbook of English Costume in the Nineteenth Century*, Faber, 1959, rev. ed. 1970
The History of Underclothes, Michael Joseph, 1951, rev. ed., Faber, 1981

Cunnington, P. *Costume of Household Servants*, A. & C. Black, 1974

Cunnington, P. and Buck, A. *Children's Costume in England*, A. & C. Black, 1965

Cunnington, P. and Lucas, C. *Costume for Births, Marriages and Deaths*, A. & C. Black, 1972
Occupational Costume in England, A. & C. Black, 1967

Cunnington, P. and Mansfield, A. *English Costume for Sports and Outdoor Recreations*, A. & C. Black, 1969

de Marly, D. *The History of Haute Couture 1850–1950*, Batsford, 1980
Fashion for Men: An Illustrated History, Batsford, 1985

Edwards, R. and Ramsey, L. G. G. (eds) *The Connoisseur Complete Period Guides to the Houses, Decoration, Furnishing and Chattels of the Classic Periods*, The Connoisseur, London, 1968 (chapters on Textiles, Costume and Jewellery in 'The Regency Period 1810–1830' and 'The Early Victorian Period 1830–1860')

Farrell, J. *Umbrellas and Parasols*, The Costume Accessories Series, Batsford, 1985

Flower, M. *Victorian Jewellery*, Cassell, 1951

Foster, V. *Bags and Purses*, The Costume Accessories Series, Batsford, 1982
A Visual History of Costume: The Nineteenth Century, Batsford, 1984

Gernsheim, A. *Fashion and Reality 1840–1914*, Faber, 1963. Reprinted as *Victorian and Edwar-*

dian Fashion: A Photographic Survey, Dover, New York, 1981

Gibbs-Smith, C. H. The Fashionable Lady in the Nineteenth Century, HMSO, 1960

Ginsburg, M. Victorian Dress in Photographs, Batsford, 1982

Goldthorpe, C. From Queen to Empress: Victorian Dress 1837–1877. Exhibition at the Costume Institute, Metropolitan Museum of Art, New York, 1988

Jarvis, A. Liverpool Fashion: Its Makers and Wearers. The Dressmaking Trade in Liverpool 1830–1940, Merseyside County Museums, 1981

Levitt, S. Victorians Unbuttoned: Registered Designs for Clothing, their Makers and Wearers, George Allen & Unwin, 1986

Mackrell, A. Shawls, Stoles and Scarves, The Costume Accessories Series, Batsford, 1986

Manchester City Art Galleries Women's Costume 1800–1835 (1952); 1835–1870 (1951); 1870–1900 (1953)
Children's Costume (1959)
Wedding Costume 1735–1970 (1977)

Moers, E. The Dandy: Brummell to Beerbohm, Secker & Warburg, 1960

Moore, D. Langley The Woman In Fashion, Batsford, 1949
The Child in Fashion, Batsford, 1953
Fashion Through Fashion Plates 1771–1970, Ward, Lock & Co., 1971

Newton, S. M. Health, Art and Reason: Dress Reformers of the Nineteenth Century, John Murray, 1974

Ribeiro, A. Dress and Morality, Batsford, 1986

Rose, C. Children's Clothes, Batsford, 1989

Rothstein, N. ed. Barbara Johnson's Album of Fashions and Fabrics, Thames & Hudson, 1987

Steele, V. Fashion and Eroticism: Ideals of Feminine Beauty from the Victorian Era to the Jazz Age, Oxford University Press, 1985

Swann, J. Shoes, The Costume Accessories Series, Batsford, 1982

Tarrant, N. The Rise and Fall of the Sleeve 1825–1840, Royal Scottish Museum, Edinburgh, 1983

Great Grandmother's Clothes: Women's Fashion in the 1880s, Trustees of the National Museums of Scotland, 1986

Taylor, L. Mourning Dress: A Costume and Social History, George Allen & Unwin, 1983

Tozer, J. and Levitt, S. Fabric of Society: A Century of People and their Clothes 1770–1870, Laura Ashley Publications, 1983

Walkley, C. and Foster, V. Crinolines and Crimping Irons. Victorian Clothes: How They Were Cleaned and Cared For, Peter Owen, 1978

Walkley, C. The Ghost in the Looking Glass: The Victorian Seamstress, Peter Owen, 1981

The Way to Wear'em: 150 Years of Fashion in Punch, Peter Own, 1986

Waugh, N. Corsets and Crinolines, Batsford, 1954
The Cut of Men's Clothes 1600–1900, Faber, 1964
The Cut of Women's Clothes 1600–1930, Faber, 1968

Costume Society Publications

Papers delivered at the Society's Annual Conferences:
The So-Called Age of Elegance. Costume 1785–1820 (1970)
Early Victorian. Costume 1830–1860 (1969)
High Victorian. Costume 1860–1890 (1967)
La Belle Epôque. Costume 1890–1914 (1967)

Designs of Modern Costume engraved for Thomas Hope of Deepdene by Henry Moses, 1812. Introduction by J. L. Nevinson, Extra Series No. 4, 1973

Working Class Costume from Sketches of Characters, 1818, ed. P. Clabburn, Extra Series No. 3, 1971

Benjamin Read's Splendid Views 1829–1839. Introduction by A. Buck and Notes by R. Hyde and A. Saunders. Guildhall Library and the Costume Society, 1984

Costume. The Annual Journal of the Costume Society (published since 1967) includes a number of articles on aspects of nineteenth-century dress.

Index